The Perennial Philosophy

Series

World Wisdom
The Library of Perennial Philosophy

The Library of Perennial Philosophy is dedicated to the exposition of the timeless Truth underlying the diverse religions. This Truth, often referred to as the *Sophia Perennis*—or Perennial Wisdom—finds its expression in the revealed Scriptures as well as the writings of the great sages and the artistic creations of the traditional worlds.

Introduction to Sufism: The Inner Path of Islam appears as one of our selections in the Perennial Philosophy series.

The Perennial Philosophy Series

In the beginning of the twentieth century, a school of thought arose which has focused on the enunciation and explanation of the Perennial Philosophy. Deeply rooted in the sense of the sacred, the writings of its leading exponents establish an indispensable foundation for understanding the timeless Truth and spiritual practices which live in the heart of all religions. Some of these titles are companion volumes to the Treasures of the World's Religions series, which allows a comparison of the writings of the great sages of the past with the perennialist authors of our time.

Introduction to Sufism

The Inner Path of Islam

by

Éric Geoffroy

Translated by
Roger Gaetani

World Wisdom

Introduction to Sufism: The Inner Path of Islam
© 2010 World Wisdom, Inc.

Library of Congress Cataloging-in-Publication Data

Geoffroy, Eric.
 [Initiation au soufisme. English]
 Introduction to Sufism : the inner path of Islam / by Éric Geoffroy ; translated by Roger
Gaetani.
     p. cm. -- (The perennial philosophy series)
 Includes bibliographical references and index.
 ISBN 978-1-935493-10-5 (pbk. : alk. paper) 1. Sufism. I. Gaetani, Roger, 1954- II. Title.
 BP189.G28713 2010
 297.4--dc22
                                                                    2010011130

Printed on acid-free paper in the United States of America.

For information address World Wisdom, Inc.
P.O. Box 2682, Bloomington, Indiana 47402-2682
www.worldwisdom.com

CONTENTS

TRANSLATOR'S FOREWORD

Why is there a need for yet another book on Sufism, the mystical path of Islam? Let us look to the great Sufi poet and spiritual master Rūmī for some clues. He wrote, "Do not look on that Beauteous One with your own eye: behold the Sought with the eye of seekers. Shut your own eye to that sweet-eyed One; borrow an eye from His lovers." Although we may simply be interested in learning something about Sufism, and not in pursuing the deep spiritual fulfillment to which the quote from Rūmī refers, the same principle still holds: our best chance at understanding what Sufism really is comes through surveying the thoughts of the great theoreticians of Sufism, who sought to articulate the ways of and to God, and through glimpsing something of the hearts of the great Muslim mystics, who tried to communicate their rapture in God to posterity. The task, then, for a worthy survey of Sufism must include selecting and transmitting authentic key voices of Islamic mysticism in a way that is comprehensible and stimulating to contemporary readers. This book admirably accomplishes all this, but it also adds an important new voice in the study of Sufism for many readers of English: that of Éric Geoffroy.

Dr. Geoffroy is a prominent French scholar and writer who specializes in the study of Sufism. The publication of this, his first full book translated into English, brings a unique and authoritative perspective on Sufism to our attention. For those who have spent some time in Muslim lands where authentic Sufism can still be found, as well as for those who have studied intelligent and objective writings on the subject, Geoffroy's facts and insights will ring true. He has done the work for us of amassing fourteen centuries of oral and written history and then condensed this into a cohesive survey covering multiple dimensions of a body of knowledge and practice that, by its own admission, must resist final comprehension by reason alone. Beyond the flow of facts, which is impressive enough in this book, a fuller understanding of any mysticism will require some degree of intuition on the part of the reader, and the author has provided us with many opportunities to experience something of the "taste" of authentic Sufism. In addition, there is a refreshing candor in Dr. Geoffroy's writing. He does not whitewash the abuses within Sufism, nor does he harbor any hidden agendas: his Preface to this book is a model of simplicity, clearly revealing his objectives and his major themes, which are then delineated and expanded upon throughout the survey.

Introduction to Sufism: The Inner Path of Islam unfolds elegantly. The organization of the work is highlighted by the numerous sections and subsections. This helps us to appreciate the remarkable scope of the book, which strikes an excellent balance between theory and practice, and early and late historical developments. We can also sense Geoffroy's objectivity in giving equal say to the divergent movements and personalities that have contended for prominence, or sometimes even dominance, in Sufism's long and colorful history. And readers will certainly find more than a little of that color in these pages. We think both seekers and scholars will find that this book, besides being wide-ranging and well researched, has a rare attribute: by articulating so well the disputes between the scholars of the letter of the divine Law and Sufis, and then between different currents within Sufism itself, Dr. Geoffroy has given us a book that lends itself like few others to discussion and debate. We can easily imagine lively conversations, whether in college classrooms or in readers' living rooms, framed by the contents of this volume.

We have alluded to the authenticity of Geoffroy's approach. It should probably be noted that his consistent focus on the role of the Prophet Muhammad in Sufi spirituality and on the essential link between Sufism and the Koran places, and keeps, Sufism within its proper context. Without this context, there is no longer any real Sufism to be studied, only its counterfeits. By keeping true to this very real grounding of Sufism in the Prophet and the Koran, Geoffroy keeps true to his subject. This is the real Sufism that is found in the ancient treatises and in the meeting rooms of the dervishes. There is no real Sufi who does not love the Prophet and the Koran. The story of the endless search for a balance between the "outer" path (Islam) and the "inner" Path (Sufism) to God is the very real story that must be accurately portrayed by any religious history, just as it must be intensely re-lived by each spiritual traveler in the here-and-now. Going beyond the dispassion of the facts alone, Geoffroy shares with us the very human passion of the torments and triumphs that have made both the history and the practice of Sufism so compelling to those of us beyond its geographical homelands.

A key to drawing the reader into this text is its attention to universal aspects—of which we can find many—that speak powerfully to non-Muslims as well as to Muslims. There is a great deal of attention paid to interpreting the particular language and symbols of Sufism and Islam for readers who are most likely Christians living in the modern West. The author's efforts in this regard may not be obvious, but all the better. Certain sections will be more explicit on such concepts as the "transcendent unity of religions" within Sufism, but throughout the book readers will find references that are meaningful in the field of comparative religion, and ideas or stories that may relate closely to their own religious backgrounds.

This is all to say that we have found this book a worthy addition to the writings that offer an introduction to Sufism, and well worth the effort of translation for the English-reading public. It is our pleasure to introduce the writing of Éric Geoffroy to a broader audience; it is our regret, on the other hand, that we could not capture the full flavor of his writing despite all our efforts. His phrasing can sometimes be quite lyrical, and fertile imagery often abounds. However, this will not always work in the same way in English, and we accept all blame for places where the text does not equal the eloquence of Dr. Geoffroy's French. The text follows the original French as closely as possible, but we have inserted a few notes where we thought it necessary for the English reader.

In closing, it only seems right to give a line missing from Rūmī's thought quoted above. He wanted to entice seekers after God to go beyond any mysticism that they might learn from book or human master. The passage concludes, "Nay, borrow eye and sight from Him, then look on His face with His eye." This is a threshold beyond which no book can pretend to take the reader, and the master must also leave the seeker there to cross it for himself or herself. In that realm the "secret" which we all bear within ourselves is fully divulged. To the extent that we can sense the whisperings of this secret within ourselves, we will understand, and enjoy, the words in this book.

—Roger Gaetani

TRANSLITERATION SYSTEM
FOR ARABIC CHARACTERS

ء	' (except initially)
ب	b
ت	t
ث	th
ج	j
ح	h
خ	kh
د	d
ذ	dh
ر	r
ز	z
س	s
ش	sh
ص	s
ض	d
ط	t
ظ	z
ع	'
غ	gh
ف	f
ق	q
ك	k
ل	l
م	m
ن	n
ه	h
و	w
ي	y

The article al- and l- (even before "sun" letters)

Short vowels		Long vowels	
ˊ	a	ا ى	ā
ˋ	u	و	ū
ِ	i	ي	ī

PREFACE

Sufism, a key expression of the spirituality of Islam, asks of the initiate that he devote himself to the greater *jihād*,[1] that is, to the struggle against the various passions and illusions which assail him. This is so that he can find an inner space in which he can contemplate the realities of the Spirit. Sufism depends upon an initiation in order to transmit the spiritual blessings which flow from the Prophet, through a Sufi master, to a disciple.

A true Sufi shaykh is, in fact, connected to a spiritual lineage which reaches all the way back to Muhammad. Starting in the twelfth century, several great Muslim saints created paths (*tarīqa*) that ensured the transmission of the initiatory discipline which every aspirant must follow. These paths use different methods to arrive at divine knowledge, for, as the Sufis say, "There are as many paths leading to God as there are sons of Adam." In the course of time, these paths were institutionalized and became brotherhoods (or, "orders"); as the centuries passed, some declined, while others reassessed and then renewed themselves.

Sufism, however, goes far beyond the framework of the brotherhoods. Having the Koran as its source, it is based on the example of the Prophet. Therefore, it in no way rejects either the law or the rites of Islam. To the contrary, it illuminates them from within, continually renewing their meaning for the faithful. Far from being a marginal or deviant phenomenon, Sufism is at the heart of Islamic culture. Over the course of centuries, millions of Muslims have followed this path which today is often viewed as an antidote to dry and lifeless interpretations of the religion.

This book is based on the conviction that Islam and Sufism are intrinsically linked together. It depends upon the venture that the inward-directed approach of Sufism is not incompatible with a critical analysis. Sufis themselves have defined their discipline as a "spiritual science": we have supported this perspective by putting the doctrines and practices back within their proper contexts.

In this book, we have quoted only a few works or articles in foreign languages because we are addressing French readers. In the interest of brevity, we have given the sources of quotations only when we have thought this to be important. Whenever possible, we have given the names of the transmitters of *hadīths* (words of the Prophet) in parentheses. The indexes at the end of this volume should make it easier for readers to find their way around.

---

[1] Translator's Note: An Index of Technical Terms provides concise definitions of the major Islamic and Sufi Arabic terms used in this book.

Chapter 1

FUNDAMENTALS

DEFINITIONS AND OBJECTIVES

"Sufism is nothing but idolatry, for its purpose is to preserve one's heart from all that is not God; but, there is nothing other than God."

—Shiblī

"Sufism is a reality without a form."

—Ibn al-Jalā'

"Anyone who would express his thoughts on Sufism is not a Sufi; anyone who bears witness to Sufism is not a Sufi. In order to live Sufism, one must be 'absent' from it."

—Ibn Bākhilā

It is said that there are a thousand definitions of Sufism. Let us make an initial attempt at one. In Islam, the polarization between exoterism and esoterism is very pronounced. In the Koran, God presents Himself as, at the same time, the Outer (*al-Zāhir*) and the Inner (*al-Bātin*),[1] under seemingly opposite Names which the Sufi will have to reconcile during his spiritual search. Are not the human soul and the cosmos in God's image? For the Sufi, the outward proceeds from the inward, as the peel of a fruit encases the pit. Thus, Sufism represents the living heart of Islam, the inner dimension of the Revelation given to Muhammad, and not an arbitrary form of occultism.

Sufism can also be defined as an aspect of the eternal Wisdom. In several instances, the Koran mentions the "immutable Religion" (*al-dīn al-qayyim*): this is the primordial religion, without name, from which all historical religions spring. The purpose of Islam, the last revealed message, was to highlight the divine Oneness,[2] of which Adam was the first messenger. The Spirit bestowed Itself upon Islam as it had done before with other religious forms: In referring to Christian or Jewish spirituality, certain Muslims speak of

---

[1] Koran 57:3.

[2] Translator's Note: Readers will encounter this term, "Oneness," throughout the book. It is a theological and philosophical term that refers to the indivisibility of God's nature, or His Unity which allows no compromise or qualification. Thus, it also applies to the Uniqueness of God. If we think through this concept fully, which is precisely what many Sufi sages have done, its ramifications upon the nature of creation and upon our own existence cannot be underestimated.

"Christian Sufism" or "Jewish Sufism." Authentic Sufism is played out in a harmony which the initiate must continually restore between the body and the spirit, and between religion as it was established on earth and its inner reality.

A Mysticism?

Sufism is commonly called "Muslim mysticism." This expression does have a certain relevance if one understands it as the knowledge of the "mysteries," as a communion with the divine through intuition and contemplation. The Koran, which distinguishes the "world of Testimony" (*'ālam al-shahāda*), i.e. the perceptible world, from the "world of Mystery" (*'ālam al-ghayb*), asks the faithful to believe in this Mystery, the *ghayb* (literally, "that which is not accessible to sight)." One of the goals of Sufism, precisely, is to pierce through the opacity of this world in order to contemplate spiritual realities that lie beyond simple faith.

In the Christian world, the term "mysticism" has been extended to apply to cases which are imbued with individual subjectivism. According to René Guénon, mysticism is passive; the Sufi, however, actively undertakes "labors" in order to reach spiritual realization. Thus, Sufism is, essentially, an initiatory[3] path in which the master-disciple relationship enables the regular transmission of spiritual blessings (*baraka*). Provided with this protection, the aspirant can progress along the path in order to go beyond the limits of individuality—potentially or in actuality—and to reach deliverance. It has been said that "Sufism is a state in which all human traces have vanished,"[4] and "Sufism is freedom."[5]

The Sufi does not seek to withdraw from the world. His destiny is to achieve realization here and now, possibly even "in the midst of the crowd."

---

[3] Translator's Note: In translating the French word "initiatique" we have chosen to use the standard English term "initiatory" rather than the term "initiatic" because the former should be more familiar to readers. However, it should be pointed out that when Dr. Geoffroy uses the term it is almost always in reference to a formal "initiation," which is to say a process that transmits an esoteric spiritual influence or blessing from master to disciple. It does not refer, as the English term "initiatory" commonly does, to something that helps something else commence, such as an initiatory speech at a conference. In this book, "initiatory" will usually refer to one of the many processes, actions, or states that are involved in the spiritual life of a disciple who has formally been initiated into the Sufi path.

[4] Qushayrī, *Risāla* (Beirut, 1986), p. 283. (English edition: *Al-Qushayri's Epistle on Sufism: Al-risala al-qushayriyya Fi 'ilm al-tasawwuf* [Garnet Publishing, 2007].)

[5] Hujwirī, *Kashf al-mahjūb* (Beirut, 1980) (translated from Arabic), p. 239. (English edition: *Kashf al-Mahjub*, titled *Revelation of the Mystery*, translated into English by Reynold A. Nicholson [Pir Press, 1999].)

As the "son of the moment," he must develop his spiritual qualities within the circumstances in which God has placed him. For all that, Sufism does display genuine "mystical" features. First of all, Sufis believe that it is God who takes the initiative in making them travel towards Him, and that their progress depends upon His grace. The aspirant (*murīd*, "one who desires God") moves along the path only because God "desired" (*murād*) him beforehand. The following *hadīth qudsī*[6] expresses this: "If he [man] draws nearer to Me a hand's span, I draw nearer to him an arm's length. If he draws nearer to Me an arm's length, I draw nearer to him a fathom's length; and if he comes to Me walking, I hasten toward him."

Sufism distinguishes between spiritual "states" bestowed by God and initiatory "stations," and so it depends on this subtle interaction between activity and passivity. The spiritual "states" are clearly of a passive nature: One example is "rapture" (*jadhb*), by which God "uproots" the Sufi from this world by withdrawing his mental faculties from him.

Knowledge and Love

Sufis deduce the reasons for the creation of the world from God's desire to make Himself known. "I was a hidden treasure that longed to be known, so I created the world" says a *hadīth qudsī*. Sufism is truly situated within the dual perspectives of "knowledge" (*ma'rifa*) and of "love" (*mahabba*). For Sufis, these two approaches to the divine are strongly complementary and each strengthens the other. "Love is the annihilation of individual being in spiritual delight, and knowledge is the contemplation, in bewilderment [of the mystery of the divine Oneness]," said a master.[7] The way of love is "mystical" through the Sufi's desire for union, which galvanizes him. But this attitude is not only devotional: it also rests on contemplation.

At times, Sufis employ love and knowledge one following the other, and at other times simultaneously. Many agree in stating that they are identical. For, how is one to love God without knowing Him, and how is one to hope to know Him without loving Him? "The spiritual life is not a choice between light and heat."[8] The great masters of Sufism have preached different paths: Junayd and Ibn 'Arabī turned to metaphysical knowledge, while Hallāj and Rūmī turned instead to the intoxication of love. However, throughout the history of Sufism a certain balance has been maintained between these

---

[6] A divine saying, uttered by the Prophet, in which God speaks in the first person.

[7] Qushayrī, *Risāla*, p. 327.

[8] M. Chodkiewicz, *Le Sceau des saints* (Paris, 1986), p. 63. (English edition: *Seal of the Saints: Prophethood and Sainthood in the Doctrine of Ibn 'Arabi* [Islamic Texts Society, 1993].)

two ways, on both the individual and collective levels. The path of knowledge can be placed beneath the banner of the divine "Majesty" (*jalāl*), and the path of love beneath the banner of "Beauty" (*jamāl*). According to Islamic tradition, both are reabsorbed within the divine "Perfection" (*kamāl*).

Who is the Sufi?

The word "Sufism," which first appeared in the nineteen century, is a translation of the Arabic word *tasawwuf*, which refers to the action of being *sūfī*, or, rather, of striving for *tasawwuf*. According to most writers on spirituality, the essence of the term *sūfī* is too subtle for it to have an established and unambiguous etymology. Among the meanings which they propose, two are linguistically plausible, as well as being complementary.

The first is both intangible and more accepted than the other. It is derived from the Arabic verb *sūfiya*, "it was purified." "He whom love has purified is merely 'pure' [*sāfī*], but he whom the Beloved has purified is *sūfī*."[9] Qushayrī, one of the great authors of Sufism, cites a scriptural source for this quest for purity (*safā*'): "There is no longer purity in this world," said the Prophet. "Only stains remain. From now on, death is a gift for Muslims."[10] The major goal of Sufism is to return man to his original purity, to the state in which he was not yet separated from the spiritual world.

The Sufi is thus the perfect initiate, the *yogī* of the Hindu tradition, the being who has succeeded in climbing back up the arc of divine manifestation and who has "reached God" (*wāsil*). According to one of Rūmī's images, he has transformed the copper from which man was made into gold. He acts as a "spiritual hero" (*fatā*), because few people affiliated with Sufism achieve this supra-individual state. One thus distinguishes the *sūfī*, the "realized" man, from the *mutasawwif*, the aspirant who still undergoes the tribulations of the Path and who makes an effort through spiritual discipline to reach the state of the *sūfī*. During the first centuries of Islam, shaykhs seldom called themselves *sūfīs*, so much did this word presuppose the existence of extraordinary qualities. The Iranian master Kharaqānī (d. 1033) "was in the almshouse with forty dervishes one day. They had not had anything to eat for a week. A stranger knocked on the door. He had brought a bag of flour and a sheep. 'I have brought this for the Sufis!' the man shouted. Having heard the news, the Shaykh declared 'Let anyone who claims to be a Sufi accept them! As for me I do not have the audacity to make a mockery of Sufism.' All tongues

---

[9] Hujwirī, *Kashf al-mahjūb*, p. 230.

[10] *Risāla*, p. 279.

were silent, and the man departed with his flour and his sheep."[11]

According to the second etymology, the word *sūfī* was derived from the word *sūf*, wool. The Prophet used to suggest that his disciples wear patched woolen robes as a sign of spiritual poverty (*faqr*). "Wear wool," he is reported to have said. "In your heart you will feel the gentleness of the faith" (Hākim). This positive aspect of *faqr* is based on a Koranic verse: "O ye men, ye are the poor in your relation to God, whereas He is the All-sufficient, He, the Owner of Praise" (Koran 35:15); it consists of "ridding oneself of everything but God."[12] Even up to the present day, the followers of an initiatory way are often called *fuqarā'*, the "poor in God." As did the prophets who preceded him, Muhammad wore clothing of wool,[13] and his Companions would have followed his example with the same concern for humility. The first ascetics of Iraq were criticized for wearing wool clothing, as well as for their inclination to self-mortification, supposedly because the Christian monks of that time and place shared these practices. It is possible that the term *sūfī* was used in Arabia even before the advent of Islam.[14] The Umayyad caliph Mu'āwiya (d. 680) is said to have used it to describe an ascetic of his times,[15] and this practice was confirmed at the time of Hasan Basrī (d. 728). It is the case that since the earliest days of Islam, wool has symbolized purity: a disciple of Basrī, Mālik Ibn Dīnār (d. 744), declared himself unworthy to wear wool clothing because he had not yet reached the state of inner purity. From Kufa and Basra (Bassora), where the first Iraqi Sufis lived, the term *sūfī* was passed on to the Abbasid capital, Baghdad, where in the ninth century a school of spirituality was called *tasawwuf*, "the fact of clothing oneself with wool." Summarizing the close bond that links the two meanings mentioned above, a master of this school defined the *sūfī* as "one who has covered his purity with wool."[16]

A Reality without a Name

Many Muslims are suspicious of Sufism for the sole reason that the terms *sūfī* and *tasawwuf* are not found in the Koran and may not have existed during

---

[11] Kharaqānī, *Paroles d'un soufi*, presented and translated from the Persian by C. Tortel (Paris, 1998), p. 91.

[12] According to Shiblī, quoted in the *'Awārif al-ma'ārif* of Suhrawardī (Beirut, 1983), p. 53.

[13] According to his servant, Anas Ibn Mālik.

[14] See for example Sarrāj, *Luma'* (Leyden, 1914), p. 22.

[15] M. Z. Ibrāhīm, *Usūl al-wusūl* (Cairo, 1995), p. 321.

[16] Kalābādhī, *Traité de soufisme* (Paris, 1981), p. 29. (English edition: *The Doctrine of the Sufis*, translated by A. J. Arberry [Cambridge University Press, 1977].)

the lifetime of the Prophet. In their eyes, it is a question of a "blameworthy innovation." Ibn Khaldūn, who himself was not a Sufi, replied that at the time of the Prophet it was not necessary to give a particular name to Islam's interior path. The new religion was then being lived in its fullness, the exoteric along with the esoteric, because the Companions of Muhammad were witnessing the model of "realized" man in the Prophet. This spiritual companionship (*suhba*) was able to concentrate within itself all of the spiritual benefit that the Prophet's entourage drew from him. In this proximity to the luminous prophetic source, terminology and doctrine didn't have a place. A shaykh of the tenth century stated that "Sufism once [at the time of the Prophet] was a reality without a name; it is now a name without a reality."[17] For Shiblī, who was one of the great masters of Baghdad and one who loved a paradox, the fact that Sufis had been given a name resulted from their having fouled their egos. If they had been really "transparent," devoid of their own attributes, no name could have been attributed to them.

The doctrine and terminology of *tasawwuf* took on their essential form in the ninth century, during the time of the "collecting" or "codification" (*tadwīn*) of Islamic doctrine, which from then on was formed into different sciences. These (i.e. the "fundamentals of law," the "fundamentals of religion," "comparative law," "terminology of *hadīth*," and "Koranic commentary") did not exist during the time of the Prophet any more so than did "Sufism." The term *salafī* designates modern Muslims who claim to be like the first believers (*salāf*); the modern *salafīs* reject all later doctrinal, and especially mystical, contributions. The term itself emerged over the course of centuries and does not have any greater claim to scriptural support than "Sufism."[18] It is therefore incumbent upon contemporary Muslims to remember to bring to Sufism a respect similar to the one that they show for the other disciplines of Islam.

The Science of Spiritual States[19]

If Sufism does have a place within the domain of Islamic sciences, this doesn't mean that it has lost any of its individual character. Because its

---

[17] Hujwirī, *Kashf al-mahjūb*.

[18] This observation summarizes the thinking of some Sufi shaykhs, but also of some contemporary Muslim scholars.

[19] Translator's Note: This is an opportune point at which to examine the term "science" used throughout this book. The French word "science," along with its Arabic equivalent, can be used to designate the English word "science" in the sense of an area of study undertaken with empirical or scientific rigor. However, in these other two languages, the same term also designates an individual's knowledge, or a body of knowledge that we may not consider entirely "scientific" in modern English usage, with Sufism being the most pertinent example. It might

essence is subtle, it has been called since its beginnings the "knowledge of hearts" or the "knowledge of spiritual states" as opposed to the formal disciplines such as the law. Being the "knowledge of the inner" (*'ilm al-bātin*), as opposed to exoteric knowledge (*'ilm al-zāhir*), it proposes an alternative and paradoxical explanation of the world, which most often is incomprehensible to exoterists. The Prophet Moses, representing the Law, experiences this at his own expense when he meets Khadir, the enigmatic character who appears to some saints in order to initiate them.[20] Following his example, Sufis are content with making "allusion" (*ishāra*) to the spiritual realities to which they have access.

Sufism distinguishes itself once again by its *supra-rational*—not *irrational*—character, whereas theology and law rely on discursive reason and dialectical thought. Sufis do not reject the other disciplines of Islam, but they use them as a springboard, explaining that the word *'aql*, which means "reason" or mind, also means "shackle." Because the spiritual world does not obey the laws of duality, it is indeed by the union of opposites that the Sufi realizes the divine Oneness.

The Sufi method of investigating spiritual realities rests on inspiration and "unveiling." The works of Ibn 'Arabī, along with the orisons and poems of many other masters, are considered to be inspired directly by God or indirectly by the Prophet. We must here distinguish inspiration (*ilhām*) from revelation (*wahy*), which only prophets receive, even if Sufis do consider the former to be heir to the latter. As for "unveiling" (*kashf*), it is for Sufis the principal mode of access to the supra-sensible world. As the fruit of an exacting discipline, it permits the raising of the veils that the world of the senses (*mulk*) throws over man, thus allowing him to reach the world of the spirit (*malakūt*), or even the world of the Divine (*jabarūt*). Often described as a bolt of lightning that illuminates the consciousness and fixes itself upon the latter through its intense flashing and clarity, this "unveiling" leads to the vision of certainty (*yaqīn*) and to the direct perception (*'iyān*) of spiritual realities, which evaporates the doubt associated with the speculative sciences. It has its foundation particularly in Koranic verse 50:22: "You were heedless of this; now have We removed from you your veil, and piercing is your vision this day." Ghazzālī (d. 1111) was the first to insist on "unveiling" as a method of cognition but it has reappeared so frequently in *tasawwuf* that one

be noted that this fuller definition of "science" can include ways of systematically coming to know or grasp things which escape the limits of simply rational thought. We have sometimes translated the term "science" as either "knowledge," or "science," or "skill," according to the varying contexts.

[20] See the Koran 18:65-82.

can speak of it as "Sufi epistemology."[21]

The knowledge bestowed by divine Grace (*al-'ilm al-wahbī*) eludes the usual operations of reason. It distinguishes itself from knowledge acquired through individual effort (*al-'ilm al-kasbī*), and can by this fact come upon an unlettered, simple farmer or craftsman because he knows nothing of the pretensions and the ratiocinations peculiar to many humans. In Sufism, these unlettered people figure among the greatest saints. *Tasawwuf* has also been defined, notably by Ibn Khaldūn, as "the knowledge that comes directly from God" (*al-'ilm al-ladunī*), in reference to verse 18:65: "We taught him [Khadir] a knowledge [emanating] from Us."

Even in its most speculative dimension, Sufism cannot be reduced to a theoretical philosophy. The aspirant can, of course, derive more benefit from his master's presence than from the reading of any mystical treatise. Sufism is above all a matter of "tasting" (*dhawq*). When one of his disciples informed him that some criticized Sufism because it didn't depend on argumentation, Ibn 'Arabī gave him this answer: "If someone enjoins you to prove the existence of the 'knowledge of divine secrets,' demand that they in turn prove the smoothness of honey. He will answer you that this is a question of a knowledge derived through taste. Reply to them that it is the same for Sufism."[22] It is in that same sense that one must understand this Sufi adage: "Only the one who has tasted knows." Sufism is a path of awakening, a path destined to develop the higher states of consciousness of being, starting with daily life, with the world of forms, and with rites.

The Initiatory Path

Though it is of an intuitive nature, the Sufi experience rests on rules and proven methods. Far from pertaining to some "natural mysticism," it depends upon an initiation. Under a master's direction, the aspirant follows an inward journey that must lead him to climb the ladder of the universal hierarchy of Being, just as the Prophet was carried at the time of his nocturnal Ascent (*mi'rāj*) up to the divine Presence.

This initiatory path proceeds from the Koran, which defines itself as a "guidance" (*hudā*). Beginning with the first *sūra*,[23] the *Fātiha*, the believer asks God to guide him on the "straight path" (*al-sirāt al-mustaqīm*). Sufis also frequently refer to this verse: "As for those who strive [spiritually] in Us, surely We shall guide them to Our paths: God is with those who search for

---

[21] A. Knysh, *Islamic Mysticism* (Leyden, 2000), p. 311.

[22] Ibn 'Arabī, *Tadbīrāt al-Ilahiyya* (Leyden, 1917), pp. 114-115.

[23] Translator's Note: A *sūra* is one of the 114 chapters of the Koran.

excellence" (Koran 29:69). To define the initiatory Path, masters use the geometric symbol of the circle. The circle represents the divine Law (*Sharī'a*). Most people remain within this limit all their lives, which is to say that they are content with an outer observance of the religion. Only some undertake the initiatory journey that will lead them to the center, where they have access to the inner Reality (*Haqīqa*) of the divine message and, beyond, of all manifested things.

"As many paths (*tarīqa;* pl. *turuq*) as [there are] sons of Adam":

One can travel a path toward the Real (*al-Haqq*),
God, from any authentic spiritual tradition.

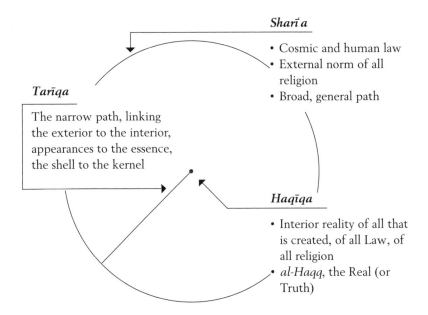

Sharī'a
- Cosmic and human law
- External norm of all religion
- Broad, general path

Tarīqa
The narrow path, linking the exterior to the interior, appearances to the essence, the shell to the kernel

Haqīqa
- Interior reality of all that is created, of all Law, of all religion
- *al-Haqq*, the Real (or Truth)

Etymologically, the terms *Sharī'a* and *Tarīqa* each mean "path." The *Sharī'a* is the "broad path," marked out by the prophets, which all Muslims must follow—it being understood that for Islam every kingdom and every community follows its own individual *Sharī'a*. The *Tarīqa* designates the "narrow path" to which only those who have some predisposition are called. It is the path of the Sufis and it is for this reason that they perceive themselves as the spiritual elite (*al-khāssa*). In this sense, they distinguish themselves from the commonality of believers (*al-'āmma*) who will only know God in the world beyond, after their death. Propelled by Love, the Sufis seek to know God in this world: through the "initiatory death" they anticipate that encounter.

Reality is immutable, but it is obvious that man can have access to It only while following the *Sharī'a*: in Islam as in all other traditions, it would not be possible to have authentic esoterism without exoterism. The symbol of the circle not only shows the intrinsic orthodoxy of Sufism in relation to the religion that is its support, but it also explains why Sufi masters see in Sufism the heart, the "kernel" of Islam.

As the Sufi progresses on the Way, he ascends a double ladder, one of "initiatory stations" (*maqām*; pl. *maqāmāt*) and one of "spiritual states" (*hāl*; pl. *ahwāl*). The former are the fruits of spiritual discipline (*mujāhada*), and once secured they stay that way for the one who has attained them; the latter are divine favors which are granted to the mystic without his having caused them and which therefore assume a fluctuating and elusive character. Through his spiritual work, the initiate can "master" this ephemeral state and can transform it into a "station," the goal being for him to dominate his *hāl* and not the other way around. Sufis assign to the term *maqām* this scriptural origin: "There is no one among us who hath not a designated station (*maqām*)" (Koran 37:164). The first to have suggested initiatory degrees, this one in ten stages, was Imam 'Alī,[24] but the formulation of the stations and states of the Way is more often attributed to Dhū l-Nūn Misrī (d. 859).

Among the stations are "repentance," "renunciation," "destitution before God," "endurance," and "contentment." Among the states are "desire for God," "love," "contemplation," "proximity to God," and "intimacy." Given the ambivalent nature of human consciousness, certain states or stations are presented in pairs which are at one and the same time opposites but also complementary: "the fear of God" is coupled with "hope" placed in Him, "constriction" with "dilation," etc. These classifications are just "broad outlines," as René Guénon reminds us,[25] because the number and the order of the stations and states vary considerably from one author to another. Some Sufis are able to make out "one thousand stations" or "innumerable stations." The initiatory Path, indeed, is not exempt from optical illusions: "Every time that I thought I had come to the end of the Path," confesses Abū Yazīd al-Bistāmī, "it was made known to me that this was the beginning of it."[26] In the same way, what one Sufi defines as a "station" can be considered a "state" by

---

[24] Sarrāj, *Luma'*, p. 130.

[25] *Initiation et realisation spirituelle* (Paris, 1980), p. 195. (English edition: *Initiation and Spiritual Realization* [Sophia Perennis, 2004].)

[26] Sulamī, *Tis'a Kutub* (Beirut, 1993), p. 381.

another. Therefore, it is necessary to take a nuanced view of the opposition between these two forms because they are, in fact, interdependent. Ansārī Harawī groups the two together under the term "dwelling places" (*manāzil*). When the Sufi reaches a certain initiatory degree, he is freed from duality; for him "there is no longer state nor station."[27] When touching upon this subject, Ibn 'Arabī speaks of "non-station" (*lā maqām*), which is within the domain of divine grace alone.[28]

In a more immediate way, all masters emphasize the sincerity and purity of intention (*sidq, ikhlās*) required of the aspirant. The latter will have to track down within the recesses of his soul any traces of self-satisfaction toward himself and toward the works of devotion that he accomplishes. The difficulty resides in the fact that until he reaches a certain level of contemplation, he perceives himself as adoring God, as being sincere, etc. To get out of this labyrinth he must endeavor to subdue the soul's fixation upon itself.

To this end, the aspirant will first have to practice "trusting self-abandonment in God" (*tawakkul*), a major station and a cardinal virtue. He will thus perceive that it is God who "wants" (*murīd*) His servant to come closer to Him. Whatever may be the asceticism to which he gives himself over, whatever may be his degree of spiritual aspiration, the disciple must never forget that first he "is wanted" by God (*murād*), and that it is love alone that provides him with energy.[29] Within this relationship, two complementary paths exist: the "traveler" (*sālik*) progresses in a conscious way, while the one "overjoyed in God" (*majdhūb*), is drawn into Him and traverses the path as though lit by flashes of lightning, or as if he were distanced from himself. The *majdhūb* is generally considered to be inferior to the *sālik* because he rarely has the capacity to help others to accomplish this journey. It is the role of the spiritual guide to let the novice share in the guide's own experience.

Goals of the Sufi

According to their various spiritual experiences, Sufis assign several goals to their discipline. Fundamentally, the Sufi wants to react against the spiritual degeneration that has affected humanity—and therefore himself as well—since the creation of the world. While following the initiatory Path, he recovers the state of "union" that was his in the spiritual world, and at every moment he renews the Pact (*mīthāq*) sealed between God and man before

---

[27] Ibn 'Abbād, *Al-Rasā'il al-Kubrā* (Fes, 1902), letter no. 14.

[28] *Futūhāt Makkiyya*, cited by D. Gril in *Les Voies d'Allah* (Paris, 1996), p. 100.

[29] Cheikh Khaled Bentounès, *Le Soufisme, coeur de l'islam* (Paris, 1996), p. 72.

man's incarnation on earth.[30] More conscious than others of this contract, the Sufi attempts to regain his initial purity while fighting against bodily and worldly attachments.

For this purpose, the Koran and the Prophet frequently put the believer on guard against the snares that his carnal soul (*nafs*) sets for him. Echoing the Prophet's words, "Man's fiercest enemy is the carnal soul that lies hidden within him," one of the earliest masters defined Sufism as a discipline "leaving no part for the ego." This is the basis of the "greater holy war" (*al-jihād al-akbar*) extolled by the Prophet and of the different forms of struggle against the passions of the soul to which Sufis have dedicated themselves throughout the centuries.

— *Purifying the Soul.* Sufis agree on the necessity of devoting oneself to the purification of the soul (*tazkiyat an-nafs*), which is the only way that can bring about the emergence of a noble character (*khuluq*) and the proper inward and outward attitude (*adab*) in a human being. In doing this their intention is to follow the model of the Prophet: "Surely thou art endowed with a tremendous character (*khuluq*)," says the Koran addressing the Prophet (68:4). The noble virtues (*akhlāq*, pl. of *khuluq*) that Sufis endeavor to acquire are therefore the same as those of Islam, but Sufis give them particular weight by bringing them to life within themselves; thus these virtues are transmuted into initiatory stations. This type of Sufism, it goes without saying, has been accepted by most of the *ulama*.[31] In this perspective, it represents one of the three parts of the religion, along with the dogma ('*aqīda*) and the Law (*Sharī'a*). He who travels the Path would not try therefore to experiment with supernatural phenomena but would try instead to ascertain the truth of the Law and to perfect his submissiveness to God.

— *Knowing God.* Other Sufis, going further, considered purification to be just a means and not an end in itself, since its goal is to arrive at the knowledge of God in order to better worship Him. "They have not appreciated God equal to His true measure" (Koran 6:91). According to Qushayrī, this

---

[30] See the Koran 7:172.

[31] Translator's Note: We use the simplified spelling *ulama* here for the term '*ulamā'*. It is the plural of the Arabic term '*ālim*, meaning "scholar." Thus, the *ulama* are Islamic scholars who might specialize in law, theology, philosophy, Koranic interpretation, etc. The word is used extensively throughout the book, so it is important to understand that the root form of the term refers to knowledge; thus, *ulama* refers in general to the body of learned people within the Islamic community who have acquired or been granted knowledge, for which they are usually held in high esteem.

verse means "They did not know God in His true measure." The doctrinal seeds of "knowledge," of gnosis (*ma'rifa*), are present in the first masters, and it may be that it is necessary to see in this the beginning of a Neoplatonic influence which would later provide Sufism with conceptual tools. According to Ma'rūf al-Karkhī (d. 815), who was regarded as the founder of the Sufi school of Baghdad, Sufism consists in "seizing upon Divine Realities (*haqā'iq*) and forsaking all that comes from creatures (*khalā'iq*)." During this same period, al-Bistāmī affirms that the "knower," the gnostic, "flies towards God, while the ascetic only walks," and Ruwaym says that "the hypocrisy of gnostics is better than the sincerity of aspirants [who aspire only to purification]."[32] Knowledge is a mirror, adds Ruwaym, in which the gnostic sees God revealing Himself. Dhū l-Nūn insists on this direct grasping of God: "How did you (come to) know your Lord?" someone asked him. "I knew my Lord through Himself."[33]

Inspiration and unveiling are indispensable for he who wants to clear a path towards this God who appears as "the Light of the heavens and the earth" (Koran 24:35). All Sufis have, therefore, sought to make room in themselves for the "radiation" (*tajallī*) of this light. Unblocking human nature from its opacity, just as the sun drives away darkness,[34] this theophany[35] reveals God to the heart of man. As-Sarrāj observes that the simple believer sees by the light of God, while the gnostic sees by God Himself.[36] Later, Ibn 'Arabī would explain how multiplicity is spread from its start in Oneness through a succession of uninterrupted theophanies that take innumerable forms. The Sufi thus sees God in all being, in every manifested thing. *Unlike the ascetic, he does not reject the world, because to him it is illuminated by the divine Presence.* "Beings were not created so that you would see them, but so that you would see their Master in them," said Ibn 'Atā' Allāh.[37] Again and again the Koran encourages man to decipher the "signs" (*āyāt*), to contemplate God by contemplating His Manifestation. "We shall show them Our signs in the universe and in themselves until they see that it is the Truth [God]" (Koran 41:53).

---

[32] Qushayrī, *Risāla*, pp. 315-316.

[33] Ibid., p. 315.

[34] See Koran 92:2.

[35] Translator's Note: A "theophany" is a visible or perceptible manifestation of God within creation.

[36] *Luma'*, p. 41.

[37] *La Sagesse des maîtres soufis*, translated from the Arabic (to French) by É. Geoffroy (Paris, 1998), p. 51.

— *Union with God, or "Extinguishing Oneself" in Him?* The ultimate goal of the mystical life cannot be to know God but to be united with Him. However, in Islam one cannot speak of a *via unitiva* in the same sense as in Christian theology. From the point of view of the central dogma of *tawhīd*, which focuses only on "the divine Oneness," the very concept of "union" with God is eminently paradoxical. Indeed, union presumes the coming together of two entities, of two substances. Now, the profession of faith (*shahāda*) of Islam affirms: "There is no god but God." For the Sufi, this negative assertion actually means: "Only God is," since that which is created, the contingent, vanishes in the face of the Absolute.

Thus, the Sufi doesn't live in a state of union, strictly speaking, since in Islam there is no continuity of substance between God and creation. His goal is "extinction in God" (*fanā'*). Removed from the various temptations of the world, the initiate then knows the intoxication of immersion in the divine Presence. Being completely unaware of himself as subject-consciousness, he becomes a mirror in which God contemplates Himself. One can illustrate this state, which is accompanied by a temporary withdrawal from the perceptible world, by an example:

> One day Junayd was at home with his wife when Shiblī entered. His wife wished to veil herself again, but Junayd told her: "He is not aware of your presence, remain as you are." Junayd spoke for a moment with Shiblī, and the latter began weeping. Junayd then said to his wife: "Veil yourself now, for Shiblī has just come out of his state of being absent."[38]

This state paradoxically opens up the horizons of Knowledge, for man can only have access to divine realities when his ego no longer interposes itself in his contemplation, that is to say when divine Being shows through in him.[39]

This experience of extinction in God, which is the essential paradigm of the mystical life in Islam, transmutes the exoteric "testimony" (*shahāda*) of Islam into contemplation (*mushāhada*). It was validated by exoteric scholars, who saw in it the inward realization of the fundamental dogma of the divine Oneness. However, *fanā'* was interpreted by Sufis in a variety of ways. Cultivating the paradox, some, upon coming out of their ecstasy, let it be thought that they had really been experiencing union with God (*ittihād*) or,

---

[38] Junayd, *Enseignement spirituel*, translated by R. Deladrière (Paris, 1983), p. 197.

[39] See, for example, Ansārī, *Chemin de Dieu*, translated by S. de Laugier of Beaurecueil (Paris, 1985), p. 120; Ibn 'Arabī, *Le Livre de l'extinction dans la contemplation*, translated by M. Vâlsan (Paris, 1984), pp. 48-49.

worse in the eyes of Islam, the incarnation of God in themselves (*hulūl*). This is not, however, what they would profess on the dogmatic plane in their moments of lucidity. The jurists of Islam obviously didn't take such nuances into consideration.

— *Dying to Oneself, and Living Again Through Him.* In order to react against the slippery slope created by the "intoxicated" mystics, other Sufis, called "temperate," emphasized that in the ecstatic state of *fanā'* man always had to keep a glimmer of lucidity, especially as this state, being paroxysmal but still transient, was only the prelude to a more complete experience, that of *baqā'*: having burnt away his individual attributes, the initiate "subsists" henceforth in and by God so that it is the divine Attributes that now act in him. According to a *hadīth qudsī* frequently cited by Sufis, God becomes "the ear with which he hears, the sight through which he sees, the hand with which he grasps, and the foot with which he walks." In the first phase, the one of *fanā'*, a person doesn't see anything outside of God; in the second, the one of *baqā'*, he sees Him in everything. After the intoxication of immersion in God comes the soberness that allows the initiate to be with God and with the world at the same time. Letting God do with him as He will, he achieves ontological servitude (*'ubūdiyya*) while at the same time putting himself at the service of men.

This double experience of *fanā'/baqā'* is so essential in Sufism that Junayd thought that it is this experience alone which defines it. "*Tasawwuf*," he said, "is summed up thus: the Real [or, the 'Truth,' i.e. God] makes you die to yourself, and causes you to come alive again through Him."[40] This theme is the transposition onto a mystical plane of the Koranic verse: "All that is on [earth] is passing away (*fān-in*). There remains (*yabqā*) but the Countenance of your Lord of Majesty and Munificence" (Koran 55:26-27). The initiatory death, as implied by the experience of *fanā'/baqā'*, is a response to the Prophet's injunction: "Die before dying!" Specifically, it is inscribed in the example of Muhammad, he who was "sent" among men to guide them.

Extending the dogma of the divine Oneness and the spiritual "tasting" of *fanā'*, some Sufis explained that God is One in the sense that He alone possesses Being: in manifesting creatures, He endowed them with an existence emanating from His Being, but this has only an ontological content that is at best relative, or even non-existent. Many exoteric scholars have fought against this metaphysical formulation, which is known as the "oneness of Being" (*wahdat al-wujūd*) because it has seemed to them to deny divine transcendence.

---

[40] Qushayrī, *Risāla*, p. 280.

For all those that travel the path of Sufism, purification is therefore an obligatory part of the passage: the initiate must consider the murky depths of his ego simply as a darkness that is stopping him from receiving the light of gnosis or from being united with the divine. Similarly, for the men and women who follow *tasawwuf*, they aspire to live Islam fully, in all its dimensions, and not only by adhering to its dogma or law. In no case can Sufism be assimilated into some other mysticism or into some other esoterism that is either similar or dissimilar to Islam. If some Sufis, in reaction to the authoritarian formalism of jurists, have adopted oppositional and provocative attitudes, they have always remained—except for some notable "deviations"—within the sphere of Islam.

Bibliography

Many definitions of "Sufism" are found in the manuals in Arabic of Sufism that we have cited. Only two manuals have been translated into French (Translator: Only English editions are given below):

Kalābādhī, *Doctrine of the Sufis*, translated by A. J. Arberry (New York, 1977).

Hujwirī, *Kashf al-Mahjub* (titled *Revelation of the Mystery*), translated by Reynold A. Nicholson (Pir Press, 1999).

See also:

Titus Burckhardt, *Introduction to Sufi Doctrine* (World Wisdom, 2008).

René Guénon, *Insights into Islamic Esoterism and Taoism* (Sophia Perennis, 2004).

DIVERSITY IN SUFISM

A Rich Pallet of Spiritual Types

"Water takes its color from the color of its container."[41] By means of this rather roundabout saying, Junayd, the great Sufi of Baghdad, especially wanted to show that there are multiple paths into Sufism. Indeed, according to a Sufi proverb, "There exist as many paths leading to God as there are sons of Adam." Thus, each person progresses on the *Tarīqa* according to his own predispositions. In the tenth century, Sarrāj explained this diversity by citing the following saying of the Prophet: "The divergences between [Muslim] scholars are a source of mercy." Sarrāj applied this to those "learned in inwardness," meaning the Sufis. Each Sufi may speak according to the spiritual degree which he has attained (i.e., according to the sum of his experience at a given moment), but all will profit from this exchange.[42]

---

[41] Ibid., p. 316.

[42] *Luma'*, p. 107.

This tendency to pluralism is related to the Islamic principle of "divergence" (*khilāf*), which is particularly evident in Islamic law. Far from blurring differences, the first authors of manuals on Sufism (tenth-eleventh centuries) readily highlighted them because they illustrated the richness and the subtlety of Sufi experience. Thus, it will be seen that Sufis may not always agree on the terminology of their doctrines and that they sometimes even disagree on theological points.[43]

These early authors very quickly formulated several prototypes of spiritual life; these were, most often, in the form of pairings of opposites: intoxication/sobriety; renunciation of the world/adopting it (the better to transcend it); "learned" mystic/"illiterate" mystic, etc. Some authors further distinguished between the "renunciate" or ascetic (*zahid*), the "poor in God" (*faqīr*), the "blameworthy man" (*malāmatī*), and the *sūfī* properly so-called. In the eleventh century, Hujwirī refined this classification and enumerated twelve Sufi schools according to the specific spiritual qualities of their masters, or according to the doctrines which they espoused: for example, Bistāmī exemplified spiritual intoxication, Junayd clear-headedness, Muhāsibī the acceptance of destiny, Hakim Tirmidhī sanctity, Kharrāz *fanā'/baqā'*, and so on.[44] The future initiatory paths, or "brotherhoods," would later also be drawn to a particular spiritual temperament over others. The manuals also distinguish between the one who is "traveling" (*sālik*) and the one "entranced by God" (*majdhūb*). The former, we have seen, traverses the Way propelled by *his* own will, or at least he believes that he does so: According to the words of a Persian master, he "volunteers to follow the divine Will." As for the second, God has attracted him through His Will.

Sufi masters also specified several degrees along the scale of holiness. Indeed, for Sufis the world is governed by the saints (*awliyā'*). Within a hierarchical system, each saint has functions that correspond to his spiritual degree: the Pole of the saints (*qutb*) is surrounded by two associates (*imāms*); further below are the four pillars (*awtād*), then seven—or forty, according to different authors—surrogates (*abdāl*), etc. Thus, there would be a hundred and twenty-four thousand saints, which is the same as the number of prophets known to humanity. When one of them dies, he is replaced at once by another saint of the category below his own.

In this hierarchy, only the Pole has an intimate knowledge of all the spiritual abodes. A simple initiate thus is not necessarily able to recognize the authority of those who are superior to him and who have reached a

---

[43] Ibid., p. 212; Kalābādhī, *Traité de soufisme*, pp. 38-46.

[44] *Kashf al-mahjūb*, pp. 403-508.

level of "realization" which he has not been able to reach. Some Sufis think that they have reached the height of holiness because they minimize or are unaware of the spiritual realization of other initiates: "If Abū Yazīd [Bistāmī] were among us," said Shiblī a century after the death of that saint, "he would learn his Islam from one of our novices!"[45] Many declarations of this kind are sprinkled throughout the history of Sufism.

This variety of spiritual behaviors can also be explained by some basic points of Sufi doctrines. The doctrines of prophetic heritage (*wirātha*) first appeared among the earliest Sufi authors and were later more fully articulated by Ibn 'Arabī. According to these doctrines, Muslim saints receive the spiritual heritage of past prophets, starting with the Prophet Muhammad, who recapitulated and encompassed all of the previous prophetic types. Thus, a Muslim saint will be "noetic" (i.e., gifted in intellectual perception) "Abraham-like," "Moses-like," or "Christ-like," with such an identification being temporary or permanent. This heritage acts like a kind of "genetic inheritance" which "imprints itself upon the behavior, the characteristic virtues, and the charisma of the *walī* ("saint") in specific and visible ways."[46] When inheriting the spiritual characteristics of a prophet in this way, the degree of holiness of the "heir" corresponds to the rank of the prophet: For example, some were simply a "prophet" (*nabī*), while others were a "messenger" (*rasūl*) who brought a new law or a message to all of humanity.[47] Sufism has thus known Moses-like saints who, like the Prophet Moses coming down from Mount Sinai, veiled their faces so that the intense light which streamed from them would not blind or kill those who saw them.[48] There have also been "Christ-like" saints who would have had the ability to resurrect people from the dead, as Jesus did.

The doctrine of the "theophany of the divine Names" (*tajallī al-asmā'*) and of their manifestation in created beings, which was developed by Ibn

---

[45] *Luma'*, p. 397.

[46] M. Chodkiewicz, *Le Sceau des saints*, pp. 96-97.

[47] Translator's Note: This is an important distinction within Islam itself, not just in Sufism. A "prophet" is someone who communicates in a more or less direct way with the divine realm and then communicates this to a group of people, most often without any resulting addition to a scripture. A "messenger" is of a more elevated station in that he both communicates with the Divine and then is charged with instituting religious changes in his own community or in larger groups according to the revelation which has been entrusted to him. In the case of the Prophet-Messenger Muhammad, he was the conduit for the revelation of a scripture, the Koran, which would found a new religion. Obviously, the number of prophets far outnumbers the number of messengers. It should also be noted that Muslims believe that many of prophets were found in all periods and places in pre-Islamic history, not just in Arabia.

[48] Ibid., pp. 95-96, 106.

'Arabī and by other masters as well, provides another explanation of the diversity of spiritual temperaments. It is known that in Islam God makes Himself known to men through His Names, of which the canonical number is ninety-nine. The number of these is actually infinite, since created beings are so numerous. However, they all are contained in the Name of the Essence, *Allāh*. They each have the function of being an "isthmus," that is, a place of exchange between the Named and man, each Name being for the human being a "personal lord" who gives him access to the Divinity. For example, the person to whom God appears as the "Apparent One" (*al-Zāhir*) will not be like the person upon whom the Name the "Interior" (*al-Bātin*) has been bestowed.

Sufi Literature

The diversity of Sufism also comes from the contrast between an ethical kind of Sufism ("to acquire the noble Koranic and prophetic virtues") and a theosophic or metaphysical kind of Sufism based not only on scriptural sources but also on Neoplatonic and gnostic doctrines. Between these two well-defined levels, there is room for a whole range of intermediate possibilities.

This gradation is easily found in Sufi literature. Authors like 'Abd al-Qādir Jīlānī and 'Umar Suhrawardī refuse to touch on any metaphysical dimension in their work, preferring instead to concentrate on the practical aspects of the Path. They believed that esoteric teaching can only be done orally, because it is intended for a restricted circle of disciples. They base their thinking on *hadīths* (reports of the Prophet's words and actions) which warn against unwarranted esoterism: "Speak to men according to their degree of understanding. Would you want God and His Prophet to be contradicted?" (Bukhārī).[49]

Certain Sufi authors gave way to moralism and sentimental pietism, perhaps through prudence, or simply through conformism. It is this kind of writing which the metaphysician Frithjof Schuon (d. 1998) had in mind when he spoke about "average Sufism" or "mitigated esoterism."[50] The concessions to exoterism here are too significant for one to be able to use the term *tasawwuf*. Some, too concerned with "legalizing" Sufism, have trivialized the terminology by robbing it of any esoteric or initiatory content. The

---

[49] Translator's Note: As mentioned in Dr. Geoffroy's preface above, the name in parenthesis following the *hadīth* refers to the transmitter, in this case Bukhārī, who was one of the major early scholars to collect and verify the authenticity of prophetic statements.

[50] *Le Soufisme, voile et quintessence* (Paris, 1980), p. 110. (English edition: *Sufism: Veil and Quintessence, A New Translation with Selected Letters* [World Wisdom, 2006].)

trend of *zuhd* ("renunciation of the world," "asceticism"), which preceded Sufism historically, has in fact been kept alive through a kind of religiosity that is colored by spiritual virtues and includes explorations of a theosophical nature. Strictly speaking, this kind of religiosity has touched the mosque-going public, whom preachers have targeted, more so than Sufis. On the other hand, metaphysicians such as Yaḥyā Suhrawardī and Ibn Sabʿīn have always been marginalized within Sufism. The case of Ibn ʿArabī, however, is different. Drawing extensively upon the heritage of Sufism, his work gave further depth to some Sufi doctrines, which then was redistributed to later Sufism, introducing into it a vein of esoterism.

This "average Sufism" is undoubtedly found in the manuals of Sufism of the tenth and eleventh centuries. These cast the doctrines of the earliest masters in such a way as to have them conform to Sunni orthodoxy, following the adventure of Hallāj. For all that, these manuals did not put an end to allusive, illuminist, or even paradoxical dimensions of Sufism, but they did tend to codify them. One then saw treatises of "codes of conduct" multiplying, intended for the increasing number of people who felt called to the practice of *tasawwuf*. These expressions of average Sufism were enhanced by the work of Ghazzālī (d. 1111), who reconciled Sunni pietism with Neoplatonic metaphysics. Then, starting in the thirteenth century, they were replaced by the literature of the great initiatory paths (in particular the Kubrawiyya, Shādhiliyya, Khalwatiyya or Naqshbandiyya Sufi orders), which disseminated their teachings to varying degrees. Intended primarily for disciples on the path, the aim of these teachings was initiatory and practice-based, but they can be applied at various levels; the esoteric doctrines were prudently distilled into them in order not to offend the ordinary people who sometimes listened in on the lessons of a shaykh, as well as not to attract the attention of censors.

The golden age of Sufi literature was in the thirteenth century. It was during this time that the great doctrinal works of prose were written, but also mystical poetry, short initiatory treatises, manuals concerning the rules of life, collections of aphorisms, devotional texts, historical dictionaries including the mystical life, hagiographic accounts of saints' lives, etc. Many masters, however, did not write a single text on Sufism—some of whom were, in any case, illiterate—either because they had not received the "unveiling of expression" (*kashf al-ʿibāra*) or quite simply because they thought that written formulations of the doctrines can be obstacles to the immediate apprehending of spiritual realities. The many genres of Sufi literature illustrate the diversity of mystical experience in Islam. A tendency to develop models also emerged: for example, Junayd representing "sobriety" and Hallāj "intoxication"; however, these states are often experienced one after the other by the same person, thus producing not one model but several models. If these are not given life from within, they degenerate into stereotypes; this is particularly true in the spiritual realm, where routine can have a corrosive effect.

Inward Alchemy

What relations did Sufism maintain with the occult sciences, including some rather varied disciplines (e.g., astrology, alchemy, talismans, "science of letters,"[51] as well as endless methods of divination)? The Sufi masters accepted the validity of some of them, but feared that they might be corrupted for magical purposes. As regards sciences such as alchemy or the esoteric science of letters (*'ilm al-hurūf*), confusion can indeed arise around their purposes and levels of practice: the latter one stays situated at the psychic level if the disciple gets involved in a mentality of magic, while it becomes spiritual if his intention is initiatory. This is why masters have insisted on an inner alchemy which "transmutes" the heart and not matter; for example, Ibn 'Arabī took an oath never to use the power of letters for purposes of divination.[52]

Throughout history, Sufis have often involved themselves in such activities, especially in the Turco-Persian world or in Morocco. Today, along the outer edges of the Muslim world, particularly in areas where there are animistic tendencies, the mentality of magic and its applications (e.g., possession, divination, geomancy, protection through talismans, etc.) are still very much alive. This is rejected by some Sufis, for whom God is the only real Agent in this world. Shamanism, for example, is far from having disappeared among Turkish populations from the steppes of Turkestan to the Anatolian plateau, and one might speak of a "Sufized shamanism."[53] One is here a thousand leagues, obviously, from the policed mysticism of the cities of the Arab world in particular. Furthermore, the Islamic brotherhoods continue to play a crucial mediating role between local customs and Arab Islam in Black Africa.

---

[51] Translator's Note: The "science of letters" mentioned here refers to an esoteric study in Islam similar to the numerology applied to the Kabala or to similar disciplines in other traditions. In its Islamic form, numerical values are assigned to Arabic letters, which are then used in various ways to reveal meanings hidden in scriptures, etc. The usage most distasteful to the majority of Sufi masters has been in divination, in the foretelling of future events. It is not surprising that such a study would attract practitioners within Islam, which is a religion founded on the miracle and the power of the Word of God embedded in the Koran.

[52] On Ibn 'Arabī's work concerning the science of letters, see the chapter of D. Gril in *Les Illuminations de La Mecque* (Paris, 1988), pp. 385-487.

[53] T. Zarcone, "Le brame du saint. De la prouesse du chamane au miracle du Sufi," in *Miracle et karāma. Hagiographies médiévales comparées* (Paris, 2000), p. 416.

The pluralism of Sufism is also illustrated in the various relations with the Law which Sufis have maintained: the approach to the Law taken by some may appear disconcerting, but it can also appear to be quite genuine. This is illustrated by the many debates which have taken place in the Sufi world around questions of (a) initiatory techniques (e.g., should one practice the invocation, the *dhikr*, aloud or in a lowered voice? Is it spiritually advantageous to spend time listening to song and music?); (b) the orthodoxy of Ibn 'Arabī and the doctrines of the "oneness of Being"; (c) relations with other religions (from a complete openness based on shared metaphysics, to an exclusion based on denominational incompatibilities), etc. If today Sufism is to a great extent the inheritor of the spiritual humanism and universalism of Islam, there is also a "fundamentalist" Sufism, which has arisen as a reaction to the materialism of the West. Given all these variations, we might wonder if there is anything in common between, for example, the self-restraint of a mystic partaking of the doctrines of the elite and the gatherings held in certain popular brotherhoods, or between a solidly Sunni Sufi scholar and a local dervish intoxicated with mystical rapture and perhaps a little hashish. . . .

Ultimately, if Sufism offers multiple paths, it is because Sufism emanates from Islam, which itself has multiple aspects. Just as there is no supreme authority in Islam equivalent to the pope, there is no singular spiritual authority in Sufism: Ibn 'Arabī was called the "Great Master" (*al-Shaykh al-Akbar*) by only some Sufis, and his work remains controversial; Jalāl al-Dīn Rūmī was regarded as another pole of Islamic spirituality, even though this was very often the cause for rivalry between their respective disciples. This kind of situation, no doubt, inspired the following saying of Ruwaym, which has been repeated over the centuries by several masters: "The Sufis will continue to do well as long as they have divergent positions."[54]

Bibliography

Frithjof Schuon, *Sufism: Veil and Quintessence A New Translation with Selected Letters* (Bloomington, 2007) (concerning the various levels of Sufi literature).

SUFISM AND SHI'ISM

Doctrinal Affinities

Not all Islamic spirituality and esoterism is represented by Sufism. Shi'ism (the "party of 'Alī"), which is followed by approximately ten percent of today's Muslims, appeared from the beginning as a movement in which political claims and esoteric doctrines co-mingled in support of each other. This alliance crumbled when established Shi'ite powers, such as the Safa-

---

[54] Qushayrī, *Risāla*, p. 282.

vids, emerged. From that time on, the exoterist Shi'ite clergy has shown itself to be as intolerant towards mystics as the Sunni "jurists."

Therefore, one could not compare Shi'ism and its various currents in time and space to pure gnosis, as Henry Corbin suggested. Like any religion, Shi'ism is intransigent in regard to its dogmas, with its clerical hierarchy imposing its norms, its common religious practices and, of course, its esoterism. Although it is a minority within Islam, it is much more divided than Sunnism since there are many groups within it which are considered by Shī'as themselves to be "heterodox"; many of these center on Twelver Shi'ism, which was the state religion in Iran at the beginning of the sixteenth century. Imam 'Alī had had to draw back from some of his disciples who were so dedicated to him as to divinize him; this tendency to the deification of a human being, proscribed in Islam, was a recurrent situation among certain Shi'ites known as "extremists" (*ghulāt*). Furthermore, there is in common Shi'ism a taste for "passion" and a morbid mournfulness, neither of which is very compatible with the idea of gnosis; in the actual experience of Sunni Muslims, it is rather the prevailing legalism and the weight of customs which are the obstacles to knowledge.

Basically, Sufism and Shi'ism share in the same Muhammadian inheritance which is transmitted through esoteric teachings. Most of the initiatory chains (*silsila*) of the Sufi orders pass through 'Alī, but Sunnis also look to this saying of the Prophet: "I am the city of knowledge, and 'Alī is the door" (Tabarānī). Thus it is not surprising that throughout the centuries the Imams Ja'far Sādiq, Mūsā Kāzim, and 'Alī Ridā, who were descendants of 'Alī, should act as spiritual masters to Sufi masters such as Bishr, Bistāmī, and Ma'rūf Karkhī, and that the latter should in turn appear in the initiatory chains of the Sufi orders. Ja'far Sādiq, especially, has been recognized by all as a spiritual authority, particularly in the field of esoteric interpretation of the Koran. Doctrinal and initiatory affinities between Sufism and Shi'ism are undeniable, especially the idea that the cycle of "initiatory sainthood" (*walāya*) is the successor to that of prophecy (*nubuwwa*), which guarantees the ever-living presence of an esoteric path in Islam.

Shi'ites detect in these affinities an influence of their own doctrines on Sufism, influences which Sufis generally deny. In doing this, Sufis call upon the early origins of their esoterism and their initiatory attachment to the family of the Prophet. The investiture of the "cloak" (*khirqa*), which was practiced for a long time in Sufism, actually has as its source the gesture of the Prophet covering 'Alī, Fātima, and their children Hasan and Husayn with his cloak. But the Prophet was no more "Shi'ite" that he was "Sunni," and Shi'ites are not the only ones to venerate the family of the Prophet (*ahl al-bayt*).[55] In turn, some of the *ulama* and Sunni thinkers thought that they detected elements of crypto-Shi'ism in Sufism. Thus, Ibn Khaldūn thought that the *khirqa* was borrowed from the Shi'ite tradition; the concept of the "spiritual Pole" (*qutb*) of Sufism also seemed to have much in common with the Shi'ite concept of the Imam, the inner guide for faithful Shi'ites who is himself the pole of the universe. Again, according to Ibn Khaldūn, the propensity of some Sufis to proclaim themselves to be the *Mahdī* (the "Rightly-Guided," a figure who was descended from the Prophet and who must come at the end of time to fight against the Antichrist in order to prepare for the return of Christ on earth) was due to the influence of Shi'ism.

In fact, primitive Shi'ism and Sufism drew from the same source and were therefore influenced by parallel experiences. The influence of the Andalusian Ibn 'Arabī was very clearly absorbed into Shi'ite gnosis, helping, for example, to fashion the Shi'ite doctrine of *walāya*. Imam Khomeini himself admitted to this influence.[56] The main character in the spread of Ibn 'Arabī's ideas throughout the Shi'ite world was Sadr al-Dīn Qūnawī (d. 1273), Ibn 'Arabī's son-in-law and disciple, who was linked chiefly to the Iranian philosopher Nāsir al-Dīn Tūsī. In the wake of this, an osmosis developed between Sufism and Shi'ite gnosis. Thus, for Haydar Amolī, a spiritual Twelver Shi'ite who lived in Baghdad at the end of the fourteenth century, every true Sufi is a Shi'ite, and every true Shi'ite is a Sufi; he exhorted the two groups to recognize each other in the same way.

Some Sufi initiatory paths (*tarīqa*) in Iran were developing at the same time, and these would eventually slip into Shi'ism. In general, Iranian Sufism has fluctuated between Sunnism and Shi'ism for the reason that their identities have not always been sharply defined. One example concerns the Ismā'īlis, a branch of Shi'ism that is characterized by a pronounced esoterism. During a time when they were being pursued by the Sunni authorities, some of them went underground and joined Sufi *tarīqas*. And then there is the Bektashi brotherhood in Turkey: their dogmas have fluctuated a great deal, and Sufis have generally considered them to be heterodox.

Two Rival Esoterisms

In spite of their doctrinal affinities, Sufism and esoteric Shi'ism have

---

[55] Sunnis, whether they be Sufis or not, usually have a dim view of Mu'āwiya, who usurped the power of 'Alī, and of his Umayyad successors, who persecuted the Shi'ite imams; they were no less "Sunni" for this criticism since their doctrine, too, referred to the *Sunna* of the Prophet.

[56] C. Bonaud, *L'Imam Khomeyni, un gnostique méconnu du xx`siècle* (Paris, 1997).

through the centuries had relations that have been far from idyllic. There has generally been an incompatibility between these two forms of esoterism, precisely because they are so close to each other. The founding masters of Sufi orders were frequently descendants of the Prophet themselves, which demonstrates that it is not the prerogative of the Shi'ites alone to be related to the Prophet through 'Alī. The differences in perspective lie above all within the respective models themselves: Sufis venerate 'Alī and the Shi'ite Imams for being members of the family of the Prophet and for their great spirituality, but their ultimate reference point is Muhammad. In the tenth century, Hallāj himself, whose activities appeared rather confused to many Sunnis, did not leave any ambiguity on this point: the Prophet is *the* guide. Later, Ghazzālī, writing against the Ismā'īlis, would emphasize that same axiom. As for Ibn 'Arabī, the scholar of Islam Henry Corbin would arrive at the conclusion that he had been greatly influenced by Iranian gnosis;[57] however, Ibn 'Arabī made some rather harsh comments about Shi'ites and demonstrated his attachment to Sunni Islam on several occasions.[58] In addition, his Shi'ite disciples admitted that there were insurmountable doctrinal divergences between them and him, which appears to be altogether logical.

Sufis, who often were part of the Sunni *ulama*, generally expressed animosity toward Shi'ites and even approved the execution of Shi'ite "extremists," whose heterodoxy was made much of here and there in various reports. Since approximately the eleventh century (i.e., since Shi'ism began to pose a political danger to Sunnism), most Sufi orders came to the aid of Sunni regimes in their fight against Shi'ites. In the thirteenth century, Shi'ites were accused of having made a pact with the Mongols, who were then pouring into all of the Muslim east. Only a few Persian and Turkish brotherhoods refrained from the anti-Shi'ite mood. This was very much the case with the Naqshbandiyya order, which is especially widespread throughout the eastern territories of Islam and is thus in geographical contact with various forms of Shi'ism.

For their part, the Shi'ites were not to be outdone. They believed that the sole source of authority is the Imam, who alone possesses the power to interpret texts and to intercede (with God) for the faithful. Any other source

---

[57] H. Corbin, *En islam iranien*, p. 156. Henry Corbin considered it to be a "disequilibrium" that Sufis believe the Prophet to be the sole source of the "charisma" which Shi'ites, on the other hand, divide up between the Prophet and their Imam. (*La Méthode spirituelle d'un maître du soufisme iranien, Nur Ali-Shah*, by M. de Miras [Paris, 1973], preface, pp. 9-10).

[58] M. Chodkiewicz, *Le Sceau des saints*, p. 191; C. Addas, *Ibn 'Arabī ou la quête du soufre rouge* (Paris, 1989), p. 281. (English edition: *Quest for the Red Sulphur: The Life of Ibn Arabi* [Islamic Texts Society, 1993].)

of authority, such as that of a Sufi master, is therefore seen as a usurpation. It is for this reason that the Shiʿite clergy, contrary to the general attitude, have usually condemned not only Sufism, but also philosophy. The Sunni *ulama,* on the other hand, have rejected Sufism because of the relativism that it has seemed to them to introduce into the Revelation. Shiʿite communities have, in general, been reluctant to be in close contact with Sufis. In the twelfth century under the Ayyubids, when establishments for Sufis were created in Aleppo, the Shiʿites became worried: they considered the Sufis to be "idle people" and denounced them as "spies."[59]

Everywhere that Shiʿism became politically established, Sufism ended up by being either suppressed or pursued. This was the case in Fatimid Egypt, and even more so in Safavid Iran. The founder of the Safavid dynasty, Shāh Ismāʿil (fourteenth century), banned the term *tasawwuf* in favor of the term *ʿirfān* ("gnosis") and followed this up by tracking down Sufis and destroying the mausoleums of several of their saints. His successors continued the same policy, obliging the Iranian Sufi orders to emigrate. The attacks against Sufism also came from Persian Shiʿite theosophists such as Mullā Sadrā, who in the seventeenth century readopted the doctrines of Ibn ʿArabī but rejected any other form of Sufism. The Iranian dervishes of this time were often lax and eccentric, and so they did give a very misleading impression of *tasawwuf.* By stigmatizing the "Sufis," the theosophists were also trying to avoid the attacks of the Shiʿite exoterist clergy upon themselves. Still today, certain Iranian Shiʿites hold the term *tasawwuf* under suspicion, and the Islamic Republic of Iran regularly persecuted Sufis. Some of them, such as S. H. Nasr and J. Nūrbakhsh, became exiles. However, interest in Sufi masters such as Ibn ʿArabī and Rūmī continues in current-day Iran.

Differences in religious sensibilities, the gap between their dogmas, and political interests (consider the ancient antagonism between the Ottomans, who were fervent defenders of Sufism, and the Safavids) were too important to both sides for the two forms of esoterism to merge. The traditional mistrust which characterized the relationship between Sufis and Shiʿites is currently becoming blurred within the framework of an ecumenism; the fact remains, however, that Sufism must be defined in principle, as it has been historically, as the mystical or esoteric dimension of Sunni Islam.

---

[59] A. M. Eddé, *La Principauté ayyoubide d'Alep* (Stuttgart, 1999), p. 426.

Bibliography

Mohammad Ali Amir-Moezzi, *Le Guide divin dans le shī'isme originel* (Lagrasse, 1992).

Henry Corbin, *En islam iranien*, vol. III (Paris, 1972). (English edition: *The Divine Guide in Early Shi'ism: The Sources of Esotericism in Islam* [State University of New York Press, 1994].

Seyyed Hossein Nasr, "Chi'isme et Sufisme", in *Essais sur le Sufisme* (Paris, 1980), pp. 145-169. (English edition: "Shi'ism and Sufism: Their Relationship in Essence and in History," in *Sufi Essays* [Kazi Publications, 1999].)

Thierry Zarcone, "L'Iran," in A. Popovic and G. Veinstein, *Les Voies d'Allah*, pp. 314-321.

THE ROLE OF THE FEMININE IN SUFISM

From its origins, Islam gave women a position that was incontestably better than that which was reserved for her in the other religions or societies of the time. One might want to recall that the Koran often distinguishes "Muslim women" from "Muslim men," and "believing women" from "believing men," in order to underscore the religious identity of women and their autonomy in their relation to the Divine. The Prophet lived with women all around him, and the love which he had for the fair sex must be interpreted above all on a metaphysical level, as Sufis have explained.

The old misogynist reflexes, however, quickly took over again after he died: Early on, male jurists limited the perspective which had been broadened by the Prophet. A number of women, however, made a place for themselves in Muslim society, particularly in the transmission of Islamic sciences: there were many who founded mosques or *madrasas*, and who taught Hadith or the law; more rarely, they led the prayers and preached sermons on Friday. Some were surrounded by an air of holiness, such as al-Sayyida Nafīsa (d. 824), a descendant of the Prophet who is still much venerated in Cairo. An expert in law and a remarkable contemplative, she was dubbed the "patron of those who give *fatwās* and on whom are bestowed supernatural powers" because of her complete knowledge of exoteric and esoteric sciences. She strongly impressed Imam Shāfi'ī, and Ibn Hajar attributed a hundred and fifty miracles to her.

The Eternal Feminine in Islamic Mysticism

Over the centuries, women often turned towards mysticism, where they could more easily experience some freedom, than towards exoteric sciences. Don't the various forms of spirituality involve what is known as "feminine intuition," which is in contrast to the rational religious sciences which suit men instead? Thus some suggest that Sufism would correspond to the "right brain functions" of human beings, among which is intuition, while exoteric Islam would correspond with "left brain functions," where cognition occurs.

The first ascetics and Sufis recognized the holiness of women. For example, Ibn Hanbal and Bishr Ḥāfī asked Amina Ramliyya to intercede for them, and Dhū l-Nūn Misrī considered Fātima of Nishapur his spiritual master. But it was especially Rābiʿa ʿAdawiyya (d. 801), who lived in Basra in Iraq, who marked the minds and spirits of people. She was that "witness of the love of God" whose golden legend even reached the ears of Saint Louis and his chronicler, Joinville.[60] In eleventh century Iran, women received initiation as well as men. Some fulfilled the function of spiritual master; one of them, it is said, had five hundred disciples from both men and women. Starting in the twelfth century, some *ribāts* (places dedicated to the contemplative life) which were reserved for women appeared in several Islamic urban centers.

Mystical poets of the time showed that they were very attuned to the female element of the divinity. In Arabic literature, Laylā incarnates the divine Lover, who initiates one into a higher and transcendent love. For Ibn al-Fārid, she designated God, who veils and unveils Himself at one and the same time to men. But there is also Salmā and many others. Rūmī saw in woman "a ray of the divine light" and perceived her as "more creator than created being." Ibn ʿArabī, an "Heir to Muhammad," underscored the spiritual stature of woman and her role in the contemplative life of male mystics. According to his doctrines, God, as the point of conjunction between opposites, contains the principles of both male and female, principles which take part equally in that cosmic union which is realized in any coupling, whether of plants, animals, humans, or other. Ibn ʿArabī even accords preeminence to the female element, which corresponds to the "primordial Nature" from which all forms of existence result. In his eyes, the contemplation of God through woman can be more perfectly realized than in any other support of divine Manifestation, and the love of woman is an integral part of the Muhammadian example. Rābiʿa was regarded as the "diadem of the men of God." What could such a statement signify? Ibn ʿArabī affirmed that spiritual "virility" (*rujūliyya*) is not connected to the human biological condition (and thus more to men): women have access to spiritual perfection, and thus to all the degrees of sanctity, including that of the Pole. That is why they can lead the prayer, according to Ibn ʿArabī; Mary (Maryam), the mother of Jesus, is the model for women in this respect, and some scholars or Sufis have accepted her function as that of a prophet (*nubuwwa*). The *Shaykh al-Akbar* counted two women among his masters in Andalusia. Of fifteen of his disciples whom he invested with the initiatory mantle (*khirqa*), fourteen were women, and he saw in Nizām, the young Persian woman who inspired him to write a col-

---

[60]   On Rābiʿa, see *infra*, pp. 68-69

lection of poems, a fully realized theophany.[61]

The Effects of the Male Ambience

It is not the privilege of all Sufis to have such an opening to the feminine element of spirituality. Throughout the centuries, average Sufism has often adapted itself to the ostracism of women who asserted themselves in Islamic culture. Women saints thus were generally marginalized, even being omitted from collections of accounts of saints, and women would sometimes be excluded from certain "orthodox" Sufi orders, which led them to take refuge in popular Sufism, which is more tolerant, and in the 'worship' of saints. Nowadays, many barriers have fallen, and a growing number of women play major roles in Sufism, giving spiritual direction to men and women, whether the place is Tunis, Beirut, Istanbul, or Delhi.

Bibliography

Nelly and Laroussi Amri, *Les Femmes soufies ou la passion de Dieu* (Saint-Jean-de-Braye, 1992).

Michel Chodkiewicz, "La sainteté féminine dans l'hagiographie islamique," in *Saints orientaux* (Paris, 1995), pp. 99-115.

Annemarie Schimmel, *Le Soufisme ou les dimensions mystiques de l'Islam* (Paris, 1996), pp. 518-531. (English edition: *Mystical Dimensions of Islam* [The University of North Carolina Press, 1975]. In particular, see Appendix 2, "The Feminine Element in Sufism.")

————. *Mon âme est une femme. La femme dans la pensée islamique* (Paris, 1998). (English edition: *My Soul Is a Woman: The Feminine in Islam* [The Continuum Publishing Company, 1997].)

SOME PREJUDICES REGARDING SUFISM

Prejudices towards Sufism are most often due to ignorance, but sometimes they are combined with intellectual dishonesty. Two of them seem to be particularly stubborn.

Sufism is a Kind of Quietism, and is the Egotistical Search for Individual Salvation

For about a century, this first prejudice has been the most frequent objection in the writings of certain Muslim reformists. They have forgotten that the great reformist thinkers of the past learned and borrowed ideas from Sufism and never disavowed it. From the point of view of history, their charge is not

---

[61] See *infra*, p. 92

valid. Although spiritual seekers of all religions withdraw more or less from the world for a while, the Sufi's vocation is to return among people and to put himself at the service of humanity. The Sufi is here following, as in the other aspects of his life, Muhammad's model of the contemplative engaged in the world.

The first Sufis specifically distanced themselves from Muslim "ascetics" who rejected the world. For centuries, Sufi initiatory paths have been very active in Muslim societies. Their members come from all social classes: a minister or a president (formerly an *emir* or a *sultan*), as well as a simple craftsman or peasant, or someone from the middle class or from the circle of the *ulama*, any might be in a Sufi order. Sufism was, and remains, a central reality within Islamic culture. Here are a few indications of Sufism's activities: Because of its flexibility, it was able to help a great deal in the spread of Islam, particularly in outlying areas such as the Balkans, the steppes of Central Asia, Black Africa, and Southeast Asia. In many cases, Sufis were merchants or businessmen. They also played their part in the defense of the territories of Islam as participants in the "lesser *jihād*"; in doing so, they kept the association between it and the "greater *jihād*," or the battle against the ego.[62] Some Sufi groups were celebrated for opposing European colonialism or Soviet, and even Chinese, imperialism.

Within Muslim societies, the influence of Sufi masters extended to several levels. Thus, the miracles that were attributed to them were almost always aimed at the community (e.g., cures, making food multiply, making money appear in order to donate it, etc.). In high demand by the population, shaykhs were privileged intercessors for the people with their leaders—sometimes to their own detriment. They arbitrated conflicts (between Muslims and Christians, for example). They had the responsibility of welcoming and accommodating travelers, including those on the fringe or excluded from society, in their *zāwiyas* (establishments for Sufis). They also often had the role of therapist (they took diseases onto themselves, cured madness, dealt with possession, etc.). This "pivotal role"[63] which they played, that of mediator between people and God and between people and temporal powers, does not mean that the shaykhs interfered in the direct relationships that Muslim believers maintained with the Divine, or worse, that they sought to "make themselves partners with God": the role involved channeling the spiritual

---

[62] See, for example, our *Jihād et Contemplation. Vie et enseignement d'un soufi au temps des croisades* (Paris, 2002) (re-edited).

[63] According to a formulation of the historian Peter Brown, which he had applied to late Antiquity (*The Cult of the Saints: Its Rise and Function in Latin Christianity* [University of Chicago Press, 1982]).

energies of individuals and, when it was needed, the fervor of the populace.

Some groups undoubtedly practiced these forms of community charity for propaganda purposes or to secure patronage or improved standing. It is also true that some acted like parasites and benefitted from the credulity of the people, especially in rural areas. But the great initiatory paths have always stressed the virtues of work: the aspirant must earn his living through ordinary means. Formerly, begging was a spiritual exercise aimed at self-examination and entrusting oneself to God; however, it was meant to last only for a while; some masters always opposed it, as well.

Sufis built, and still build, a number of mosques, hospitals, and old people's homes and, nowadays, centers for vocational training. In past centuries, they contributed to social cohesion by instituting certain religious celebrations and various celebrations of saints' days. To this day, such activities have encouraged most Muslim countries to lend unquestioning support to the social actions of the Sufis. These days, Sufis often take the initiative on cultural, artistic, and publishing projects, and are active in inter-faith dialogue. These examples prove that Sufis are people who are familiar with the realities of daily life and who are concerned with the problems of others, and are not isolated "mystics" immersed in a kind of spiritual self-centeredness.[64]

Sufism is a Popular Religion, Conceived as a Reaction to the Legalism of "Orthodox" Islam

This second common prejudice has the following history: In the early days of their path, Sufis were seen as a spiritual elite (*al-khāssa*) and as the successors to the prophets: the inspirations and the "unveilings" of which they were recipients came after the Revelation, which closed with the death of Muhammad. In spite of their initial reservations, many of the *ulama*, who fought against the incursion of Hellenistic rationalism into Islam, recognized the prophetic lineage and thus the orthodoxy of Sufism. Beginning in the twelfth century, Sufism was promoted as the "heart of Islam," and became the path of spiritual realization within the religion. But its success also led to a paradox: it was not only the clerics who participated in Sufism, but also broader sectors of the population. The "narrow path," previously limited to the heroes of the spiritual journey, became popularized. The recognition of Sufism made it possible for the doctrines and the common practices of Islam to be spiritualized, but a particular kind of *tasawwuf* evolved to include aspects of pietism; it generated and organized what from then on would be

---

[64] Some specific examples concerning the medieval Middle East can be found in our book *Soufisme en Égypte et en Syrie sous les derniers Mamelouks et les premiers Ottomans* (Damascus, 1995), pp. 109-119.

an increasingly popular religiosity, with all the excesses that this can entail. The prestige of shaykhs was great, and so it was tempting for pseudo-Sufis to benefit from this fact. From about the fifteenth century, several regions of the Muslim world experienced a cultural decline, and Sufism lost some of its eminence, as was the case for other areas of Islamic life, too.

Even so, some of the initiatory paths maintained their bearings and kept up their demanding spirituality. Some masters saw to the replacement of the "elders" whom they claimed to represent, deploring the degeneration which had befallen Sufism. Sufism, however, was often able to retain both its initiatory content and, following Ibn 'Arabī's school of thought, the loftiest metaphysics, which continued to be found in writings or oral teachings. But this kind of Sufism was more discrete, and so many outside observers were more captivated by the spectacular displays of some than with the quiet inner experiences of others. For example, it was Westerners who came up with the term "maraboutism" to designate the semi-magical, semi-spiritual charisma of some Maghribian[65] or African shaykhs. However, Sufi doctrine stresses the need for detachment for those who have received initiation: it must not be used to satisfy any worldly desires, even of a subtle nature, and could not be used to assist in obtaining "proceeds" for anyone.

Since the end of the nineteenth century, Sufism has been shaken up, first by reformist thought and then by the rapid social change that has confronted the entire Muslim world. It has gone through a purification from all of this, and believers now participate in it because of conviction, not mere custom. The elite of the *ulama* are still often connected to it. It would therefore be incorrect to describe Sufism as simply a free space which can be used as a counterbalance to the dryness of the Islamic religion. Historically, Sufism and Islam have found themselves and their doctrines in opposition to each other only when they misunderstood each other, or when there was a conflict of authority, with one criticizing the other in order to keep control of its own flock.

---

[65]   Translator's Note: The Maghreb (alt. Maghrib) is the Islamicized area of northwestern Africa, including such present-day countries as Morocco, Mauritania, Algeria, Tunisia, etc.

Chapter 2

SUFISM AND ISLAM

TWO NAMES FOR A SINGLE REALITY

The Fundamentally Koranic Character of Sufism

Sufism, conveyed by Islam, contributed through its many aspects to the broad perspective which had been opened by the Islamic concepts concerning prophets and prophecy. The new religion had immediately found itself transplanted into history, in the sense that it had established itself in lands where other religious or philosophical substrata had previously prevailed. Over several centuries, and sometimes lasting until our own times, these various substrata have been maintained by and have coexisted with Islam, whether they be Iranian Mazdeism, the Neoplatonism of Alexandria, or Eastern Christianity. At that same time, Islam came into contact with Hinduism and Buddhism along the eastern edge of its domain. As it expanded westward from Arabia, it found itself in the middle of the Old World and came into contact with the most diverse spiritual climates. One of the meanings of the following verse refers to this phenomenon: "We have made you a middle (also "midmost" or "intermediate") community" (Koran 2:143).

External influences thus intervened during the development of the new religion. Certain orientalists have too hastily deduced from this that Sufism was of foreign origin, that it was non-Islamic. They wondered how such a rich and universalistic spirituality could emanate from "the religion of Muhammad." These orientalists competed to find either a Christian source, or a Hindu source, or a Hellenistic source for Muslim mysticism. In a study published many years ago, and which remains a valuable reference, Louis Massignon (d. 1962) refuted these allegations one by one, highlighting the fundamentally Koranic character of Sufism. "It is from the Koran, constantly recited, contemplated, and practiced," he declared, "that the origin and development of Islamic mysticism springs forth."[1] In his famous thesis, *The Passion of Hallāj*, he recognized that "There are real seeds of mysticism within the Koran, seeds suitable for an autonomous development without any

---

[1] See Massignon's *Essai sur les origines du lexique technique de la mystique musulmane*, 3rd edition (Paris, 1999), p. 104. (English edition: *Essay on the Origins of the Technical Language of Islamic Mysticism* [University of Notre Dame Press, 1997].)

foreign insemination."[2]

Following this, Islamicists explored a great number of unpublished texts of Sufi literature and deepened their knowledge of the work of the masters: their work reaffirms the intuitions of Massignon and establishes, in one way or another, that Sufism is a major axis within Islam.[3] One of Massignon's students, Paul Nwyia, who provided solid foundations for the study of Islamic hermeneutics (i.e. the science of interpreting sacred texts, etc.), sought "to show, through the study of the earliest Muslim attractions to mysticism, how this interiorization of the Koranic vocabulary took place and how the technical lexicon of Sufism was gradually formed."[4] More recently, Michel Chodkiewicz investigated the essential relationship between the doctrines of Ibn 'Arabī (d. 1240) and the Koran. In *An Ocean Without Shore*, Chodkiewicz created a meticulous report showing that the Koran provided the structure for both the foundation and the framework of the great Andalusian's work.[5] One might thus conclude that this debate is over, particularly since the recurring polemics engendered by it are something of an "irritant," as Paul Nwyia noted. But some Islamicists still maintain that Sufism was the recipient of multiple foreign influences and to such an extent that nothing properly Islamic would remain in it.[6]

It is very likely and even logical that the philosophy of Philo of Alexandria (first century after Christ) or the Neoplatonism of Plotinus (third century after Christ) indirectly nourished Sufi metaphysics and cosmology, or that ascetic behavior was stimulated by the example of the Christian hermits, or that certain initiatory methods of eastern Sufism developed through contact with Indian yogis or Buddhist monks.[7] This heritage, it goes without saying, had to be assimilated without being openly acknowledged. Yahyā Suhrawardī (twelfth century), however, was condemned by the Sunni authorities specifically for having explicitly drawn from pre-Islamic Iranian sources.

---

[2] *Passion* (Paris, 1975) (new ed.), III, 21. (English edition: *The Passion of al-Hallāj*, four vols., Princeton University Press, 1982.)

[3] See, for example, M. Molé, *Les Mystiques musulmans* (Paris, 1965), p. 24; S. Trimingham, *The Sufi Orders* (Oxford, 1971), p. 2; A. Schimmel, *Mystical Dimensions of Islam* (Chapel Hill, 1975).

[4] *Exégèse coranique et langage mystique. Nouvel essai sur le lexique technique des mystiques musulmans* (re-edited in 1991), p. 13.

[5] *Un océan sans rivage: Ibn 'Arabī, le Livre et la Loi* (Paris, 1992). (English edition: *An Ocean Without Shore* [State University of New York Press, 1993].)

[6] See J. Baldick, *Mystical Islam* (London-New York, 1989).

[7] On the other hand, the supposed influence of Vedantic philosophy upon Abū Yazīd Bistāmī, advanced a few decades ago, is now generally called into question.

In return, Sufism influenced other mystics. Limiting ourselves just to the Hispanic world, the diffusion of the texts and methods of Sufism into the spiritual lives of medieval Andalusian Jews has been proven.[8] Perhaps through the intermediary of these Jewish mystics, St. John of the Cross may have been influenced by the Shādhilī spirituality of North Africa, and Saint Ignatius of Loyola's *Spiritual Exercises* may have been similarly inspired by Sufi initiatory disciplines.

One could find numerous examples of this cross-fertilization in either direction.[9] The speculation of such borrowings, however, does not add anything of great substance to the subject, particularly since these borrowings have often occurred quite late. In reality, analogies between the doctrines and practices of different traditions are traceable to factors common to the psychological and spiritual experiences of all human beings. Thus, "surprising affinities" that exist between Hinduism and Islam are due to the fact that "the two religions together share a similar vision of the major topics of metaphysics."[10] The reciprocal influences which have occurred over the centuries between these two spiritual traditions do not explain anything about their closeness regarding fundamental principles. The practice of the extinction of "ego" in the divine "Self," for example, represents a necessary passage within any initiatory process that leads a disciple to deliverance, enabling him to go beyond the consciousness of the ego. The Sufis have expressed it in terms of *fanā'*, the Hindus in terms of *nirvāna*, and Christian mystics have spoken of the "annihilation of the heart in God." Each spiritual seeker sees his practice within the mold of his own tradition, which gives him a particular orientation and "foretaste," but which accomplishes this according to prototypes that apply to all the "sons of Adam."

THE KORANIC MODEL

"To Combine One's Flesh and Blood with the Koran"

Junayd, the master from Baghdad (d. 911), stated: "Our science [i.e. Sufism] is intimately linked to the Koran and the model of Muhammad (*Sunna*)."[11]

---

[8] See O. and D. Maïmonide, *Deux Traités de mystique juive*, translated by P. Fenton (Lagrasse, 1987).

[9] P. Fenton, "Les traces d'Al-Hallāj, martyr mystique de l'islam, dans la tradition juive," *Annales islamologiques* 35, IFAO, Cairo, 2001, pp. 101-127: this article illustrates quite well the stamp of the Sufi of Baghdad upon Jewish mysticism.

[10] D. Shayegan, *Hindouisme et soufisme. Une lecture du "Confluent des Deux Océans"* (Paris, 1997), p. 20.

[11] Qushayrī, *Risāla*, p. 431.

One should not read into this statement a "petition of principle" (i.e. circular reasoning or begging the question), or a trick intended to divert the animosity of the "scholars of the Law," but a reality which is illustrated by the abundant mystical literature of Islam. It is obvious that the doctrinal treatises of the Sufi masters, just like the spiritual lessons that they give in mosques or other places, are nourished by the Koran and *Hadīth*. Sulamī points out that mystical knowledge can find a valid foundation only within the scriptural sources of Islam, because these are not prone to human deficiencies.

The legalism attributed to Islam does not come from the Koranic text, but rather from the development of a legal casuistry, which might be a legacy of the Semitic mentality: as it moved away from the light of the Koranic Revelation, the message of Islam, which was primarily spiritual, solidified into prescriptive language. Even so, the verses of the Koran which could properly be considered legalistic amount to just a few (between 4-6%).

The Koran is strewn with verses which have an obvious spiritual or esoteric dimension. "He [God] is with you wherever you are" (2:115); "We [God] are closer to him [man] that his jugular vein" (50: 16); "On the earth there are signs for those who have certain vision. . . . And within yourselves, do you not see?" (51: 20). In the *sūra* "The Cave," the superiority of mystical knowledge, "emanating directly from God" (*al 'ilm al-ladunī*) is affirmed in comparison with human thought.[12] The Koran also includes many parables. Sometimes, their meaning is intentionally enigmatic, and it is necessary to resort to exegesis. Thus, the celebrated "Verse of Light" (24:35) has been the subject of multiple interpretations, ranging from the most metaphysical (*The Niche for Lights* of al-Ghazzālī[13]) to the most scientist (some modernists have read within it the principle of electricity). All of these verses fed the meditations of Muslim mystics and simple believers alike. For them, the entirety of the Koran, even within its very letters, is Spirit, since it emanates directly from God. Whether it concerns stories of the prophets, moral precepts, eschatological warnings, or even legal regulations, each verse contains a divine "secret" (*sirr*). The believer perceives intuitively that the significance of each verse infinitely exceeds its obvious meaning, even if this does not allow easy access.

It is thus the entire texture of the Koran that provides the structure for the initiatory Path in Sufism. In the tenth century, Abū Tālib Makkī proposed that "The [Sufi] aspirant only deserves this appellation if he finds the

---

[12] See *infra*, p. 61.

[13] Translation of the *Mishkāt al-anwār*, by R. Deladrière (Paris, 1981). (English edition: *The Mishkat Al-Anwar* [*The Niche for Lights*] by al-Ghazzali, translated by W.H.T. Gairdner, various publishers and editions.)

goal of his aspiration within the Koran, deducing from it his own deficiencies and his sole recourse, which is in God."[14] All Sufis, certainly, do not fulfill this requirement, but they do tend to "combine their flesh and their blood with the Koran," according to the formula of Dhū l-Nūn Misrī. One example is Emir 'Abd al-Qādir: in his *Kitāb al-Mawāqif*, he had 372 spiritual "halts" inspired by Koranic verses, which he quoted as epigraphs.

The Sufi Travels His Path Through the Book

We saw that the *Tarīqa* has "stations" (*maqāmāt*) and "states" (*ahwāl*) marked out along its progress. In his *Luma'*, one of the major manuals of Sufism, Sarrāj (tenth century) established very explicitly that both of these are grounded in the Koran. From the beginning to the end of his initiatory journey, the Sufi thus walks "through the Book." For example, the station of "trusting surrender to God" (*tawakkul*) is based specifically on "Put your trust in God, if you are believers!" (Koran 5:23), the state of "proximity" (*qurb*) on "When My servants question you concerning Me, [say to them that] I am near" (2:186), and that of "love" (*mahabba*) on "God will soon bring men whom He will love and who will love Him" (5:54). The Koranic terms describing "stations" and "states" quickly became prototypes of the Path, templates which would form the mystical practices of Islam as well as Sufi terminology.

The Arabic root W-L-Y[15] found in the Koran is an important one, since it occurs 227 times there. It found great favor not only in Sufism, but also in all of medieval Islamic culture, which was imbued with mysticism. From this root with its multiple embedded meanings come the terms *walāya* ("holiness") and *walī* ("friend of God," "near to God": a saint). *Al-Walī* is a divine Name which establishes a relationship shared with all beings, yet only saints are conscious of it. Indeed, only saints reflect the divine *Walāya*, God's "support" for His creation, or the care He takes of it, from which the "proximity" between God and man arises. The saint is one "brought close" in the sense that he has been admitted into intimacy with the Divine. In the eyes of exoterists, this establishes a supposed competition between "saints" and prophets of Islam. This criticism initially cast a shadow over the doctrines of *walāya*, but they quickly gained recognition in Muslim societies.

Over the centuries, the meanings of certain Koranic terms thus grew richer through a great accumulation of doctrines, as masters and various mys-

---

[14] *Qūt al-qulūb* (Cairo, 1961), vol. I, p. 119.

[15] M. Chodkiewicz, *Le Sceau des saints*, pp. 34-39. (English edition: *The Seal of the Saints. Prophethood and Sainthood in the Doctrine of Ibn 'Arabi* [Islamic Texts Society, 1993].)

tical movements gave them a particular flavor and substance. In the eleventh century, Hujwirī characterized each of the twelve Sufi schools of his time through a doctrinal feature, generally drawn from Koranic terminology: thus, he associated the school of Tirmidhī with *walāya* or "proximity-holiness," that of Muhāsibī with *ridā* or "contentment," that of Sahl Tustarī with the battle against the passions of the ego, etc.[16]

One can follow the progress of a Koranic term through the time and space of Sufism. For example, from the Koranic point of view, *tawakkul,* or "trusting surrender to God," is without question a cardinal virtue; however, Sufis endow it with an ultimate meaning: it then refers to one who aspires to God but who no longer directs himself, depending instead on the divine Will (*isqāt al-tadbīr*). This theme, which can be found among the first masters (Dhū l-Nūn, Tirmidhī), became a major element of Shādhilī doctrine in the thirteenth century.[17] According to the Koran, *murāqaba,* or "constant vigilance," is exerted by God with regard to His creatures. This is also widely echoed by "sober" Sufis, who apply themselves to the practice of vigilance in their relationship with God. One could cite many such examples to show that the Koran nourished Sufi practice and shaped its expression.

A Multitude of Meanings: Sufi Exegesis

Sufis did not draw their terminology only from the Koran; they developed specific hermeneutics (i.e. methods of interpreting spiritual texts) which have taken their place among the disciplines of Koranic exegesis. In the languages of Revelations (Sanskrit, Hebrew, Arabic), certain terms have the ability to reflect increasingly higher realities, moving from the concrete to the universal. This is because the process of Revelation retraces that of manifestation, which also involves a multiplicity of degrees. The structure of sacred languages, which is "woven of symbolism, is able to transmit, through a series of resonances, meanings which extend from the world of man to the world of spirits and eternal ideas."[18] In this respect, a number of factors straightaway make a case for a reading of the Koran on many levels: the polysemy (i.e. the capacity for having multiple meanings) of the old Arab language, the underlying connections that the roots weave between

---

[16] Hujwirī, *Kashf al-mahjūb,* p. 403 *et seq.*

[17] One Shādhilī master, Ibn 'Atā' Allāh (d. 1309), even devoted a work to this: *Al-Tanwīr fi isqāt al-tadbīr,* translated by A. Penot under the title *De l'abandon de la volonté propre* (Lyon, 1997). (English edition: See *The Book of Illumination,* which includes *Kitab al-Tanwir fi Isqat al-Tadbir* [Fons Vitae, 2005].)

[18] J-L. Michon, *Le Soufi marocain Ahmad Ibn 'Ajība et son Miraj. Glossaire de la mystique musulmane* (Paris, 1973), p. 143.

themselves, and even the ambiguity of some of these roots. There should be no surprise, then, that with the changing of periods, sensibilities, and trends within Islam, different readings of the Book would be proposed. Here we should call upon the authority of the Prophet:

"Nobody reaches a true understanding of the Koran if he does not discover many 'aspects' (*wujūh*) within it" (reported by Suyūtī).

"The Koran has multiple 'aspects'; thus, read it while applying the best of these" (Ibn 'Abbās).

"Each verse has an outer meaning and an inner meaning; every letter has a boundary and every boundary has a point of ascension" (al-Hasan).

Concerning this profusion of meanings suggested by the Prophet, the Sufi method of awakening the intelligence is to try to confound human reason and to point out its weaknesses. Sahl Tustarī (d. 896) said, "[Even] if man received a thousand degrees of understanding for each letter of the Koran, this would not exhaust all the meanings which are contained in just one verse." The Word of God, he explains, is in the image of God Himself: Infinite and Uncreated; therefore, how could it be comprehended fully by man, who is an ephemeral creature?[19]

The Koran itself informs us that "no-one other than God knows its interpretation" (Koran 3:7). It follows then that man can achieve this only through divine inspiration, and not by reasoning. This is why the Koran shows the way, inviting man to a gradual comprehension of its language and terminology. For example, in the Koran, man can arrive at "certitude" (or "certain vision," *al-yaqīn*), in three progressive stages: from a kind of "knowledge" that is still outward (*'ilm al-yaqīn*), the initiate will pass to the "eye of certainty" (*'ayn al-yaqīn*), but then only the "reality of certainty" (*haqq al-yaqīn*) will give him access to certitude-knowledge. In the context of the Koran, these expressions do not have an expressly spiritual meaning, but they do lead to this. In mystical circles, the term *yaqīn* found in the Koran means the going beyond, or rather the flowering forth of faith. Following long inward effort, the initiate will have access to spiritual realities thanks to the progressive lifting of the veils which masked those realities: the "certain vision" is the fruit of this process which abolishes all duality between the contemplator and the Contemplated.

Thus, for a single term, the Koran inspires the layering of meanings to which corresponds a hierarchy of the levels of consciousness. These various meanings, it goes without saying, neither conflict with nor neutralize each other; they harmonize with and complement each other in an integrated knowledge. Sometimes, a single idea is referred to with different words, thus

---

[19] *Luma'*, p. 74.

bringing about a gradual deepening of the meaning. This is the case with the Heart, the spiritual center of man: in order of increasing inwardness, the *qalb*, an organ that is still physical, is transmuted into *fu'ād*, and then into *hubb*.[20] The progression, one will notice, generally is divided into threes, whether it is a question of the Koran, of the prophetic traditions, or of Sufi literature. The number three is the first to express multiplicity as an odd number, the latter always being preferred in Islam. This three-tiered hierarchy emanates from universal principles of metaphysics, such as the three degrees of human nature (body, heart, spirit), or those of universal manifestation (the sensible world, the intermediate world of spirits, and the world of divine Sovereignty).

Ja'far Sādiq (d. 765), a major spiritual figure in Islam and the sixth Shi'ite Imam, is one of the first to systematize the esoteric interpretation of the Koran and to apply the aforementioned hierarchy of meaning to the degree of understanding attained by people of the Revelation. Based on verse 35:32, where three categories of believers are mentioned, Sufis came to distinguish between ordinary believers (*al-'āmma*), the spiritual elite (*al-khāssa*), and the elite of the elite (*khāssat al-khāssa*). Only the latter attain a full understanding of the Koran, and reach the peak of each initiatory station. "Your degree of understanding of the Koran," warned Abū Sa'īd Kharrāz (d. 899), "depends on your degree of proximity to God."[21]

Thus, the Sufi interpretations of the Koran extend the Book's multiple levels of meaning, resulting in meanings which fit one within the next. This kind of interpretation follows several processes: First of all, there is *istinbāt*, a Koranic term (4:83) which means, in ordinary language, "the drawing of water from a well"; the Sufis perceive the need for bringing the hidden meaning of a verse to the surface. However, Sarrāj points out, mystics do not possess the sole privilege of *istinbāt*: because of the multiplicity of "aspects" contained in the Koranic text, both doctors of the Law and theologians "draw" meanings from it that conform to their own readings.[22]

Ishāra, "allusion" or "allusive intimation," plays a fundamental part from the Sufi point of view because it conveys all of the subtlety and the necessary

---

[20] Translator's Note: The first two are Arabic terms which are commonly translated by our word "heart." The first, *qalb*, is typically used in common speech and also refers to the physical organ. The next term, *fu'ād*, applies to the innermost heart, and is thus not at all physical. The final term in the hierarchy, *hubb*, means "love," telling us that the heart itself has been transcended and that there is a complete union of subject and object in undifferentiated "love."

[21] Ibid., p. 89.

[22] Ibid., p. 106.

keenness of perception required in this inward discipline. *'Ibāra*, or "explicit speech," is usually considered its antonym. The greatest masters never claimed that they were offering complete explanations which covered all of the dimensions of the Koran to some extent or other. They presented to a reader's consciousness "esoteric allusions," but this does not abrogate the literal reading of the Book, which imposes itself on these masters as much as on ordinary believers. They did not defy the outer meaning, but rather invited readers to discover the other meanings which a verse may conceal.[23] *Ishāra* is content to suggest meanings, to cause resonances at subtle levels of being.

The spiritual exegesis of the Koran is more generally known under the name of *ta'wīl* ("interpretation"), in contrast with *tafsīr*, the literal, grammatical, historical, or theological "explanation" of the Book. The term *ta'wīl* means "to restore the initial meaning to [the verse]," that is, to its true origin, or from its form to its essence. It would soon come to designate all "inner" (*bātinī*) commentaries of the Koran which were valued for their mystical, symbolical, or esoteric content. For Shi'is, the use of *ta'wīl* has constituted a fundamental scriptural principle ever since the beginning.

Let us give an example of esoteric interpretation, sometimes attributed to Ja'far Sādiq, sometimes to Abū Yazīd Bistāmī, and approved by later Sufis. "When kings enter a city, they corrupt it, and make poor wretches of its noblest inhabitants" (Koran 27:34). Over the apparent meaning of this verse another one is layered for Muslims of deeper spirituality: "When gnosis (*al-ma'rifa*) penetrates the heart of man, it expels or burns up all that is found there [i.e., passions and illusions that the ego maintains]."[24] Certain doctors of the Law, such as Ibn al-Jawzī, made a point of denouncing these interpretations as arbitrary; according to these scholars, they produced allegories which were not justified by the letter of the Koran.[25]

In any event, in his exegesis Ibn 'Arabī gives evidence of the most scrupulous attention to the letter, even to the form, of the divine discourse. Unlike some of his disciples—who are often indirect—he begins with the initial meanings, with the etymology of the Koranic terms, and he challenges the interpretations of symbolists.[26] Generally speaking, Sufis have warned against the meanderings of unrestrained spiritualistic interpretations, and they stipulate that no suggested reading should clash with the obvious meaning of the

---

[23] One modern reformist who is a specialist of exegesis agrees with this (A. Mérad, *L'Exégèse coranique* [Paris, 1998], p. 71).

[24] *Luma'*, p. 92.

[25] Ibn al-Jawzī, *Talbis Iblīs* (Cairo, n. d.), pp. 319-325.

[26] M. Chodkiewicz, *Un océan sans rivage*, p. 177.

text. They fear becoming like the *bātiniyya* (Ismailis, but also with other esoteric currents typically derived from Shi'ism), who give preference to the hidden meaning of the Book to the detriment of the literal meaning; in fact, these groups depend upon their hermeneutics in order to annul the external Law. Al-Ghazzālī used all his powers as a scholar in order to dissociate Sunni Sufism from such tendencies, and Ibn 'Arabī condemned the *bātiniyya* more than once in his work.[27]

The search for a balance between exoterism and esoterism, to which Sufi exegesis testifies, can be summarized in this saying from the Iraqi Sufi and scholar Alūsī (d. 1853), who was the author of a very complete commentary on the Koran: "He who claims to know the secrets of the Koran before having mastered the exoteric commentaries of the Book can be compared to one who claims to have reached the innermost part of a house without having passed through its door."[28]

The Hadīth Qudsī, *or "Divine Utterance"*

In Islam there is a scriptural category intermediate between the Koran and *Hadīth*. These are the "holy utterances" (*hadīth qudsī*) of divine origin; they were related by the Prophet himself and do not belong to the body of the Koranic Revelation. Moreover, the style of the speech is unlike that which dominates the Koran. As if in a tone of confidentiality, and most often in the first person, God addresses at times man in general, at other times He addresses His religious servants, and still at other times He addresses His elect.

In fact, some *hadīth qudsī* build a pedagogy of mysticism in which God takes the initiative to make the believer enter into His intimacy and His proximity. They reveal "truths which were not intended for the entire religious community, but only for the contemplatives."[29] Thus, throughout the centuries, these were a subject for contemplation by the Sufis, and they are among the most quoted scriptural texts. The one which is most loved by Muslim spiritual adepts is: "Whosoever shows hostility to one of My 'elect' [saints], I declare war upon him. My servant does not cease to approach Me by supererogatory works until I love him. And when I love him, I am his hearing by which he hears, his eyesight by which he sees, his hand with

---

[27]   C. Addas, *Ibn 'Arabī et le voyage sans retour* (Paris, 1996), p. 123. (English edition: *Ibn 'Arabi: The Voyage of No Return* [Islamic Texts Society, 2000].)

[28]   Al-Alūsī, *Tafsīr rūh al-ma ānī* (Beirut, 1987), vol. I, p. 7.

[29]   T. Burckhardt, *Introduction aux doctrines ésotériques de l'islam*, p. 43. (English edition: *Introduction to Sufi Doctrine* [World Wisdom, 2008].)

which he seizes, and his foot by which he walks" (Bukhārī). This *hadīth qudsī* is often cited among Sufis in order to account for an advanced spiritual state, a state of transparence to the divine Being, a state of total obliteration of the individual ego which is aware, from that point on, of being nothing but the instrument of the divine Might.[30]

Bibliography

Henry Corbin, *L'Imagination créatrice dans le soufisme d'Ibn 'Arabī* (Paris, 1958). (English edition: *Creative Imagination in the Sufism of Ibn 'Arabi* [Routledge, 2007].)

Eric Geoffroy, "Mystique," in *Dictionnaire du Coran* (Paris, 2007).

Denis Gril, "Exégèse mystique," in *Dictionnaire du Coran* (Paris, 2007).

Pierre Lory, *Les Commentaires ésotériques du Koran* (Paris, 1980).

THE MODEL OF MUHAMMAD

"Sufis are Those Who Follow the Path of the Messenger of God and Strive to Acquire His Noble Virtues."[31]

The message of Islam was revealed in order to be followed by men. The Koran, however, is a text that is packed with layers of meaning and it is often symbolical. It is not a guide that is explicit enough to cover all aspects of the lives of believers. The Prophet, whose "nature was that of the Koran itself" (according to his wife 'Aisha), was obviously the person best suited to embody this message, and consequently he was the best model for Muslims to follow. The Companions and the first generations which followed them thus were preoccupied with carefully recording not only his acts and words (*hadīth*), his personal qualities, his habits of daily living and his tastes, but they also noted his tacit approval of practices or customs and his reserve or silence on various matters. The "path" marked out by the Prophet thus makes up the second source of Islam: this is the *Sunna*, which draws its authority from the Koran itself: "Obey God and His Messenger" (3:132).

"You have in the Messenger of God a beautiful model" (Koran 33:21). Does this model require nothing more than an outer conformity to the teaching of the Prophet, or to a code of conduct, or to guidelines of hygiene, etc., or does it also include an inner dimension? The *Sunna* is not only an important legal reference point, which is what it is often understood to be;

---

[30] One can refer to the French translation of 101 *hadith qudsī* chosen by Ibn 'Arabī: *La Niche des Lumières*, trans. by M. Vâlsan (Paris, 1983).

[31] Suhrawardī, *'Awārif*, p. 229.

it also shapes the worldview and the spiritual personality of Muslims. They agree on the ethical value of the teaching of the Prophet who came, in his own words, "to bring noble characters to perfection." In several places the Koran introduces Muhammad as a messenger come to purify men.[32] But, in the hereafter, what is the true nature of the Prophet, which the Koran describes as "sublime" (68:4)? Muhammad referred specifically to this when he said: "I was already a prophet when Adam was between spirit and body"[33] (Tirmidhī). Sufis and Muslim spiritual adepts in general developed doctrines of the primacy and preeminence of the Prophet in relation to the whole of creation from such scriptural sources.

The Prophet as Primordial Light

The cosmos emanates from the Light of Muhammad (*al-nūr al-muhammadī*), the refraction of the divine Light. This light had progressed from one prophet to the next prophet until its final "incarnation" in the historical figure of Muhammad. It is reported that he said: "I am the first man to have been created, and the last to be sent [as a prophet]." Thus, metaphysical time ("the first man") shows itself to be a perspective which is the opposite of physical time ("the last to be sent"). This inversion appears clearly in the following verse: "When We concluded a covenant with the prophets, with *you*, with Noah, Abraham, Moses, and Jesus, son of Mary. . . . A solemn covenant! " (Koran 33:7).

Muslim spiritual figures interpreted several verses as allusions to the Light of Muhammad: "A light and a clear Book came to you from God" (5:15); "O Prophet, We have sent you as a witness, as a bearer of glad tidings, and as a warner, as one who summons unto God—by His leave–and as a lamp that illumines" (33:45-46). All creatures owe their existence to the *nūr muhammadī*, just as all the prophets of humanity have drawn their own light from it. In a famous prayer, Muhammad asks God to envelop him in light.[34]

This topic calls to mind the concept of the Christian Logos or the *avatāra* of Hinduism. But, here again, theories related to borrowings appear insufficient.[35] This is not a question of some doctrine which resulted from "devia-

---

[32] Koran 62:2, 2:129, 2:151, 3:164.

[33] Or, "I was already a prophet when Adam was still between water and clay," but this version is not recognized as authentic by all scholars.

[34] É. de Vitray-Meyerovitch, *Anthologie du soufisme* (Paris, 1978), p. 151.

[35] M. Chodkiewicz, *Le Sceau des saints*, p. 84. (English edition: *Seal of the Saints* [Islamic Texts Society, 1993].) In Chapter 4 of this work, the reader will find a comprehensive treatment of this question.

tions" occurring within Sufism, because the doctrine appeared as early as a disciple of Hasan Basrī (d. 728), and is implicit in the work of one of the first exegetes of the Koran, Muqātil (d. 767). According to Sahl Tustarī (d. 896), who made the doctrine explicit, the *nūr muhammadī* has a dimension that is cosmic but also mystical, since this "light" establishes a link between God and man: "The primordial Muhammad represents the crystal which draws the divine light upon itself, absorbs it into its core, projects it unto mankind in the Qur'ānic scripture, and enlightens the soul of mystic man."[36] Indeed, those Sufis who apply themselves to the spiritual retreat (*khalwa*) are able to experience the inner vision of the *nūr muhammadī* in one form or another.

The Reality of Muhammad, Mediator between the Divine and Human Realms

The subject of the "Light of Muhammad" was quickly integrated into the broader doctrines of the "Reality of Muhammad" (*al-haqīqa al-muhammadiyya*), of which Muhammad is the final and perfect historical manifestation. "The prophets who were sent one after the other to mankind are each intermittent and fragmentary manifestations of the 'Reality of Muhammad,' which is deployed integrally only in the person of Muhammad, whose Revelation embraces and completes those which preceded it."[37] The earliest masters alluded to this esoteric dimension of the Prophet which escapes common understanding. "That which created beings are able to grasp of the reality of the Prophet," affirmed Abū Yazīd Bistāmī, "is comparable to the drops of water which seep out of a full water-bag," meaning, that it amounts to very little indeed.[38] Al-Hallāj believed that only Abū Bakr al-Siddīq, who was very close to the Prophet and was the first caliph of Islam, perceived this reality.[39] The doctrine of the Reality of Muhammad spread into the mystical literature of Islam starting in the thirteenth century. It found its formal expression in the work of Ibn 'Arabī (d. 1240) and successive representatives of his school.

The Reality of Muhammad is an essential metaphysical principle which acts as a mediator between the divine and human spheres, and it consequently takes various forms. It is particularly identified with the "universal Man" (*al-insān al-kāmil*), i.e., the Prophet considered not in his human in-

---

[36] G. Böwering, *The Mystical Vision of Existence in Classical Islam* (Berlin-New York, 1980), p. 264.

[37] C. Addas, *Ibn 'Arabī et le voyage sans retour*, p. 26.

[38] Al-Kalābādhī, *al-Ta'arruf* (Damascus, 1986), p. 70.

[39] See his *Kitāb al-Tawāsīn* (Paris, n. d.), p. 3.

dividuality, but as the "image of God" (*nuskhat al-Haqq*) in creation. "He who sees me sees God," the Prophet was reported to have said (Muslim). In the Akbarian school of thought, i.e., the one connected to the *Shaykh al-Akbar*, Ibn 'Arabī, the Reality of Muhammad is thus the mirror of God; from this standpoint, Muhammad has divine attributes such as the First and the Last, the Manifest and the Hidden, and so on. In the fifteenth century, 'Abd al-Karīm al-Jīlī on several occasions revisited this assertion in his work and, more recently, Emir 'Abd al-Qādir (d. 1883), who was buried near Ibn 'Arabī in Damascus, showed himself to be very daring on this point. In his spiritual summation entitled the *Book of the Halts* (*Kitāb al-Mawāqif*), the latter practically identifies *al-Haqq* (God) with the *haqīqa muhammadiyya.*[40] Such doctrines, however, alarmed the learned doctors of Islam, for whom the fact of "associating" somebody or something with God (*shirk*) constitutes the most serious sin of all.

Thus, it is necessary to distinguish between the early formulation of the "Light" of the Prophet, which has solid support in the scriptures (the Koran and especially in *hadīths*), and his metaphysical extension as a "Reality," which is less likely to be grasped by the average person. Thus, during a time when the Ismailis were attributing the source of light first and foremost to the Shi'ite Imam, and the philosophers to the Prime Intellect, al-Ghazzālī (eleventh century) was basing his doctrines on the *nūr muhammadī* in order to highlight the cosmic preeminence of the Prophet: in his *Niche for Lights* (*Mishkāt al-anwār*),[41] he called upon these doctrines to reinforce Sunnism— i.e. fidelity to the *Sunna*—which had been disrupted by various dissidents. In the opinion of Ibn Taymiyya, too, the *nūr muhammadī* assisted the cause of Sunnism because it confirms the preexistence of Muhammad; he stipulated, however, that the Prophet was created of clay, not of light.[42]

The further one progresses through the medieval period, the more the esoteric dimension of the Prophet appears in general works, which were read by a rather large audience. The Egyptian Suyūṭī (d. 1505), who was thought of as an authority on various Islamic sciences during his lifetime, addressed this reality many times in his work, in which he quoted this *hadīth qudsī*:

---

[40] *Le Livre des Haltes*, translation by M. Lagarde (Leyden, 2000), vol. I, particularly pp. 241-256, 290-294.

[41] Translated by R. Deladrière (Paris, 1981). See also the "Book of the Noble Attributes of Prophecy," attributes inherited by the Prophet, in *al-Ihyā' 'ulūm al-dīn* by the same al-Ghazzālī.

[42] Ibn Taymiyya, *Fiqh al-tasawwuf* (Beirut, 1993), pp. 62-65; M. al-Tablāwī, *Al-Tasawwuf fī turāth Ibn Taymiyya* (Cairo, 1984), pp. 218-220.

"If you were not, I would not have created the heavens!"[43] This saying is often considered to be apocryphal, but several scholars hold that its sense is authentic.

The *Inner* Sunna

According to Suyūtī, the profound nature of the Prophet showed through in many aspects of his daily life. He maintained that Muhammad's judgments were determined according to the exoteric Law, but also according to esoteric Reality. For example, the regard in which he held people was not due to how they appeared, but to how they would be in the future, which he knew through a kind of spiritual revelation.[44] For the most demanding Muslims, the *Sunna* could not be limited to a formal imitation of the Prophet; rather, it consists in inhabiting, as far as possible, his inner states. Muhammad, as a divine Messenger, had to address all people, but the holiness with which he was invested—and which is of surpassing excellence to his function of prophet—was apparent only to some. Thus if the Prophet is "the unsurpassable model of all sanctity,"[45] there is an inner *Sunna* to which the spiritual elite are invited. Sarrāj explained that theologians and jurists drew their arguments and statutes primarily from the example of the Prophet. Sufis, on the other hand, focused on absorbing his "noble virtues."[46] This enabled Suhrawardī of Baghdad to declare that Sufis are the true Sunnis.

It is for this reason that Sufis see themselves as the successors of Muhammad. The saying of the Prophet, "The heirs of the prophets are those with knowledge," caused a division between exoterists and esoterists. What kind of knowledge did these "heirs" to Muhammad and the former prophets possess? Is it a question of religious knowledge, which explains the Law, or of spiritual knowledge, which reveals divine realities? Obviously, the two are inseparable, but, according to Sufi masters, the Sufis involve themselves in both, while the "men of the letter" only have access to the former. Even such great *ulama* as Ghazzālī and Suyūtī acknowledge that the heir is he who attains the *inner state* of the person from whom he inherits.

For all that, the Sufis have never claimed to reach the spiritual level of the prophets. The "quotes" attributed to some of them were, it is true, suspicious in the eyes of the doctors of the Law and, in the tenth century, Hakīm

---

[43] Suyūtī, *Ta'yīd al-haqīqa al-'aliyya wa tashyīd al-tarīqa al-shādhiliyya* (Cairo, 1934), p. 102.

[44] Suyūtī, *al-Bāhir fī hukm al-nabī bi l-bātin wa l-zāhir* (Cairo, 1987).

[45] P. Nwyia, *Exégèse coranique et langage mystique*, p. 183.

[46] *Luma'*, p. 95.

Tirmidhī fostered a certain confusion regarding the relationship between prophecy and sanctity. Later Sufis therefore strove to clarify their position on this point: a saint (*walī*) who is not also a prophet will never be able to be the equal of a prophet (*nabī*); this is the case for all Muslim saints since the closing of the cycle of prophecy by Muhammad. On the other hand, the *nabī* considered also from his quality as *walī* is superior to the *nabī* envisaged from the quality of prophet alone.

The "inner *Sunna*" begins with an outer, and often meticulous, adherence to the example of Muhammad. The greatest of such practitioners see this observance as a support for blessings and spiritual realization. As he was dying, Shiblī was performing his final ablution and he asked someone close to him to pass his wet fingers through his beard for him because such was the habit of the Prophet.[47] Far from immersing oneself in a murky mysticism, this approach to the *Sunna* draws sustenance from the slightest details of the life of the Prophet. One example was Jīlī, for whom certain major events in the life of Muhammad determined the initiatory stations of the Path; such references will be interiorized according to a disciple's own capacities. Thus, in Islam, the Prophet's ascension to the heavens (the *Mi'rāj*) represents the prototype of all spiritual experience or of any initiatory passage. As mentioned in the *sūra* of the Star (*al-Najm*), let us recall that during his ascension the Prophet, after being transported by night from Mecca to Jerusalem, was raised up to the divine Throne. His guide, the archangel Gabriel, goes no further, but Muhammad is allowed into the proximity of God, "at a distance of but two bow-lengths or nearer" (Koran 53:9). "Muhammadian" saints have this possibility of experiencing a mystical ascension. However, masters distinguish between the *mi'rāj* of the Prophet and that of saints: the former accomplished his ascension in both body and spirit, while the latter have only accomplished it in spirit. The first Muslim spiritual figure to whom one attributes a *mi'rāj* is Abū Yazīd Bistāmī. Thereafter, this subject becomes almost commonplace in Sufi literature, but one should note the special case of Niffarī (d. circa 977), a little-known visionary who, at the end of his initiatory path became the "confidante of God."

Sufism and Prophetic Tradition (Hadīth)

The attachment of Sufis to the model of Muhammad, which has both exoteric and esoteric aspects, results in the interest which they have always shown in the science of *Hadīth*. This interest is very understandable: in order to better love and imitate the Prophet, it is necessary to know his

---

[47] Ibid., p. 104.

words and actions. Thus, some great figures of primitive Sufism (including Ibn Mubārak, Dārānī, Ahmad Nūrī, Ma'rūf Karkhī, Hakīm Tirmidhī, and others) were also "traditionnists" (*muhaddith*), i.e., scholars of prophetic Tradition. In his *Luma'*, Sarrāj based the entirety of Islamic mysticism upon five words of the Prophet and he revealed the spiritual meaning given by the first Sufis to certain *hadīths*.[48] In the eleventh century, Sulamī, who was as much a *muhaddith* as a Sufi, put together a collection of *Forty Hadīths on Sufism*. His disciples Abū Nu'aym Isfahānī and Qushayrī were also distinguished in this field, and the celebrated "Epistle" (*Risāla*) on Sufism by the latter is clearly influenced by the science of *Hadīth*. This science subsequently became a central discipline in the teaching of the *madrasas* of Iran and then Iraq. Ghazzālī adorned his mystical writings with *hadīths*, and Ibn 'Arabī continued his study of the prophetic Tradition until the end of his life. The overlap between Sufism and the discipline of *Hadīth* grew over time among the Sufis, confirming the assertion of Junayd that "Our science [Sufism] is closely related to the prophetic Tradition."

This kind of osmosis is not surprising, inasmuch as the Sufi "chains of guarantors" (*isnād, silsila*) represent the esoteric counterpart of the "chains" of the traditionnists. In the science of *Hadīth*, a word or an act of the Prophet is reported by various transmitters who followed one another in time; one can thus go back to their source, which is generally a Companion or a wife of the Prophet. Similarly, in Sufism the spiritual flow from the Prophet (*baraka*)—most often transmitted through 'Alī but also through Abū Bakr—is spread from master to master, and then from master to disciple over the course of generations. The chains of *Hadīth* and Sufism thus ultimately point back to the person of the Prophet. In both disciplines, the rites of transmission, such as the "handshake" (*musāfaha*), are similar: they seal a pact, sometimes exoteric, sometimes esoteric, between he who transmits and he who receives. Let us point out that genealogy has always played a fundamental role in Arab culture.

Some Sufis undoubtedly forged spiritually charged *hadīths* to serve their own agendas, and one must call them to task on this point, but the various currents within Islam have all made use of these "white lies" to varying degrees. Critics have also reproached Sufis for employing traditions whose chain of transmission is considered to be "weak": according to the prevailing opinion, such *hadīths* cannot be used for legal bases, but they nevertheless maintain all of their spiritual value. Exoterists were also upset by Sufis when the latter sometimes claimed to have received through their dream-visions

---

[48] Ibid., pp. 103, 116-118.

confirmation or invalidation from the Prophet of the authenticity of his words. The perception of *hadīths* by means of "spiritual unveiling" (*kashf*) was, however, acknowledged by recognized scholars, in particular by some shaykhs of al-Azhar University.[49]

The Master of Masters

The initiatory relationship between master and disciple plays a fundamental role in Sufism. All shaykhs, whether they belong to a brotherhood or not, are aware that they draw their spiritual power (*baraka*) from the Prophet; they do nothing more than to represent him in this post-prophetic phase of mankind. One mystic wrote that Sufi masters are like numerous moons reflecting the sunlight of the Prophet onto the earth. Those of them who are most deeply "realized" maintain a subtle link to Muhammad, the "Seal of the Prophets," and they receive from him both spiritual teachings and instructions on how to conduct themselves in this world. We have seen how, in the initiatory paths, the chain (*silsila*) guarantees from generation to generation the regular transmission of the divine influx, and then the *baraka* of Muhammad. As the trustee of this *baraka*, the shaykh makes it radiate upon his disciples and beyond. When the disciple makes the pact with his master, he reenacts what the Companions did with the Prophet at Hudaybiyya.[50]

During his lifetime, the Prophet shared esoteric teachings with some of his Companions. What he said to the first Bedouin who came to question him on Islam had little in common with what he said, for example, to Abū Bakr, who was an intimate of his. He exchanged evocative words with Abū Bakr which remained incomprehensible to the other Companions. The "People of the Bench" (*ahl al-suffa*), who numbered about three hundred, lived in the mosque of the Prophet and dedicated themselves to their religious practices. They, too, benefited from special teachings. The Prophet repeatedly stated that he had to adapt his speech to the people with whom he spoke, and that it is not good to speak about each and every truth: "If you knew what I know, you would laugh but little, and you would cry much. . ." (Bukhārī). He responded to the same question in different ways, depending on the person with whom he was speaking. His Companion Abū Hurayra made the following acknowledgment: "I received two vessels of knowledge from the Messenger of God. I have shared one; if I had done the same with the second, my throat would have been cut" (Bukhārī). Therefore, it is necessary to distinguish between the exoteric aspect of the Prophet, the "Mes-

---

[49] See our *Soufisme en Égypte et en Syrie*, pp. 100-101.

[50] See *infra*, p. 154.

senger" sent to all created beings and who appeared accessible to all, and his esoteric aspect, which was oriented towards God and was entirely holy.

Sufis have often been reproached for venerating their masters, but they have done so only by way of imitating the Companions in their relations with the Prophet: it is said that the Companions remained motionless in front of him "as if birds were perched on their head" (Bukhārī) and, for some of them, even included some excessive expressions of reverence. From the term "Companion" (*sāhib*; pl. *ashāb* or *sahāba*) is derived the term "spiritual companionship" (*suhba*), meaning the initiatory relationship which links master and disciple or, more generally, two people traveling the Path together. Due to this proximity, the individual Companions who were especially close to the Prophet embody various models of sanctity, and are regarded as "Imams of the Sufi Path."[51] Some examples of this are: Abū Bakr, seen as the model of "truthfulness"; 'Umar as the model of one "inspired" by God and prone to many "unveilings"; 'Alī is a figure of whom the Prophet said: "I am the city of knowledge, and 'Alī is its door"; and Abū Dharr Ghifārī who was the first to speak on what would be the future Sufi doctrine of the extinction of the ego in God (*fanā'*); as well as other Companions.

The Prophet thus appeared in the writings of early Sufism (starting in the ninth century) as the sole guide to whom initiates direct an exclusive kind of love.[52] He quickly became the model from whom Sufi aspirants copied all their rules of life (*ādāb*), from the most practical to the most spiritual. Didn't Junayd say that "the doors [of spiritual realization] are closed to men, except those who follow the footsteps of the Messenger of God"?

These types of expressions would thereafter acquire the name of the "Path of Muhammad" (*al-tarīq al-muhammadiyya*): beyond some features that distinguish a given spiritual group or a particular "brotherhood" from others, Sufis have been aware up to the current day that they belong to one and the same Path started by the Prophet and continued by his "proxies," the masters of *tasawwuf*.

Taking this into consideration, the personality of a disciple's shaykh should matter little to that disciple, since the true master is the Prophet. Thus Shiblī once stated to a disciple of his that he was Muhammad, the Messenger of God. Such an attitude appears scandalous in the eyes of those who cannot comprehend the essential identification of a master with the Prophet. Many Sufis have declared that they have had the experience of what has been called (since the eighth century) "extinction in the Messenger" (*al-fanā' fī l-rasūl*), a state in which one's individuality becomes blurred because

---

[51] Hujwirī, *Kashf al-mahjūb*, p. 267 *et seq.*

[52] See, for example, the *Kitāb al-Sidq* of Kharrāz, and the *Kitāb al-Tawāsīn* of Hallāj.

it has been occupied by the spiritual being (*rūhāniyya*) of the Prophet. This extinction can occur during a visit to the Prophet's Mosque in Medina—as was the case with Emir 'Abd al-Qādir—but also under any other circumstances. Before he can abolish his ego in God (*al-fanā' fī Llāh*), the initiate must first extinguish himself in the Messenger, who is the mediating presence, the "isthmus" between divine and human realities. Thus, all forms of holiness or spiritual mastery in Islam are of significance only if they have been enlivened by the subtle bond that attaches the initiate to the spiritual being of the Prophet. It is in this context that we can understand the following saying of a master: "If the vision of the Messenger of God were withdrawn from me for even an instant, I would no longer consider myself to be a Muslim."

Having a vision (*ru'yā*) indeed constitutes a way to access the spiritual world. It can come about that initiates "see" masters of the past, or angels, or prophets who preceded Muhammad. Having a vision of the Prophet plays a prominent part in the spiritual life of Muslims, and not only for Sufis. "He who sees me (in a dream)," said the Prophet, "has truly seen me, because Satan cannot take my form" (Bukhārī). A Moroccan saint of the eighteenth century, 'Abd al-'Azīz Dabbāgh, explained that the Prophet can take up to two hundred forty-eight thousand forms, and that he frequently appears to disciples under the guise of their master.[53] If having a vision of the Prophet during sleep (*manām*) seems almost ordinary to Sufis (with various formulas existing that can bring this about), only some are able to receive visions during the waking state (*yaqaza*). These are not necessarily "visionaries" or other ecstatics, but they are saints who sometimes receive an order to found an initiatory path, or scholars who are authorities on a subject: Suyūtī claimed to have seen the Prophet more than seventy times while awake.[54]

Through having had one or the other kind of vision, a number of spiritual adepts have declared that the Prophet alone has been their master. Although they may be attached to a living shaykh, they have, in reality, been initiated by the Prophet. This privileged modality, which is rightly called "the Path of Muhammad," pertains to the *uwaysī* type of initiation, to which we will return.

Direct initiation by the Prophet is often the fruit of an intense practice of the prayer on the Prophet (*al-salāt 'alā l-nabī*). This is not a canonical prayer, but a formula of sentence length which one usually repeats by counting the repetitions on a rosary. According to the Koran (33:56), God—as well as His angels—shower blessings on the Prophet, and He commands believers to

[53] Ibn al-Mubārak, *Kitāb al-Ibrīa* (Damascus, 1984), vol. I, pp. 280-281.

[54] Sha'rānī, *al-Tabagāt al-sughrā* (Cairo, 1970), p. 29.

devote themselves to the same. Muhammad himself described the value of doing this, thus alluding to the Reality which lived within him. This prayer takes various forms in order to call upon different aspects of the Reality of Muhammad. It is recommended for those who do not have, or who no longer have, an earthly master;[55] for some, it can replace the master. Most of the founding saints of Sufi orders claim that the particular litanies or prayers which their disciples recite were received from the Prophet.

Devotion to the Prophet

Starting in the twelfth century, a broad movement of devotion to the Prophet appeared in Muslim countries, often with the source coming from Sufis. The circles of mystics became attached to the practice of the prayer on the Prophet during their evening group meetings, and the practice then quickly moved beyond just the circles of *tasawwuf*, with some *ulama* recommending it in short treatises, writing that it helps in the granting of prayers to God, in protecting oneself from the plague, in putting an end to quarrels, etc. This form of prayer, which since that time has entered into the everyday language in certain regions of the Muslim world, has inspired an extensive devotional literature. The *Burda*, a poem of praises to the Prophet in which the Light of Muhammad shows through, and the *Dalā'il al-khayrāt*, a group of formulas aimed at increasing the blessing linked to the prayer on the Prophet, are the work of such Sufis as Busīrī (thirteenth century) and Jazūlī (fifteenth century), while the *Shifā*, a model of the genre, comes from an Andalusian sage of the twelfth century, the *qāḍī* 'Iyyāḍ. Up to the present day, the *Burda* and the *Dalā'il* are frequently recited in the mosques and other public places of Islam.

Starting in the twelfth century, the celebration of the Prophet's birthday (*mawlid; mouloud* in Maghrebian dialect), which originally was brought about as much by the authorities (both Shi'ite and Sunni) as by the Sufis, quickly became an established holiday. This celebration is certainly an "innovation" (*bid'a*) in Islamic life, but the scholars have categorized it as a "commendable" one (not every innovation is "blameworthy". . .) and have themselves taken part in it.

Devotion to the Prophet grew in a more obvious manner between the twelfth and the fifteenth centuries, but the foundations on which it rested had been in place for a long time. This is one of the contributions of Suf-

---

[55] They can be short formulas, such as the "Prayer of the Opening" (*salāt al-fātih*) of Mustafā Bakrī, or longer formulas like the Prayer of Ibn Mashīsh or the "Pearl of Perfection" (*jawharat al-kamāl*) of Ahmad Tijānī.

ism to Islamic life: to have made the doctrine of the Light of Muhammad or the doctrine of Universal Man spread their light into the lives of Muslims. Each person, of course, draws from this what he can, according to his level of understanding, and popular piety does not aspire to rise to full gnosis. For the Sufis, however, even the most naive form of love for the Prophet carries within it an awakening to the true nature of the Messenger. During the first centuries of Islam, one concerned oneself primarily with the direct relationship between man and God; thereafter, this same relationship is experienced by aspiring to Muhammad's model of perfection.

Bibliography

Muhammad Ali Amir-Moezzi (directed by), *Le Voyage initiatique en terre d'islam* (Louvain-Paris, 1996).

Michel Chodkiewicz, "Le modèle prophétique de la sainteté en islam," in *Sociétés et cultures musulmanes—Les chantiers de la recherche. Lettre d'information de l'AFEMAM* n° 10, 1996, pp. 505-518.

Denis Gril, "Muhammad," in *Dictionnaire critique de l'ésotérisme* (Paris, 1998), pp. 869-871.

'Abd al-Karīm al-Jīlī, *L'Homme universel* (Paris, 1986). (English edition: *Universal Man* [Beshara Publications, 1995].)

Al-Kamālāt al-ilāhiyya fī l-sifāt al-muhammadiyya (Cairo, 1997).

Nikos Kaptein, *Muhammad's Birthday Festival* (Leyden, 1993).

Annemarie Schimmel, *Le Soufise ou les dimensions mystiques de l'islam* (1996), pp. 268-284. (English edition: *Mystical Dimensions of Islam* [The University of North Carolina Press, 1975].)

THE ISLAM OF "EXCELLENCE"

Islām, Īmān, Ihsān

Even if the term *tasawwuf* ("Sufism") was not current during the time of the Prophet, the Sufis recall that Muhammad employed a term of similar scope in order to call to mind the spiritual quest in Islam. To this end, they cite the famous "*hadīth* of Gabriel," which to their thinking supports their path: A man dressed all in white appeared one day to the Prophet while his Companions were all around him. He first asked the Prophet what *al-islām* ("submission") was. The Prophet answered the question by citing the five pillars of the faith: the dual attestation ("There is no god but God and Muhammad is His Messenger"), the prayer (*salāt*), the almsgiving for purification (*zakāt*), the fast of the month of Ramadān, and the pilgrimage (*hajj*). Then the man questioned the Prophet on *al-īmān* (faith). It consists, answered the Prophet, in believing in God, His angels, His revealed books, His Messengers, and in the Last Day, as well as in predestination. Finally, the man enquired about *al-ihsān* (excellence, the search for perfection). "It is that you worship God as if you saw Him, for even if you do not see Him, indeed He sees you," was the reply. After having posed other questions about the end of time, the man left. The Prophet then informed his astonished Companions: "He was the angel Gabriel, come to teach you your religion."

This *hadīth* is one of the most highly sanctioned scriptural sources within Sufism, because it gives from the outset several dimensions to what the term "Islam" commonly covers. "Islam" therefore has to be understood according to a multiplicity of layered meanings, which unfold from the most straightforward and formal to the most inward. In fact, the three degrees that surface here (*islām, īmān, ihsān*) lead to many subdivisions, which reminds us of the hierarchical levels of understanding of the Koran.

The first degree, *islām*, corresponds to outward practices, the outer form of the religion, which includes acts of worship (*'ibādāt*) and human relations (*mu'āmalāt*). Above all, it demands a "submission" to the Koranic and prophetic statutes, which is an act of obedience to the Legislator. It is not necessarily accompanied by faith: "The Bedouins say, 'We believe!' Say: 'You do not believe; rather say, "We submit." Faith has not entered into your hearts!'" (Koran 49:14). *Islām* is regulated by Muslim jurisprudence (*fiqh*).

Īmān, faith, has its seat in the heart, but at this stage the believer still acts upon convictions drawn from dogma. His faith is thus oriented and structured by dogmatic theology, which has several names in Arabic. Even so, it is no longer within the province of the "jurist."

Muslim spiritual figures identified Sufism explicitly with *ihsān*. Some Sufi "reformers" of the twentieth century decided to indicate their discipline by this term and no longer by that of *tasawwuf.*[56] *Ihsān* requires that one "worship God as if you saw Him." From this stems the central theme of Sufism: the direct perception of divine realities by "unveiling" and contemplation. Having developed "the eye of the heart," the initiate is then equipped with "certain vision" (*yaqīn*), a going beyond or rather a fulfillment of faith. The spiritual realization to which *ihsān* leads is generally the fruit of long effort, and it implies the practice of spiritual exercises and initiatory methods.

"It is that you worship God as if you saw Him": in regard to this "as if," the Sufis recall that man is able to contemplate the divine attributes, at most, but never the Essence. What good, then, is their ability to perceive inner things? It enables them to grasp the secrets (*asrār*) hidden in the letter of the Koran or behind the rites stipulated by Islam.

---

[56] See *infra*, p. 141.

Sufism Illuminates the Five Pillars

The first pillar of Islam requires adherence to the divine Oneness: "There is no god but God." This is *tawhīd*, an essential principle in the dogma of Islam. If one actually stays at the level of *islām*, *tawhīd* consists of an attestation, an entirely outward assertion. Philosophers and theologians define *tawhīd* by means of rational arguments (*tawhīd al-burhān*). Sufis do not disregard this dimension, but they approach *tawhīd* through direct, intuitive vision (*tawhīd al-'iyān*). In this way they pass from a knowledge that is still dualistic (*tawhīd* and me), which is how the exoterists see it, to a knowledge that is transforming, unitive, and real, once the ego is extinguished: God alone is, and only He can really testify to His oneness. God alone is, and this existence that we borrow from Him creates an intimate bond with Him. Some masters have helped believers to understand that, paradoxically, they would not be suitable for *tawhīd* as long as they remained prisoners of their individuality. One can "testify" only to what one has seen, and one can "see" divine realities only after passing beyond human consciousness.

The school of Baghdad, and Junayd and Shiblī in particular, did a great deal of work on the esoteric dimension of *tawhīd*. In a general way, masters have distinguished three degrees of experience of *tawhīd*, according to the process of interiorization which we have already described. However, Ghazzālī referred to a fourth and ultimate stage, that of "the extinction of the ego in Oneness" (*al-fanā' fī l-tawhīd*), whose essential points he got from Junayd. This experience also entails the esoteric accomplishment of another precept of Islam: according to the Koran (51:56), man was created to serve and worship God, which is what the rites stated in the five pillars address; for the Sufi, it is a matter of passing from the simple observance of works of worship (*'ibāda*) to a consciousness of the absolute, ontological servitude of man in relation to God (*'ubūdiyya*).

The school of Ibn 'Arabī gave a metaphysical formulation of *tawhīd* by defining it as the oneness of Being (*wahdat al-wujūd*). This definition caused a great deal of disapproval among exoterists, and even in some Sufi circles. It is a result, however, of the experience of *fanā'* and is an extension of the teachings of Junayd—according to whom "In being there is only God"—as well as those of Ansārī and Ghazzālī. All the doctors of the Law admitted the possibility of the extinction of the ego in God, which they somewhat later came to call the "unity of witness" (*wahdat al-shuhūd*), but many rejected the doctrine of the oneness of Being because it seemed to them that the doctrine created theories involving philosophical nuances, while it should have remained a personal experience. Now, let us recall that the "guardians" of Islam have always feared that philosophical elaborations would undermine the purity of the faith and would relativize the single access to Revelation.

The other pillars—mainly the prayer, the fast, and the pilgrimage—engage the body of the believer. Although modern tendencies stress the health-related aspect of these practices, they come to life for the believer through his faith and orientation towards God. For all that, the letter of the law ended up prevailing over the spirit, and some observers saw in these practices nothing but ritualism and formal gestures. But for those who perceive the inner meaning of Islam, they are, above all, ways to move towards spiritual realities. As the masters like to point out, the rites, which are "symbols put into action,"[57] have their primary justification in the remembrance of God (*dhikr*), which they bring about.

Using different methods and sometimes under various rubrics, many Sufi authors have devoted a large portion of their treatises to "unveiling" the symbolic scope of the rites.[58] "Each act of worship includes an aspect which is apparent and another which is hidden, a peel and a pulp," stated Ghazzālī. This concept of secrecy is not so much an expression of secrecy as it is an invitation to understanding the scope of the dogma better, or to abandoning the superficial approach. These spiritual texts often follow the formal framework of the legal texts. This is because *tasawwuf*, which aims at interiorizing the practice of religious duties, is linked to the exoteric norms. Thus, Sufi authors first address purity (*tahāra*), which must be accompanied by the intention of the heart, and which is a necessary condition for acts such as prayer. This purity, which is physically accomplished through ablutions, is not just "ritual" or "legal"—as it is often translated—because it has an obvious inner dimension. Thus Ghazzālī, who wrote of four levels of introspection in the teachings of Islam, moved from the purification of the body to the purification of character, then to that of the heart, and finally to that of the "innermost being," which consists in purifying oneself of all that is not God.

Next, the authors addressed in turn the prayer, which is the "spiritual ascension of the believer" in the words of the Prophet; *zakāt*, which are "purifying" alms according to the etymology of the word; the fast, which draws the spirit away from matter; and finally the pilgrimage, whose various phases have a very strong esoteric content. In the *Illuminations of Mecca* (*Futūhāt makkiyya*) of Ibn ʿArabī, the titles of some chapters could lead one to think that it is a very detailed book of Islamic jurisprudence inasmuch as the mas-

---

[57] R. Guénon, *Aperçus sur l'initiation*, p. 119. (English edition: *Perspectives on Initiation* [Sophia Perennis, 2004.])

[58] Among the best known of these, let us mention Sarrāj and his *Lumaʿ*; Abū Tālib Makkī, *Qāt al-qulūb*; Hujwirī, *Somme spirituelle*, p. 323 *et seq.*; Ghazzālī, in much of the first volume of his *Ihyāʾ*; ʿAbd al-Qādir Jīlānī, *Sirr al-asrār*, and Suhrawardī, *ʿAwārif al-maʿārif*, among others.

ter examined in it the slightest details related to the accomplishment of these rites.[59] In his *Spiritual Revelations at Mosul* (*al-Tanazzulāt al-mawsiliyya*), he engaged in a discussion of the prayer and ablution that is both extremely detailed and mystical. The Algerian shaykh Ahmad al-ʿAlawī (d. 1934) followed in his footsteps with *Minah quddūsiyya* (*Very Holy Graces*). In this esoteric commentary on a prayer book of Muslim dogma and law from the seventeenth century, the Shaykh al-ʿAlawī explicitly identified his spiritual interpretation of the pillars of Islam with the degree of *ihsān*. In this text, as in those cited above, the letter or the form is never glossed over; it is revealed to be a support of spiritual realization.[60]

Sufism, or Plenary Islam

To authors who are spiritual adepts, the Sufi is, in fact, the true Muslim, that is, he who has realized the three levels implicitly contained in *islām*. And Sufism is nothing other than Islam, both inner and outer, spirit and letter. To some extent, Sufism offers some relief from the standards decreed by Islam. Because of all this, some have suggested that it is necessary to have a Sufi orientation in order to truly understand and practice Islam: how else could one integrate the symbols employed by Islam into one's own understanding, or how could one utilize the divine Names. . . ?

In one stage or another of their lives, many scholars sought to make their personal experiences of Islam more spiritual. However, one could not limit the spiritual dimension of Islam just to *tasawwuf*. "We insisted enough on the spiritual values of Islam as such," remarked Mohammed Arkoun and Louis Gardet, "to ask ourselves whether it is not somewhat abusive to apply the term 'mystical' only to *tasawwuf*. [It is not] as if official Islam is only rigor and precise legal details, and that Sufis alone thirst for the presence of God. Many currents in the religion and many [written] works which are not related to Sufism are full of interiorizing potential."[61]

Spiritual realization (*tahqīq*) does not consist of an increase in the practice of the pillars, but of an inner awakening that illuminates and clarifies their meaning. "Abū Bakr," said the Prophet to his Companions, "does not surpass you through additional prayers or fasts, but through something which settled in his heart" (Tirmidhī). For the Sufi, the "submission" to which Islam invites Muslims will mean, for example, living the present moment

---

[59] See chapters 68-72 of *Futūhāt makkiyya*.

[60] Some excerpts of the *Minah* appear in translation in the book of Dr. Lings, *A Sufi Saint of the Twentieth Century: Shaikh Ahmad al-Alawi* (Islamic Texts Society, 1993), p. 219 *et seq.*

[61] *L'Islam, hier-demain* (Paris, 1978), p. 65.

fully, without looking to the past or the future, as God wills it. Such a realization allows the Sufi to be called "the son of the moment."

THE LAW (*SHARĪ'A*), THE PATH (*TARĪQA*), AND THE REALITY (*HAQĪQA*)

To the initiate, the Law (*Sharī'a*) and ultimate Reality (*Haqīqa*) are as inseparable as *islām* and *ihsān*. We are here in the presence of another mode of understanding which is equally essential to the lived personal experience of Sufism. We have seen that the Law is situated on the periphery, along with the part of Islam that it governs; thus, it deals in general statutes that are by necessity "outward" because the Law is addressed to everyone, simple believers and the initiated alike. Conceived as a protective framework, it falls under the great cosmic Law which governs the universe, and should not be lived as though it were a tiresome list of regulations or interdictions. One should not narrow down the *Sharī'a*, which to Muslims is of divine origin, just to Islamic jurisprudence (*fiqh*), which is a human application of it that is conditioned by a given temporal context. By limiting themselves only to the prescriptive character of the *Sharī'a*, the "jurists" have blurred some of its aspects, whether they be ethical, psychological, cosmological, ecological, etc., aspects which ultimately are much more essential.

In its principles as in its history, Sufism has clearly distanced itself from esoteric currents which have abrogated the Law and flouted the formal religious standards of Islam. For masters like 'Abd al-Qādir Jīlānī or Ahmad Zarrūq, the Law is an indispensable foundation because it alone safeguards from error. If Islam preaches a balance between matter and the spirit, between the life of the here-below and our future life, Sufism, for its part, pleads for Islam to be recognized in both its exoteric and esoteric dimensions. Creation is in the image of God, who declares Himself in the Koran to be "the First and the Last, *the Apparent and the Hidden*" (57:3).

Everything in the world of Manifestation contains an inner, subtle reality. One morning when the Prophet questioned his Companion Hāritha on his state, the latter answered that it had become believing truly (*haqq[an]*). The Prophet then said to him: "To each truth (*haqq*) corresponds an essential reality (*haqīqa*)."[62] The *Sharī'a*, which is concerned with the world of sensations, thus returns to the *Haqīqa* to which it is subordinate, and which corresponds to the world of the Spirit. To comprehend *Haqīqa* is to serve the one Real. It is by the name *al-Haqq* that the "men of the Inward" like to mention God. The *Sharī'a* has evolved and continues to evolve according to the times, and even to places; it will come to an end, like all that is created.

---

[62] Reported by Ibn Mājah.

Its life is nourished by the *Haqīqa* alone. Masters often employ this image: Reality is hidden within the Law as butter is hidden within milk; it is by churning milk that butter appears: there is no butter without milk.

In our world where spirit takes on material forms, *Sharī'a* and *Haqīqa* are inseparable. Hujwirī commented that "Their mutual relationship is like that of the body and the spirit: when the spirit leaves the body, the living body becomes a corpse, and the spirit disappears like the wind."[63] For Ibn 'Arabī, it is only while submitting to the injunctions of the Law that man can restore his original divine nature, and can come to know sanctity or proximity to God. Ibn 'Arabī worked on a total identification between *Sharī'a* and *Haqīqa*, because both share the same essence.[64] "The Law is not the clothing or the symbol of the *Haqīqa*, of a hidden truth which one could attain only by transgression. It *is* the *Haqīqa*."[65] But this equation has value only for the accomplished gnostic. For the majority of Muslims on a spiritual quest, such a transparency of the *Sharī'a* in relation to the *Haqīqa* is not a given; it is the fruit of the *Tarīqa*, the initiatory progression that consists of traversing the Path, which connects the *Sharī'a* and the *Haqīqa*.

Sharī'a, Tarīqa, Haqīqa: This is another threefold expression of the hierarchy of meaning in Islam, and it is very often comparable to *islām, īmān, ihsān*. Sufis refer to the following saying of the Prophet, although its authenticity is not formally established: "The Law is my word, the Path my acts, and Reality my inner state." Here, by way of example, is how Sufis might apply these three levels to a specific point of law, in this case, reasons for breaking the fast: The fast is broken, *according to the Law*, if a person who is fasting ingests some food; *according to the Path*, it is broken if he slanders another; and *according to the Reality* if he thinks of something other than God.

A Law for Sufis Only?

Is this to say that the Sufis follow a special Law, one which would cut them off from the community of believers? Certainly not, answers Ibn Khaldūn in his *Shifā' al-sā'il*, a work devoted to Sufism. "The endless ocean of their spiritual 'taste,'" he writes, "fits within the five pillars, in the same way that the particular fits within the general."[66] It is true that shaykhs sometimes give special regulations to their disciples concerning everyday life, such as

---

[63] *Somme spirituelle*, p. 434.

[64] *Al-futūhāt al-makkiyya*, vol. II, p. 563.

[65] M. Chodkiewicz, *Un océan sans rivage*, p. 80. (English edition: *An Ocean Without Shore: Prophethood and Sainthood in the Doctrine of Ibn 'Arabi* [Islamic Texts Society, 1993].)

[66] *Shifā' al-sā'il* (Tunis, 1991), p. 237.

prohibiting them from something that is licit for the average Muslim, or having them accomplish rites that have to be carried out at a precise hour, or perhaps applying themselves to the *dhikr* rather than to the supererogatory prayers, etc. In his *Book of the Halts* (*Kitāb al-Mawāqif*), where he transcribed his visions into dialogues, Niffarī has God say: "My Knowledge does not require that you give up My law, but that you follow some prophetic practice (*sunna*) rather than another." As the Egyptian Sha'rānī explained, each shaykh perceives the rites of Islam according to his own esoteric scope and cannot be judged by those who only have access to the outer 'peel' of the Law.

In regard to this point, Sufis point to the superiority of Khadir (or Khidr), as is suggested in the Koran, to Moses, the prophet of the Hebraic Law. In *sūra* 18 (v. 65-82) the enigmatic Khadir, who initiates the prophets and the saints, puts Moses to the test three times, by performing acts which apparently go against the Law: he sinks a boat, kills a young man, and rebuilds a wall contrary to all logic. Moses, who adheres to the outward norms of the Law, displays impatience and outrage. As for Khadir, he perceives the profound reality of things and judges them according to the *Haqīqa*: he explains the justice of his actions to Moses and then leaves him behind.

The grievance of "laxism" sometimes leveled by the doctors of the Law against Sufis generally applies only to pseudo-mystics, or to those who deliberately place themselves within a heterodox position and who are stigmatized by masters themselves. For the most part, true Sufis, who are in search of excellence or *ihsān*, often take upon themselves greater burdens than do other Muslims. Witness the following anecdote, in which a "jurist" comes to test Shiblī on his knowledge of the *Sharī'a*:

> "What is the amount of legally required alms (*zakāt*) that one must give if he has five camels?"
>
> "From the point of view of the Law," answers Shiblī, "it amounts to an ewe, but for people like us [Sufis], it is the totality of what one has that must be turned over."
>
> "From which imam did you get that?"
>
> "Abū Bakr al-Siddīq, who offered all of his possessions [for the cause of nascent Islam]; when the Prophet asked him what he had kept for his family, he answered 'God and His Prophet!'"[67]

For other Muslims, Ibn 'Arabī always searched for the most accommodating solutions; to this end he accepted diverse opinions from the founders of the schools of jurisprudence. He did this in such a way as to broaden the

---

[67]   A. Mahmūd, *Abū Bakr al-Shiblī* (Beirut, n. d.), p. 13.

possibilities. However, for himself, he followed the most rigorous regulations of the *Sharī'a*.[68]

The Science of "Unveiling," the Science of Sharī'a

Ibn Khaldūn is clear on this point: if one is unable to see a "second Law" within Sufism, a law that would be both parallel and foreign to the *Sharī'a*, it is precisely because Sufism is an integral part of the *Sharī'a*.[69] The discipline of *tasawwuf* was developed starting in the ninth century, which was during the same period as other Islamic sciences. Called the "science of hearts," it began to be called "the science of spiritual states" (*'ilm al-ahwāl*) around the tenth century. The Sufis held to specific rules and methods, just as the specialists in *Hadīth*, the law, and theology had done.[70] Like any body of knowledge, Sufism has its own terminology. Through the centuries, Muslim spiritual figures have reproached exoterists with wanting to judge their art (i.e. Sufism) without ever having learned the basics concerning either its language or its content. According to an adage, "He who is ignorant of something makes it his enemy."

To Sufis it seems that exoterists have cut the *Sharī'a* off from its full scope, from its essence. The fact that Moses asks to be guided by Khadir is proof that the initiatory search is of as much benefit to believers as the search for exoteric knowledge, which is what is usually stressed. Qushayrī stressed that if the Law is a reality which is binding on man, Reality in its turn must also be a law, since the knowledge of God, gnosis, is also binding on man.[71] Abū l-Hasan Shādhilī went so far as to say that "the person who is not imbued with the knowledge of the Sufis during his life is like one who dies without having repented of his major sins."

On the experiential level, the knowledge of the Sufis is generally presented as the fruit of "unveiling" (*kashf*). What is the relation of this "unveiling"—with which one frequently associates "inspiration" (*ilhām*)—to the Law? Sufis have somewhat divergent opinions on this subject; however, they are unanimous in affirming that it is necessary to measure mystical experience with the yardstick of the Law and to reject anything that would con-

---

[68] M. Chodkiewicz, *Un océan sans rivage*, p. 79.

[69] *Muqaddima*, translated by V. Monteil into French, under the title *Discours sur l'Histoire universelle* (Beirut, 1968), vol. III, p. 1004. (English edition: translated by Franz Rosenthal [Princeton University Press, 1967].)

[70] See, for example, Sarrāj, *Luma'*, p. 378; Kalābādhī, translated by R. Deladrière (into French), *Traité de soufisme*, p. 91.

[71] *Risāla*, p. 83.

travene it. This advice from Abū l-Hasan Shādhilī summarizes their position: "If your unveiling contradicts the Book and *Sunna*, leave the first (i.e. your "unveiling") and act in conformity with the second; [it is correct to] say that God guarantees the infallibility of these two sources, and not that of your unveiling or your inspiration."[72]

Ahmad Sirhindī (d. 1624) was an Indian reformer of Sufism who was very fastidious on this point: he believed that anything that is outside the framework permitted by the doctors of the Law must therefore fall within the domain of spiritual intoxication or ecstasy and must be systematically rejected. Others believe that mystical experiences do nothing other than to bring to light the realities already contained within the *Sharī'a*; they do not add anything to the latter. The object of initiatory advancement is only to strengthen the adept's inner conviction as to the validity of the Law. This can clear away doubts which sometimes persist when one has limited oneself to faith alone.

Most masters, however, go further: the experience of *kashf* could not end in some deviation if it results from a spiritual discipline carried out according to the rules of Sufism. Quite to the contrary, it leads man to the "very source of the primordial Law, from which all the opinions of the exoteric scholars have come."[73] In this we encounter the key issue at stake in the "science of unveiling." Although certain Sufi masters ('Abd al-Qādir al-Jīlānī and Suhrawardī, in particular) warn against attaching too much importance to *kashf* in one's spiritual life, many come up against an apparent paradox: the knowledge that comes from this unveiling, which is strengthened by "certainty" (*yaqīn*), is surer than the knowledge based only on mental conjecture, and so it should have greater legal weight. It seems to them that both this unveiling and inspiration experienced by Muslims of deep spirituality must be considered as the successors to prophetic revelation (*wahy*), which would grant them an eminent reliability.

Some scholars who are authorities on Islamic sciences, such as Ghazzālī or Ibn Khaldūn, maintain the same position. For Ibn Khaldūn, prophets and saints have in common the faculty of knowing the spiritual world through "unveiling," even though the prophets' perception of it will be much more extensive than that of the saints.[74] Another scholar, Suyūtī, went so far as to grant to the knowledge of the Sufis an almost infallible status, advocating

---

[72] Ibn al-Sabbāgh, *Durrat al-asrār* (Qéna, 1993), p. 117.

[73] Sha'rānī, *al-Mīzān al-khadiriyya* (Cairo, 1989), p. 10.

[74] *La Voie et la Loi*, p. 176.

that it be given recognition in exoteric circles.[75]

A Living Law

For Sufis, the Law was not fixed in some far-off past. There is no "dead letter" of their Law, one whose instructions would have to be recalled almost artificially. Rather, every moment it reveals itself to the believer with a kind of intimacy. "You take your knowledge from mortal scholars who follow one after the other, while we receive ours from the Living, Who does not die!" exclaimed Abū Yazīd Bistāmī to the "jurists" of his time.[76] So, the great masters have always favored the "effort of interpretation of the Law" (*ijtihād*) over the imitation of some imam in matters of jurisprudence: the gnostic who possesses inner certainty drinks directly from the source of the Law. To understand or interpret the Law, one does not have to depend on the rational argumentation of exoterists, but on one's own "unveilings" (in regard to the Law). After one attains this degree of realization, wrote Suyūtī, one can even contradict those who have transmitted exoteric knowledge to him.[77]

In other words, the mystic could not go against the Law itself, because he realizes within himself its relevance. However, he may challenge how the "doctors of the Law" have appropriated the interpretation and the administration of the Law. Here we see one more of the contributions of Sufism, namely making a distinction between the divine Law itself and its appropriation by one or another human group. One can imagine the tensions which existed and which still exist between Muslim spiritual adepts and exoterists due to their different approaches to knowledge and the Law, as well as to conflicts over authority and guardianship over the multitude of believers. Throughout the centuries, however, the *Tarīqa* will assert itself more and more from behind the *Sharī'a* and the *ulama*, and more and more it will give off the perfume of Sufism. Why and in which way did this evolution take shape?

Bibliography

Michel Chodkiewicz, *Un océan sans rivage* (Paris, 1992). (English edition: *An Ocean Without Shore* [State University of New York Press, 1993].)

Ibn Khaldūn, *La Voie et la Loi*, translated by R. Pérez (Paris, 1991).

Suyūtī, *Al-Hāwī lil fatāwī* (Beirut, n. d.).

---

[75] *Al-Hāwī lil-fatāwī* (Beirut, n. d.), vol. I, p. 342.

[76] This challenge is often cited in works of Sufism.

[77] *Ta'yīd al-haqīqa al-'aliyya*, p. 26.

Chapter 3

SUFISM IN ISLAMIC CULTURE: HISTORICAL PERSPECTIVE

THE PATH OF THE PIONEERS

For Muslims, the Prophet Muhammad embraced all aspects of life completely and harmoniously. Each believer can thus find a response to his own aspirations in the example of the Messenger. Added to this, for the Sufis, is the fact that Muhammad has an esoteric dimension, and this is the only way through which one can understand the true function of the Prophet in this world.

His Companions tended towards that same unifying consciousness: those who were close to the Prophet, such as Abū Bakr, 'Umar, and 'Alī may have managed the affairs of the community, but this did not prevent them from also being great men of the spirit. However, the Companions were oriented towards different paths, according to their temperaments. Some turned to the contemplative life, forsaking the immediate pleasure of this world for the benefits of the Koranic perspective on the Hereafter. Later, Sufis would look to Companions such as Abū Dharr Ghifārī and Salmān Fārisī as models of "the poor in God," men who would themselves have worn coarse wool cloaks, a distinctive sign of the ascetics of the first centuries.

A Foundational Attitude: The Ascetic Renunciation of the World

Until the ninth century, Islamic spirituality fit almost exclusively within the framework of *zuhd*, a word that can be translated as "detachment" or "renunciation." This inner attitude, which consists of looking at this lower world with a certain distance, has its prototype in the Prophet. The many treatises devoted to *zuhd* and the collections of *hadīths* composed during that period concerned the ethics of everyday life, which consisted of integrity and of balance and which followed the example of the prophets or the Companions.

This ascetic movement was mainly a reaction to the worldly character of the Umayyad dynasty, which governed the Muslim community from 661 to 750. It was also a reaction to the many injustices of this dynasty for which history has held it responsible, such as the usurpation of the position of Hasan, the son of Imam 'Alī, by Mu'āwiya, the first Umayyad caliph. This irreparable shift from a legitimate spiritual authority to hereditary royalty created in some people a desire to withdraw from worldly affairs. They believed that the material goods which were quickly being acquired during the military conquests of the day were likely to divert believers from the mission which was incumbent upon them in the here-below. Abū Dharr Ghifārī openly reproached Muʿāwiya for leading a luxurious life, and he did not hesitate to criticize the ruler's methods of government.

Beyond the political context, *zuhd* was firmly supported in scriptural sources. To see this, we can look to the life of Hasan Basrī (d. 728), a famous preacher from Basra in the south of Iraq, a city from which one of the principal schools of *zuhd* spread. He epitomized the cardinal virtues that many men of the spirit would try to resurrect in the following centuries: fear of God and the Judgment, the unremitting self-examination of conscience and scrupulous adherence to the Law, altruism and the duty of helping to guide one's brethren, and so on. He recommended that asceticism be moderate, and he also took part in the development of Islamic thought. Thus he was included by the *ulama* of later times as one of the group they called the "pious precursors" (*al-salaf al-sālih*), while the Sufis still view him as one of the founders of their discipline and one of the successors, via ʿAlī, of the Prophet.

Very early, however, some men of the spirit deviated from the more moderate ethics of *zuhd*, and radically removed themselves from the world. They left city, work, wife, and children to devote themselves to extreme physical asceticism. In their eyes, celibacy was a necessary state because they needed to resist women, whom they likened to the carnal heart which tempts one to evil. For these men, who were always beset with afflictions, the life of this world is an evil in itself and it inspired only distaste and aversion in them; thus it was advisable to cling to the life of this world as little as possible. The bitter fact of the base nature of their hearts and of human society drove them to tears, which earned them the nickname of "eternal weepers" (*al-bakkā'ūn*). It is true that the Prophet encouraged crying, but he had in mind spiritual emotion as the reason for it, more so than sadness; he also had in mind the positive affect of crying on the carnal heart. Even so, he preached balance in religious life and gave the body its full due; for this reason, he sometimes had to temper the ascetic zeal of one or another of his Companions. It is known that he lived his own life surrounded by women, and that he was close to his children and grandchildren. Celibacy is, in general, viewed badly in Islam, and so Sufis who do not marry are an exception. Ibn al-Jawzī, of the twelfth century, did not refrain from castigating the excesses to which the ascetics went, because these seemed to him deviations from the *Sunna*. Thereafter, Muslim spiritual adepts would often find themselves reproached for their quietism. Such reproaches are explained by those initial excesses, which came to be denounced even within Sufism.

The first ascetics, however, did not lack interest in the future of the Muslim community. They practiced the *jihād*, in the Arab-Byzantine wars in particular, and while fighting against the outer enemy, they carried out an inner combat against the ego. To that end, they withdrew to *ribāts*, buildings for military purposes which were located far from cities and thus were favorable to meditation. For example, there was Ibrāhīm Ibn Adham (d. 778), an Iranian prince who, through his aversion for the world, settled in a *ribāt* in Syria after many travels. Little by little, the *ribāts* lost their defensive functions and became like monasteries that sheltered ascetics and contemplatives. This was the case with the *ribāt* of Abadan, in the south of Iraq, in which the first Sufis stayed.

In the second half of the ninth century in Iran, the Karrāmis followed an ascetic path with displays of self-inflicted privations, insistence on giving oneself over entirely to God, begging, preaching to the common people, etc. This movement, which some of the *ulama* criticized in particular for affirming the superiority of the saints over the prophets, very quickly organized itself: the Karrāmi groups attached themselves to *khānqāhs*, establishments focused on devotion as well as on welcoming and hosting passersby. Following their example, Sufis also withdrew into the *khānqāhs*.

The "Path of Blame" (Malāma): *From Concealment to Provocation*

At the same time, the Malāmatis appeared in Nishapur, the capital of Khurasan (northeastern Iran and Uzbekistan), adopting behavior contrary to that of the Karrāmis. They advocated the "path of blame" (*malāma*), of which one of the scriptural bases is this verse of the Koran: "They will fight in the way of God; they will not fear the blame of anyone" (5:54). Like the ascetic groups, they held that the *nafs*, the carnal heart, was their most fearful enemy, following several traditions of the Prophet on this subject. But their strategy went much further, because it was entirely inward. Instead of making a public spectacle of their bodily mortifications, they sought to hide their spiritual states under the veil of anonymity. They distrusted miracles as well as mystical states (*ahwāl*), which in their eyes were illusions, they refused to let themselves be dominated by spiritual intoxication, and they wanted to preserve the intimacy between themselves and their Lord. In order to avoid attracting attention to themselves, they made themselves transparent within society, avoiding any public office which would put them on display, and they wore no clothing with which they could be identified.

Despite their opposition to a certain spiritual pretentiousness displayed by many Sufis in Baghdad, the Malāmatis quickly found that they did share some affinities with the attitude of Junayd in particular. Defying the tendency toward "intoxication" within mysticism, some Iraqi mystics were inspired by *malāmati* spirituality, and Sufism soon absorbed the spirit of *malāma*; it fascinated masters like Ibn 'Arabī because of its exacting standards and demands.

Malāma did not arouse any hostility from the *ulama* since it brought people back to the observance of the Law, stripping them of self-conceit. Sufism, said one of them in the twelfth century, consists only of "the five prayers [per day] and waiting for death." Several men of the spirit thus hid their sanctity behind their social status as exoteric scholars or grand *qādīs*.[1] But *malāma* has another aspect which consists of incurring the "blame" of its own circle, and this attracted a great deal of condemnation from the doctors of the Law and from society. This was precisely the goal sought by the Malāmatis, for whom "the best means of hiding their inner lives was to earn bad reputations."[2] They achieved this while pretending to engage in thievery, insults against morality, laxity in the application of the Law, etc. It was from their ranks that the Qalandars sprang, a group that sought to destroy social conventions in order to shock the good conscience of Muslim society. These perilous ethics brought about many abuses and counterfeits. Thus the pseudo-Qalandars—the "Kalandars" of the *Thousand and One Nights*— transgressed the Law, reversing the ideal of the Malāmatis.

From Asceticism to Mysticism

It was still in the ninth century that a certain number of Iraqi Sufis began to question the relevance of the ascetic approach. They thought that any relevance it might seem to have was, in fact, an illusion, and that people had to move beyond it. Alarmed less by the "miasmas" of their souls, these Sufis wanted to love God and to know Him. They abandoned *zuhd*—though they held to some of its virtues such as "poverty," the fear of God, and pious scruples—and turned to *tasawwuf*, the mystical search leading to intimacy with God. The Sufi Path is consequently built on the love (*mahabba*) and the knowledge of God (*maʻrifa*).[3] Later mystics very often remained "ascetics" in their daily discipline—"We did not receive Sufism by chattering, but by hunger, detachment, and the rejection of conformism," Junayd declared—, but some had a higher goal and sought to expand their state of consciousness.

Beyond any other mystic, Rābiʻa ʻAdawiyya (d. 801) of Basra, inspired others to a selfless love aimed at God alone. This mystic, who did not compromise with the created world, not even with the Kaaba which she described as an "idol adored on earth," undertook an asceticism which recommends the rejection of the world as well as the quasi-sensual desire for

---

[1]   See É. Geoffroy, "Le voile des apparences, ou la double vie du grand cadi Zakariyyā al-Ansarī (m. 926/1520)," *Journal asiatique*, n° CCLXXXII, 1994, 2, pp. 271-280.

[2]   R. Deladrière, in his introduction to *La Lucidité implacable* by Sulamī (Paris, 1999), p. 19.

[3]   See *supra*, p. 3.

paradise. For her, both paradise and the hell feared so much by ascetics, are but veils encountered in the search for God. Rābi'a rejected any spiritual authority other that God.

Yahyā Ibn Mu'ādh Rāzī (d. 872) illustrates this change in spiritual attitude very well. Although he came from the Karrāmi circle, he was resolutely optimistic, and he gave priority to hope in God rather than fear of Him, to the richness of grace rather than bitter poverty, and to the knowledge of God rather than asceticism. These ideas would come to be shared by many Sufis.

Bistāmī, the Archetype of "Intoxication"

Abū Yazīd Bistāmī (or Bastāmī, d. 875) shattered the conventional framework of *zuhd* through his dazzling mystical experiences, which were puzzling even to himself. He traveled very little from his village of Bastām, in eastern Iran. He was almost completely illiterate. Bistāmī did not make any concession to the society around him, and he delivered in raw form truths which were capable of unsettling his listeners. Though it involved an extreme asceticism, he undertook an initiatory voyage of many tribulations which brought him to divine union: "I peeled off my 'I' the way a snake sheds his skin; then I contemplated my essence: and I was Him!"[4] Bistāmī envisioned his being as having a dialogue with God and as being reflected in Him; this occurred to the extent that a substitution of the two persons resulted. The divine Presence poured into his being until he lost all consciousness of himself, causing an "overflowing" within him. This state could manifest itself in speech as *shath*. This term refers to speech which is ecstatic and paradoxical, since the created being, in this case Bistāmī, speaks in divine utterances: "Glory to Me! How great is My power!" he exclaimed under the influence of the Presence. "It is better for you to see me just one time than to see your Lord a thousand times!" he said to a disciple. After the *muezzin* proclaimed [in the call to prayer] that God is great, he went one step further: "I am even greater!"

Bistāmi made these remarks in a state of spiritual intoxication. This intoxication breaks the univocity (i.e. the "single voice") of the Law in order to restore the primary equivocity (i.e. the ambiguity and the many layers) of language and mystical experience. He wanted to grasp spiritual truths in their integral fullness, which includes their opposites. His claims regarding himself ruined any chance at conformity for him: although he practiced it scrupulously, Bistāmī declared that the Law can be a veil—as a mystic, he warned against the traps which lie all along the Path. His paradoxes made

---

[4] Cited by L. Massignon, *Essai*, p. 276.

some of his contemporaries, even in spiritual circles, say that he was more of a non-believer than was Pharaoh, who claimed divinity. History, however, would later exonerate him.

The Baghdad "School" of Sufism (Ninth-Tenth Centuries)

— **Hallaj.** A celebrated school of Sufism developed in Baghdad during the transitional period of the ninth and tenth centuries. Its most famous representative, Hallāj, is one of the most discussed Sufis. His dramatic exit from his earthly adventure—he was executed—caused a radical change in the history of Sufism. Hallāj, like other "lovers" of God, some of whom were his companions, nurtured a burning desire (*'ishq*) for God. Rather than the Koranic term *mahabba* ("love" between God and man), he favored *'ishq*, which implies a more dynamic reciprocity, but which other mystics perceived as a claim to elevate profane love to the divine level.

His cry "I am the Real [God]! (*anā al-Haqq*)" goes well beyond the expansiveness of Bistāmī.

I have become the One I love,
And the One I love has become me!
We are two spirits infused in a single body!
Also, to see me is to see Him, and to see Him is to see us.[5]

The Sufis who venerate Hallāj see in his experience a vibrant testimony of humility. "We accuse the mystic of aspiring to a lordly condition while, paradoxically, he is completely given over to speech which is foreign to him, he appears to be possessed, and he is literally insane."[6] During mystical union, such as Hallāj describes it, the duality of man-God disappears, leaving only the "divine" person; the human soul is effaced and absorbed in the Unique One.

But for the scholars of the Law, to assert such a union with God amounts to insulting the dogma of the divine transcendence. Perhaps the experience of Hallāj was a reaction to the extreme distance that Islamic theology places between the Creator and creation.[7] The jurists charged Hallāj with the same counts of indictment as those which they had used against Shi'ite extremists (who had been considered throughout the centuries as the heretics of the

---

[5]   Hallāj, *Dīwān*, edited and translated by L. Massignon (Paris, 1981), p. 117.

[6]   P. Ballanfat, "Ivresse de la mort dans le discours mystique et fondements du paradoxe," *Bulletin d'études orientales*, n° XLIX, 1997, IFEAD, Damascus, p. 46.

[7]   A. Badawī, *Shatahāt al-sūfiyya* (Kuwait, 1978), pp. 18-19.

Community). These charges were for suggesting an incarnation (*hulūl*) of God in man, a belief for which Muslims had roundly criticized Christians, and for the importance given to the esoteric meaning of the rites over their external observance, which was feared might lead to the abolition of the Law and prophetic authority (e.g. a so-called pilgrimage to the "Kaaba of the heart" exempted believers from going physically to Mecca).

Hallāj was suspected of collusion with Shiʿite groups who were threatening Abbasid power, such as the Zanj, black slaves transplanted into lower Mesopotamia who had revolted between 868 and 883, and the Carmathians, an Ismāʿīli branch who were then in rebellion. But Hallāj continued to preach his heterodox ideas, throwing gasoline on the fire. He was arrested and found guilty. His execution, in 922, thus had both religious and political motivations, as well as those of security. In his far-away province Bistāmī did not represent the same danger as Hallāj.

There was undoubtedly a bit of provocation in the behavior of Hallāj, because he seems never to have left the bosom of Sunni Islam. He may even have directed groups who claimed to represent the caliph Abū Bakr al-Siddīq and who fought against the Shiʿism of the Buyid state. All his life, Hallāj remained ambiguous. His real personality escapes us; it is certain, however, that he sought martyrdom. He also admitted to looking forward to his physical death in his desire for union:

Kill me, O my friends! For it is in death that my life is to be found, and it is in life that my death is!

Later, some masters would interpret this admission as a spiritual deficiency. According to Ghazzālī, Hallāj was the victim of an illusion. The Sufis of his time believed the same. Few defended him at the time of the inquiry conducted in Baghdad by Ghulām Khalīl, an "ascetic" preacher who was opposed to the followers of divine love. They rebuked Hallāj for revealing the "secret" and for exhibiting miracles to the crowd. Afterward, the *ulama* would assert that a man can experience all conceivable spiritual states, provided that he keeps them to himself. He is free to evolve in his inner life as long as he does not upset the creed of the simple believer. Junayd, one of Hallāj's masters, understood this well, for he had adopted the discipline of the arcane: one can only mention the secrets of the Path in front of a public capable of assimilating this teaching.

— *Junayd.* If Hallāj's quest for God was paroxysmal and appeared outrageous to Muslim society, Junayd seemed to be the model of "sobriety." He felt that the ecstatic utterances of Bistāmī were free of any artifice; apart from his moments of intoxication, the latter showed a real attachment to the Law. The ecstatic remarks of Bistāmī, he explained, are the result of the immersion of the contemplative in God. The individual consciousness, going beyond the limits of its ordinary state, experiences intoxication (*sukr*). When the "I" of the created person is crushed, destroyed, it does not interpose itself any longer as a subject in the face of God; all that remains is its divine "I," in all its majesty. Junayd was the first to claim that paradoxical remarks are excusable when they are uttered under the influence of intoxication; during these moments, the mystic is no longer regarded as a person with obligations in regard to the Law. This position would be adopted by most scholars up until our times. "They are demolished in pure oneness," wrote Ghazzālī in connection with these Sufis, "the mind is as though assailed by a stupor, they are unable to remember any other than God and unable to remember themselves." On the other hand, according to a unanimous opinion, if the mystic utters such remarks while he is lucid, or if he divulges them intentionally, he falls into unbelief (*kufr*).

Even so, Junayd, who is the model of spiritual sobriety within Sufi history and who controlled his own ecstasies, noted the immaturity of Bistāmī. He observed that it is necessary to go beyond the stage of *fanā'*—the "extinction" of self in the Self, a state in which the mystic loses his footing—to return to the world of human beings in a state which is lucid but filled with the perpetual presence of God: this is *baqā'*. From that time on, masters would often state that the quest for ecstasy is appropriate only for beginners, and that pure contemplation could not be disturbed by any state of spiritual intoxication.

Junayd was not the first to formulate the doctrines of *fanā'*/*baqā'*, which quickly became a major framework for Sufi experience, but he embodied them for the benefit of those who would follow. He was called "the lord of the [Sufi] Order (*sayyid al-tā'ifa*)" because he is considered to have achieved the ideal balance between esoterism and exoterism in Islam. His inner experience probed the mystery of the divine Oneness and led to a more elevated level of perplexity. In broad outline, the *fanā'* of Bistāmī operates through union between man and God (*ittihād*), and that of Hallāj through the infusion of God in man (*hulūl*), both of which are rejected by Islamic dogma. Only the "extinction of the ego in the divine Oneness" of Junayd (*al-fanā' fī l-tawhīd*) satisfies both the necessity of initiation and religious orthodoxy. This experience would be investigated much further by a number of currents within Sufism and would be accepted by the *ulama*. The teachings of Junayd prefigured in a certain way the metaphysics that would be developed by Ibn 'Arabī and his school; however, many in the Muslim world have rejected the hypothesis that such affinities exist.

Hakim Tirmidhī: Between Prophecy and Sainthood

Hakim Tirmidhī (d. 930), the "Sage of Tirmidh" (Termez, in Uzbekistan), was the source for the first doctrinal developments on sainthood (*walāya*), which would later be amplified and clarified by Ibn 'Arabī in particular. Tirmidhī was accused of professing the superiority of sainthood over prophecy, which obviously contradicted Islamic dogma. The ambiguity which he left in regard to the relationship between prophecy and sainthood explains why Sufi authors of the first centuries hardly mentioned him.

In particular, he is responsible for the doctrine of the "seal of the saints," which refers in Islam to a figure who brings sainthood to its ultimate perfection. This doctrine is the esoteric counterpart of the "seal of the prophets" (namely, Muhammad). The topic would arouse a great deal of questioning in mystical circles and of condemnation by exoterists.[8] Ibn 'Arabī would be called the "seal of the saints" more convincingly than other Sufis who would also claim this function. He, too, would stir up the same confusion fostered by the Sage of Tirmidh on the relationship between prophecy and sainthood: Ibn 'Arabī did this while demonstrating that Sufism is in perfect accord with the teaching of Islam.[9] Tirmidhī also developed a very elaborate spiritual cosmology and anthropology in which he recognized the preeminence of divine love. Although it seemed unconventional at first sight, his doctrine would create multiple reverberations within Sufism.[10]

Persecutions

The experiences of the first mystics explored all of the horizons, and purposely took on a rebellious character. If Sufis such as Junayd seemed prudent, it was only because an inquisition was in the air. Why? In the vast territories that had recently been conquered by Islam, seditions and schismatic movements emerged here and there, endangering the unity of the Community. However, the doctors of the Law judged that the spiritual claims of some individuals should not be allowed to challenge the politico-religious norms which they were busily establishing. A wave of persecutions followed whose impact was felt by subsequent Sufis. It was as if the doctors of the Law wanted to subpoena the entire human race as witnesses: For example, Abū Sulaymān Dārānī and Sahl Tustarī were driven out—one from Damascus

---

[8] M. Chodkiewicz, *Le Sceau des saints*, chapters 8 and 9. (English edition: *The Seal of the Saints: Prophethood and Sainthood in the Doctrine of Ibn 'Arabi* [Islamic Texts Society, 1993].)

[9] See *supra*, p. 48.

[10] Regarding Tirmidhī, one should mention the work of G. Gobillot, and notably his *Livre de la profondeur des choses* (Lille, 1996).

and the other from Tustar (Iran)—for having said that they conversed with the angels; Bistāmī had to leave his city for having spoken of his "celestial ascension"; Abū Hamza was banished from Tarsus (in the south of present-day Turkey) for having heard the voice of God in the mooing of a cow; Abū Saʿīd Kharrāz was driven out of Fustāt for having described his mystical experience, then from Mecca for having disparaged common believers; Tirmidhī was summoned to explain in front of a court the superiority which he had claimed sainthood held over prophethood, and so on. This wave of persecutions did not touch only the mystics. In the ninth century, theological quarrels created a major break between the rationalistic current of the Muʿtazilites and the traditionnists, leading to additional repressions. The Egyptian Sufi Dhū l-Nūn Misrī, for example, was taken in chains to Baghdad to defend his theological positions, not his spiritual doctrines.

Hallāj is far from being the only one to be condemned at the time of the inquisition carried out by Ghulām Khalīl. There were seventy-five other "lovers of God" who were also involved. It seemed as though someone who loved God could not also fear Him. Abū l-Hasan Nūrī especially exasperated his critics with his extravagant remarks, but he escaped the death penalty by being exiled. Ibn ʿAtāʾ, an interpreter of the Koran from a highly spiritual perspective, voiced approval of Hallāj before the judges: he was beaten to death by the guards of the caliph. Shiblī, another Sufi who was close to Hallāj, avoided the worst by feigning madness. Junayd was not interrogated because he could claim to be a "jurist."

Successors of Junayd and Hallāj

Junayd, Sufism's first apologist, knew how to adapt his language to his audience. He died about eleven years before Hallāj but he undoubtedly foresaw the kind of rupture which was caused by the execution of his ex-disciple. Theologians and state officials were attracted to him, but he shared his esoteric teachings only with some of his disciples, thus furthering the possibility of reconciling the spirit and the letter in Islam. After him, "sober" mystics set themselves to explain the various utterances of "intoxicated" mystics. Following the death of Hallāj, his disciples hid or fled towards the Eastern territories, but the school of Junayd received the support of Hanbalite or Shafiʿite *ulama*,[11] and partly absorbed the other spiritual currents. Up to the present day, the initiatic chains of most Sufi orders pass through him, and some are still simply called the "path of Junayd."

---

[11] The four schools of Sunni Islamic law are the Hanafite, the Shafʿite, the Malikite, and the Hanbalite schools.

The Sufism of "intoxication," which has its origins in Bistāmī and Hallāj, was strengthened by such great Iranian figures as Kharaqānī (d. 1033) and Abū Saʿīd Ibn Abī l-Khayr (d. 1049). The memory of Hallāj was in fact always much honored in Turco-Persian and Far Eastern Sufism. In Arab lands, people were not indifferent to the memory of the subversive of Baghdad, and some held a very special veneration for him. However, it was not possible for the community of Muslim spiritual seekers to use him as a model because any further rifts between exoterists and esoterists would undoubtedly have resulted in a true schism. Those who restored Hallāj to favor did so on their own. In regard to his spiritual temperament, Hallāj was a "Christ-like" Muslim saint, which explains why scholar Louis Massignon, who was a devout Christian, was so attracted to him. The "martyrdom" of Hallāj undoubtedly played a kind of sacrificial role in the future of Sufism. It also heralded the end of a period of unbridled exploration. It did not stop the development of mystical experience in Islam, but it did bring about much greater discretion afterward.

The ecstatic utterances of Shiblī, for example, were more measured. The *shath* did not disappear from them, but it lost something of its spontaneity and its lightning-like intensity. Sufism then entered a period of maturation, during which it established itself as a spiritual norm and became one among the other Islamic disciplines.

The Four Founders of the Legal Schools and Sufism

What was the attitude of the four founders of the Sunni legal schools, who lived in the eighth and ninth centuries, toward Sufism? Their opinions, to the extent that they can be determined, are important in the eyes of Muslims, who view these opinions as guarantees of morality and informed objectivity. It is not unimportant that later Sufis, as well as the *ulama* affiliated with *tasawwuf*, cited them as sources of authority. They regarded them as saints or, at the very least, as models of "Sufi scholars," those who knew, before others, how to link the outer and inner dimensions of the Islamic message within themselves.

The first imam, Abū Hanīfa (d. 767), frequently saw the Prophet in dreams and utilized "unveiling" in developing his legal approach. According to Hujwirī (eleventh century), he would have been a perfect Sufi, wearing a wool cloak and loving spiritual retreats.[12] Abū Hanīfa was the exoteric and esoteric master of Dā'ūd Tā'ī, and he belonged to a major initiatic chain in

---

[12] *Somme spirituelle*, p. 122.

which one would find the Sufis of Baghdad a century later.[13] His contemporary, Ja'far Ṣādiq (d. 765), the sixth Imam of Twelver Shi'ism, established Ja'fari jurisprudence in Shi'ism. Renowned for his knowledge and wisdom, he was a veritable master to several "Sunni" Sufis and he appears in various initiatic chains of early Sufism.

We have an invaluable aphorism from the second imam, Mālik (d. 795), one that is very often quoted in Sufi literature: "Anyone who devotes himself to Sufism without knowing Muslim law falls into heresy; anyone who studies the law while disregarding Sufism ends up corrupting his heart; only someone who practices the two fields of knowledge will achieve spiritual realization." Mālik had a deeply spiritual outlook on religious knowledge (*'ilm*) because, according to him, it could not be evaluated simply from the transmitted teachings: basing himself on several prophetic traditions, he presented religious knowledge as a light that God places in the heart of the scholar or sage.[14]

As for the third imam, Shāfi'ī (d. 820), he initially was hostile to Sufis, whom he had called "big eaters, ignoramuses, intruders. . . ."[15] This appraisal may have been directed at the false ascetics who were vilified by masters, too. It may also have been intended to bear witness to a growing competition between the "jurists" and the Sufis. Then, after a meeting with a Sufi, Shāfi'ī was able to separate the wheat from the chaff in early *tasawwuf*.[16] From then on, his tone changed radically: "I took two things away with me from spending time with the Sufis: 'time is like a sword; if you do not destroy it, it will destroy you' and 'if you do not occupy your carnal soul with the truth, it will keep you busy with futilities.'"[17] He made the following admission: "I like three things in this world: the absence of affectation, to spend time with people in peaceful surroundings, and to follow the way of the Sufis."[18] He is still portrayed, along with Ibn Hanbal, as relying on the intuition of spiritual adepts to solve problems which cannot be solved rationally. Future generations have regarded him as a saint and, more specifically, as a "scholar who put his knowledge into practice" (*al-'ālim al-'āmil*). For many, Shāfi'ī holds an elevated position in the esoteric hierarchy of saints and, according to Ibn Hajar Haytāmī (sixteenth century), he may have become the Pole of

---

[13] See the *Hāshiya* of Ibn 'Abidīn (Boulaq, 1905), vol. I, p. 43.

[14] Ghazzālī, *Mīzān al-i'tidāl* (Cairo, n. d.), p. 192.

[15] J. Udfuwī, *al Mūt* (Kuwait, 1988), p. 49.

[16] Hujwirī, *Somme spirituelle*, p. 147.

[17] These words are frequently cited by "Sufi sages" such as Nawawī and Suyūtī.

[18] Ajlūnī, *Kashf al-khafā'* (Cairo, 1932), vol. I, p. 341.

this hierarchy shortly before his death.[19] Even today, many Egyptians go with written requests to Imam Shāfi'ī's tomb in Cairo to ask him for intercession.

Ahmad Ibn Hanbal (d. 855), founder of the Hanbalite rite, was also behind a pious movement that strictly adhered to scriptural sources. According to many sources, he spoke in praise of Sufis such as Ma'rūf Karkhī and Abū Hamza, whom he consulted on difficult questions. He spoke against Hārith Muhāsibī (d. 857), considering him to be too predisposed to psychological introspection and the use of dialectical reasoning, but he secretly listened to him and then thanked him for his remarks. He enjoined others to "approach knowledge from above," and gave great credence to spiritual visions and miracles, as well as to the esoteric hierarchy of saints (he referred several times to this hierarchy, the *abdāl*). He has been credited with making the following suggestion to his son: "Seek the company of the Sufis, because they surpass us in knowledge, self-control, and spiritual energy."[20]

These four imams lived more than ten centuries ago, and the distortions due to the passage of time make it so that their points of view sometimes appear contradictory to us. For example, Ibn Hanbal at times seems to approve of group gatherings for *dhikr*, and hostile at other times. In any event, these imams did not denounce Sufism, whereas they criticized, for example, rational theology (*kalām*). But, if they displayed an openness to nascent mysticism, why didn't they write anything on spiritual—as opposed to simply religious—life? Sha'rānī (sixteenth century) replied that the Muslims of the first centuries, because of their proximity to the prophetic period, did not yet need such writings. For his part, Shaykh Ahmad al-'Alawī (twentieth century) observed that the imams were not able to reveal the esoteric side of their scholarly temperaments.[21]

Bibliography

Jacqueline Chabbi, "Remarques sur le développement historique des mouvements ascétiques et mystiques au Khurasan," *Studia Islamica*, n° XLVI, 1977, pp. 5-72.

Louis Massignon, *La Passion de Hallāj* (Paris, 1975). (English edition: *The Passion of al-Hallaj*, four vols. [Princeton University Press, 1982].)

Abdelwahhab Meddeb, *Les Dits de Bistāmī* (Paris, 1989).

Stéphane Ruspoli, *Le livre Tawasin de Hallaj* (Paris, 2007).

Sulami, *La Lucidité implacable. Épître des Hommes du Blâme*, translated into French by R. Deladrière (Paris, 1999).

---

[19] *Al-Fatāwā al-hadīthiyya* (compendium of *fatwas*) (Beirut, n. d.), p. 324.

[20] A. al-Kurdī, *Tanwīr al-qulūb* (Cairo, 1939), p. 405.

[21] *Risālat al-nāsir ma'rūf*, which constitutes a formal defense of Sufism (Mostaganem, 1990), p. 42.

THE CENTURIES OF MATURATION (Tenth-Twelfth Centuries)

Legal Scholars, Traditionnists, Sufis: Assertion of Identities

Starting in the ninth century, the men of religion divided themselves into three groups: on the exoteric side there were the legal scholars (*fuqahā'*) and the specialists in the prophetic Tradition (*ashāb al-hadīth*), and on the esoteric side there were Muslim spiritual adepts or seekers—who were being called "Sufis" more and more often. All were claiming to be "learned" people, whom the Prophet had said would be the successors of the prophets. They did not belong to domains that were distinct from each other because the majority of Sufis, even Hallāj, had solid backgrounds in religious fields of knowledge. But a certain distance grew up between them: the specialists in *Hadīth* reproached many spiritual seekers for their lack of competence in this discipline and for exploiting it for their own benefit; the legal scholars did not always understand an approach which operated beyond the scope of their domain; as for Sufis, a number of them moved away from the world of the *ulama*, from which they had sprung. For example, in the tenth century, Shiblī followed studies in *Hadīth* and the law; however, while he was the governor of an Iranian city, he turned to mysticism as the result of an encounter, and joined Junayd. In fourteenth century Cairo, the historian Ibn Khaldūn was a *qādī* who regretted the divide that had developed between the letter and the spirit of the law. He put the blame on the "jurists" for only being interested in the formal aspects of the religion, reminding them that the Prophet embodied both the exoteric and the esoteric sides of Islam.[22] Because of this divide, Shiblī ran, so to speak, into a brick wall when he looked to his professors for knowledge on the intimate relationship between God and man (*fiqh Allāh*). Today, Sufis still lament this reduction to "the letter of the law," which seems to them a kind of treason.

Sufis have accused jurists of restricting the term *fiqh* to mean only "law" or "jurisprudence." In the Koran, the term designates the "understanding" of ordinary things and, beyond, of spiritual realities. It encompasses all that concerns the religious life (dogma, ethics, law, etc.). According to Abū Hanīfa, the founder of the first legal school, *fiqh* is "the knowledge of the human heart, of its rights and its duties."[23] But soon the term applied only to the argumentative knowledge of legal statutes, and this usage has continued up to the present day. The Sufis wasted no time in accusing jurists of failing

---

[22] See his *Shifā' al-sā'il*, translated into French by R. Pérez under the title *La Voie et la Loi* (Paris, 1991), p. 111.

[23] A. Zaydān, *Al-Madkhal li-dirāsat al-sharī'a al-islamiyya* (Beirut, 1995), p. 54.

to understand the discipline of *tasawwuf*, while all of them, more or less, were educated in *fiqh*. "Every Sufi is a jurist [*faqīh*], but the reverse is not true," they enthusiastically claimed, though the reality of the situation did not always match their claim. This image of the Sufi scholar of the law was evident throughout the centuries that followed, but it had already been the case much earlier for Dhū l-Nūn Misrī (who studied with Imam Mālik), for Junayd, of course, and for others less well known. Ultimately, the frequent conflict between Sufis and "jurists" made it possible for challenges and questions to be leveled against both sides. But these residual tensions involve only the people who are the exponents of the doctrines, not the doctrines in themselves.

Radiance from Khurasan (Tenth-Eleventh Centuries)

After the death of Hallāj, Khurasan became the main seat of mystical activity. Iraqi Sufism superseded the other movements of the eleventh century. The temporal powers were, in fact, able to deal more easily with people established in cities, and were from then on eager to promote a reassuring image of Sufis, which was not the same for local Karrāmis, misfit ascetics, or the Malāmatis who cultivated secrecy. This new situation for Sufism manifested itself within both architecture and writing.

— **Sufism and Shafi'ism.** The Sufis adopted the Karrāmi institution of *khānqāhs*; these became places where the methods of the future Sufi brotherhoods would take shape: the communal life of disciples around a master, initiatic practices such as the making of the pact, the transmission of methods of *dhikr*, the retreat (*khalwa*), and the investiture of the "cloak" (*muraqqa'a*, *khirqa*). The relationship between master and disciple became more personal and demanding, as well as more formalized. The "master who teaches" (*shaykh al-ta'līm*) was transformed into the "master who educates" (*shaykh al-tarbiya*): a Sufism of ethics moved on to a Sufism of initiation. A more and more codified discipline became established in the *khānqāhs*. Abū Sa'īd Ibn Abī l-Khayr (d. 1049), for example, established ten rules for disciples living in the *khānqāhs* which he established.

Little by little, Sufism made its way into Sunni culture thanks to the links which developed between the spheres of the mystics and of the *madrasas*. These colleges of higher education, probably born in Nishapur in Khurasan, were targeted at promoting Ash'arite theology associated with the Shafi'ite school, and were reputedly more open to mysticism. In eastern areas, this school of law has competed with the Hanafite school, which has affinities with Mu'tazilite rationalist theology and which appears to be less approving of mysticism than was its founder. In fact, the Hanafite *ulama* were averse to

Sufism and they rejected the miracles of the saints. It is only later that they would be won over to Sufism.[24] "If the Sufis adopt the doctrines of Shāfiʻī," explained one spiritual adept of the twelfth century, "it is because these doctrines impose more restrictions [than those of Abū Hanīfa] and in practice require more rigor in the practice of religious duties."[25]

The Shafiʻite *ulama* of Khurasan introduced the discipline of Sufism as one of the subjects studied in the *madrasas,* and some Sufi masters themselves founded *madrasas.* Relations grew between the *ulama* and Sufis, giving rise to real affinities between them. Thus the initiatory chain (*silsila*) and the investiture of the "cloak" (*khirqa*) served the same ends for Sufis as the chain of transmitters (*isnād*) and the authorization to instruct (*ijāza*) for the *ulama.* For the Sufis, they attest that such and such a person has followed a spiritual discipline under the direction of an authorized master, whose initiatory chain stretches back to the Prophet.

Beginning in the eleventh century, *madrasas* were established in Iraq, where they formed the religious framework of the Seljuk state. This "official" educational system, whose programs were homogeneous from then on, had the role of imposing Sunnism above other rival ideological movements. The danger was posed, in particular, by the Shiʻism of the Buwaihids, who held the reins of power until 1055, but especially by the Shīʻa Ismāʻīlis. Their branch of Shiʻism professes a radicalism that is esoteric (i.e. of a spiritual nature) but also political, and it is active in propaganda. Its groups of missionaries were based in the north of Iran and Syria, as well as in the Fatimid state of Egypt, which was run by Ismāʻīlis. These missionaries were focused on destabilizing the Abbasid caliphate and its Turkish protectors. Consequently, Sufism was called upon by the political authorities to support the caliphate (which was the symbolic guarantor of Sunni Islam) and the temporal powers (Seljuks, Ayyubids, Mamluks, etc.) which supplied their force of arms. The grand vizier of the Seljuks, Nizām al-Mulk, was from Khurasan, and he was an Ashʻarite and a Shafiʻite. He was the first to honor the Sufis, asking them, in exchange, for their active support for the Sunni cause. In 1092, he died at the hands of the "Assassins," Ismāʻīlis from Alamut who were considered as "heretics" by the Sufis.

— *Manuals of Sufism.* The desire to integrate Sufism into Islamic culture also appeared in the manuals written in the tenth and eleventh centuries.

---

[24] It is said that treatises on the science of *Hadīth* such as by the Hanafite scholar Zaylaʻī (d. 1360) are excellent because they reflect the Sufi personality of their author.

[25] M. Ebn E. Monawwar, *Les Étapes mystiques du shaykh Abu Saʻid,* translated into French by M. Achena (Paris, 1974), pp. 38-39.

These manuals fulfilled several needs: to give organization to the spiritual heritage which the first masters had passed on, to formulate for Sufis themselves their own doctrines, and to set up Sufism as a discipline through well-developed apologetics. In these manuals, Sufis declared that they followed the same creed as other Muslims, that they would uphold prevalent theological ideas from then on and, especially, that their experiences did not contradict the scriptural sources but, in fact, were fed by those sources. These manuals also served to confer upon sainthood (*walāya*), the heir to prophecy, its full rights, and to establish a sometimes implicit equivalence between sainthood and Sufism. Lastly, the manuals have preserved for us a spiritual heritage which would have largely disappeared without them.

Most authors of manuals lived in Khurasan and in Central Asia, and stayed in *khānqāhs*. Obviously belonging to the movement of sobriety within Sufism, almost all of them followed the initiatory path of Junayd. They were very spare with comments on the excesses of "intoxicated" mystics, going back and forth between silence and justification; they sometimes also criticized the attitude of certain shaykhs in order to reinforce the orthodoxy of Sufism. Such was the case of Sarrāj (d. 988), the author of *Kitāb al-Luma'*, who showed that Sufism had its roots in the Koran and the *Sunna*. To him, the Sufis were the true successors to the Prophet. They were the only ones who fully lived the lofty message of Islam, and they represented the spiritual elite (*khāssa*) of the community. The *Kitāb al-ta'arruf*, written by Kalābādhī (d. 995), a Hanafite, is celebrated for its brevity and for its clarity of exposition. It shows Iraqi Sufism in a good light, and affirms that this quickly spread throughout Central Asia.[26] In his work *The Food of the Hearts* (*Qūt al-qulūb*), Abū Tālib Makkī (d. 996) disseminated the ethical teachings of the Sālimiyya school, which traced its origins back to Sahl Tustarī (d. 896). This manual was intended above all for beginners, to whom he suggested a daily liturgy.

In Khurasan, Sulamī (d. 1021) formed his own school. He carried out quite a remarkable synthesis of the various currents of spirituality. In particular, the synthesis was between the way of the *malāma* of Central Asia, whose doctrines he articulated (e.g., the indictment of the carnal soul, the necessity of hiding graces and mystical states, and of erasing all traces of pious works),[27] and Iraqi Sufism. It is thanks to him that the latter is permeated by the *malāmati* spirit, as well as that the term *tasawwuf* became widely used to indicate the spiritual method in Islam. His work, *The Generations of the*

---

[26] Translated into French by R. Deladrière under the title *Traité de soufisme* (Paris, 1981). (English edition: *The Doctrine of the Sufis*, translated by A. J. Arberry [Cambridge University Press, 1977].)

[27] See *La Lucidité implacable*.

Sufis (*Tabaqāt al-sūfiyya*) includes many Khurasanis otherwise unknown in *tasawwuf*. The literary genre of *Tabaqāt* (biographical collections devoted to the various specialists in a field of knowledge, such as lawyers, philologists, "traditionnists," etc.) now included Sufis as well, proof that their discipline had come to be recognized. Another proof of this recognition is that Sulamī was invited to teach his spiritual commentary on the Koran, *Inner Realities of Koranic Commentary* (*Haqā'iq al-tafsīr*), in the mosques of Baghdad.

Abū Nu'aym Isfahānī (d. 1038) was one of his pupils, and he, too, was learned in the science of *Hadīth*. In his book *The Ornament of the Saints* (*Hilyat al-awliyā'*), he put forward a scene of piety and sanctity in Islam, whose origins are traced back to the Companions and the "rightly-guided caliphs." Each saying of the saints whom he quoted is preceded by the chain of those who transmitted it (*isnād*).

The *Epistle* (*Risāla*) of Qushayrī (d. 1072), which is better organized than Isfahānī's book, remains the most-studied manual of Sufism. After devoting a section to biographical sketches of some Sufis (which owes much to the collection of Sulamī), Qushayrī addresses some of the terminology of *tasawwuf* which is so puzzling to exoterists. Then, as a good pedagogue, he explains some essential topics within Sufism: miracles, sanctity, visions, the relation of master and disciple, etc. Following Sulamī, who was his master, he reinforced the orthodoxy of Sufism by stigmatizing usurpers; this topic would become a recurring theme among later masters. He represented the alliance, which held much future promise, between *tasawwuf*, Ash'arite theology, and the Shafi'ite school. His Sufi commentary on the Koran, *The Subtle Allusions* (*Latā'if al-ishārāt*), which was also much influenced by Sulamī's, synthesized the spiritual exegesis of the earliest period. His *Gradation of Initiatic Progress* (*Tartīb al-sulūk*), which is sometimes attributed to one of his disciples, was the first treatise to explain the rules and effects of the practice of *dhikr*, which at that same time was spreading throughout the *khānqāhs*.

The first manual in Persian, *The Unveiling* (*Kashf al-mahjūb*), was written by Hujwirī (d. between 1073 and 1077). Born in what is now Afghanistan, he settled in Lahore (in present-day Pakistan) where his tomb is still visited by many pilgrims. More subjective than the *Epistle* of Qushayrī, this book is especially valuable for its accounts of the experiences of the author and the lives of the mystics of his time. Just as in the earlier manuals, this one traces the roots of Sufism to pure Islamic tradition, and presents each of the four "rightly-guided caliphs" as a particular aspect of the Path.

Ansārī Harawī (d. 1089), who was also born in what is now Afghanistan, was a unique figure due to his theological and mystical choices. As a young student, he belonged to the Hanbalite school because it refused to subject the Koran and the *Sunna* to human reason. This rigorous fideism did not prevent him from being set ablaze by Kharaqānī, that "brilliant illiterate" who was characterized by "the intemperance and incontinence of his speech."[28] Neither did it prevent him from recognizing the authenticity of the experience of Hallāj, nor from approaching the divine Oneness in monistic terms: his famous treatise of *The Stages of Travelers Towards God* (*Manāzil al-sā'irīn*)[29] closes with the ultimate stage of *tawhīd*, which is blinding and bewildering to man, since only God can definitively attest to His own Oneness. Elsewhere, Ansārī confides that man has existence only in, through, and for God. Ibn Khaldūn is considered to have seen in Ansārī a precursor to the school of the "absolute Oneness of Being" (*al-wahda al-mutlaqa*), one even more daring than Ibn 'Arabī.[30] The example of Ansārī demolishes the biased view that the Hanbalite school of law is hostile to the mystical dimension of Islam.

Ansārī went through some ordeals and was exiled for a while, but this was for theological reasons and not due to his mysticism: he fought some "innovators" too openly, namely Ash'arite or Mu'tazilite theologians. However, he finished his days surrounded by disciples in his famous *khānqāh* in Herat, finally recognized by the Seljuk leaders and the Abbasid caliph.

Ghazzālī: The Supremacy of Spiritual Intuition over Reason

The maturation of the tenth and eleventh centuries culminated in the work of Abū Hāmid Ghazzālī (d. 1111). History attributes to him the reconciliation of Sunnism, whose identity from this time on would become less restrictive, with Sufism. His major work, *Revival of the Religious Sciences* (*Ihyā' 'ulūm al-dīn*), carried out a fusion between theology, law, and mysticism and, to tell the truth, owed much to the manuals which we have mentioned above, especially to *The Food of the Hearts* by Makkī. But, unlike the latter, Ghazzālī did not measure Sufism with the yardstick of orthodoxy: he explained Islam through the light of Sufism.

Ghazzālī, as with many of the Sufis whom we have mentioned above, was from Khurasan and was both Ash'arite and Shafi'ite. Blessed with an uncommon intelligence, he was also very cultured. For this reason, he was favored by the Seljuk authorities and he spearheaded the pro-Sunni policy of

---

[28] See the cover of *Paroles d'un soufi*, sayings of Kharaqānī presented and translated into French by C. Tortel (Paris, 1998).

[29] This treatise and two others were translated into French by S. de Beaurecueil under the title *Chemin de Dieu* (Paris, 1985). (English edition of this treatise alone: *Stations of the Wayfarer* [Fons Vitae, forthcoming].)

[30] *Muqaddima*, translated into French by V. Monteil, *Discours sur l'Histoire universelle* (Beirut, 1968), pp. 1024-1025. (English edition: translated by Franz Rosenthal [Princeton University Press, 1967].)

the grand vizier Nizām al-Mulk. Because he was considered to be "an official thinker,"[31] he accompanied the movement of the Seljuks from east to west, from Nishapur to Baghdad, following the route of the Turkish conquests. His successive works seem to bring to mind military operations being launched against the doctrinal adversaries of the temporal powers. Ghazzālī taught at the famous Nizāmiyya *madrasa* in Baghdad, where he quickly achieved great celebrity; however, he then went through a serious inner crisis which resulted in a nervous ailment. He quit all of his duties and undertook a life of peregrination and spiritual retreat lasting eleven years. When considering the reasons which have been proposed to explain this crisis, it is necessary to keep in mind Ghazzālī's questioning of his own intellectual knowledge, his rejection of the legalistic approach to religion, and his need for personal experience of the divine. There is no doubt Ghazzālī was also aware of being used by the temporal authorities, whose agenda had become more and more separate from his.

Such was the exemplary nature of the career of Ghazzālī, one of the most eminent scholars of his time. After his death he came to be called "the proof of Islam." Ghazzālī mastered the most diverse doctrines in order to encourage their practice (e.g., Scholastic theology) or to refute them (e.g., Hellenistic philosophy or Ismāʿīlī esoterism), but he declared that Sufism is the supreme path leading to God and that Sufis alone can be regarded as the heirs of the prophets.[32] Although he may have identified Islam with the key elements of Sufism, he did not hold back from criticizing those whom he regarded as "pseudo-Sufis."

Ghazzālī established the supremacy of spiritual unveiling (*kashf*) and inspiration (*ilhām*) over reason. One only attains to God, he said, through a kind of knowledge that has been likened to experiencing "taste" (*dhawq*), which is the result of spiritual discipline performed under the direction of a master. One can achieve the vision of certainty (*yaqīn*) of divine realities only through contemplation and by going beyond theological hair-splitting. Ghazzālī also helped to legitimize the way of fervent love for God, which had hitherto been the subject of so much suspicion: the adept travels on

---

[31]   M. Hogga, *Orthodoxie, subversion et réforme en islam: Ghazālī et les Seljūqides* (Paris, 1993), p. 41.

[32]   See his autobiography *Al-Munqidh min al-dalāl*, translated into French under the title *Erreur et délivrance* by F. Jabre (Beirut, 1969), pp. 100-101. (English edition: *The Faith and Practice of Al-Ghazālī*, translated by W. Montgomery Watt [George Allen & Unwin, 1953].) At the end of his life, notes G. Makdisi, Ghazzālī no longer considered himself to be an Ashʿarite theologian: in his opinion, Scholastic theology was only an instrumental science which by no means ended in the knowledge of God.

his way towards God, who is pure Light, by removing the veils of darkness before him. His metaphysics of light, which he expounded in *The Niche for Lights (Mishkāt al-anwār)*,[33] clearly has Neoplatonic and gnostic elements, but it refocuses the community, which has been lured away by various deviations, on the person of the Prophet, because all beings draw their light from the Muhammadian Light (*Nūr Muhammadī*). He held that the mystical life can, and must, be lived within Sunnism, because it alone guarantees the conformity of mystical experience to the message of the Revelation.

Ghazzālī finished his life as a Sufi in Tus, his birthplace, where he founded a *khānqāh*. His *Revival of the Religious Sciences* quickly spread throughout the Muslim world because it was conceived as a complete guide to the religious life, associating traditional Sunni piety with the introspective discipline of Sufism. The book influenced the growing trend of "Sufi scholars"—who were generally Ash'arites, but also included some Shafi'ite jurists—and also many masters of "sober" Sufism. However, some spiritual figures were to be less inclined than Ghazzālī to reject dialectical reasoning or to accept the preeminence of gnosis.

The mystical thought of Ghazzālī is more complex than it seems on first sight. On the one hand, Ghazzālī does disarm the "jurists" by explaining that the desire of the Sufis to achieve union with the divine does not in any way mean that they claim to achieve union with the Substance (*ittihād*), but that they simply aim to extinguish the contingent being in the face of the Absolute, which Junayd had earlier formulated as "extinction of the ego in the divine Oneness" (*fanā' fī l-tawhīd*). This is the ultimate realization of servitude, of *islām*, and of the dogma of the divine Oneness, which should cause no objections. But on the other hand, in the *Revival (Ihyā')* Ghazzālī develops elements of the future doctrine of the Oneness of Being (*wahdat al-wujūd*). For example, he states "There is nothing that has existence if it is not God. . . . Existence belongs only to the sole Reality, to the One."[34] Some passages of *The Niche for Lights* prefigure this doctrine even more distinctly, but they have generally escaped the censure of exoterists.

The Persistence of the Mysticism of "Intoxication"

The marked tendency of the authors of manuals and then by Ghazzālī to urge moderate behavior and to avoid conflicts does gloss over another face

---

[33] *Le Tabernacle des Lumières*, edited and translated into French by R. Deladrière (Paris, 1981). (English edition: *The Mishkat Al-Anwar of Al-Ghazzali*, translated by W.H.T. Gairdner [Forgotten Books, 2008].)

[34] *Ihyā'*, vol. IV, p. 230.

of Sufism, one that is just as authentic but is purposely rebellious and even mischievous. Obviously, there is a sense of play in "intoxicated" mysticism which, by way of consequence, is susceptible to admitting many counterfeits. Hallāj was often seen as a conjurer or a charlatan. To be precise, the martyr of Baghdad left his mark upon all the Sufis mentioned here, and they all venerate his memory; some tend to identify themselves very closely with him. Shaykh Abū Saʿīd Ibn Abī l-Khayr, for example, dared to preach from the pulpit exemption from the pilgrimage to Mecca in favor of the "pilgrimage of the heart." This ecstatic mystic, with his provocative Malamatism, initially attracted the disapproval of Qushayrī, in the same way that Hallāj was criticized by Junayd, but his unique charisma and visionary gifts soon won over the admiration of his critic. Qushayrī seemed in the end to concede that Abū Saʿīd was attached to the *Sharīʿa* on the basis of *Haqīqa*, not through ordinary human rules of behavior.

The personality of Ahmad Ghazzālī (d. 1126) complemented that of his brother Abū Hāmid, the author of the *Ihyā'*. Ahmad, who was initiated into Sufism while still very young, may have had some influence in the "conversion" of his brother. An enthusiastic disciple of Hallāj, Ahmad elegantly touched on all the subtleties of the loving relationship between God and man. Thus he was seen as a pioneer of the path of mystical love in Iranian Sufism. Ibn al-Jawzī said of him, no doubt somewhat glibly, that he had an inordinate taste for the "contemplation of beautiful young men"; this practice—the *shāhid-bāzi* in Persian—was an ancient one: the beautiful face of a boy, holding a red rose in front of him, symbolized in two ways the beauty of the Beloved, and was able to guide some to union through love. Let us recall that in a society where the separation of the sexes is rather strict, women can seldom be a support for contemplation. Nevertheless, the distinction between chaste, spiritual love and profane, carnal love does not change. Most masters condemned such contemplation of beardless boys, and the presence of these beautiful young men in spiritual gatherings gradually faded away. The charge of homosexuality was all the more easy to dismiss against Ahmad Ghazzālī, who taught law in the Nizāmiyya *madrasa* of Baghdad, since he was known for his penchant for mystical love.

The favorite disciple of Ahmad was ʿAyn al-Qudāt Hamadhānī (d. 1131), who became the victim of the exoterists' lack of comprehension. A Christlike and Hallājian figure, he was martyred at the age of thirty-three years, after a secretive trial. Following the example of Hallāj, he claimed that Iblīs, the fallen angel Satan, had been rehabilitated. He did, however, accept orthodox dogma, but he formulated it in a way that was very ambiguous. Always in the vein of Hallāj, he distilled from the regulations of Islam purely mystical interpretations which the doctors of the Law could not accept. ʿAyn al-Qudāt, whose name means "the quintessence of the judges," or "the judge of the judges," was, most paradoxically, a *qādī* (a judge of *Sharīʻa* law) from the age of thirteen. . . . His *Preludes* (*Tamhīdāt*) would be contemplated and commented on by the Sufis of India, where the legacy of Hallāj has remained the most vibrant.[35]

Rūzbihān Baqlī (d. 1209), from Shiraz in Iran, removed the distance between human love and divine love: the initiate, immersed in the mystery of the divine Oneness, loses his own identity to some extent; he does not pass from a profane conception to a sacred conception of love—he is, instead, being metamorphosed or transfigured by pure love. This is the path of the "Faithful to Love," the religion of beauty which is distinguished from the dualistic religion of ascetics.[36] A rarity in Sufi literature, this ecstatic related his prolific visions of God, archangels, prophets, and celestial figures in a personal journal called *The Unveiling of Secrets*.[37] But Rūzbihān had a reference point in Muhammad, the prophet of beauty, the light of the cosmos, and the intercessor for humanity. Having mastered the Sufi legacy in both its "sober" and "intoxicated" dimensions, Rūzbihān proposed an orderly vision of sanctity, one closely linked to prophecy.[38] His theophanic experiences fed into his doctrinal teachings in a harmonious way.

Bibliography

Denis Gril, "Spiritualités," in *États, sociétés et cultures du monde musulman médiéval—Xe-x^{ve} siècle* (Paris, 2000), vol. II, pp. 421-452.

Margaret Malamud, "Sufi Organizations and Structures of Authority in Medieval Nishapur," *International Journal of Middle East Studies*, Cambridge, 1994, n° 3, vol. 26, pp. 427-444.

POETRY AND METAPHYSICS

Iranian Mystical Poetry (Twelfth-Fifteenth Centuries): ʻAttār, Rūmī, and Others

Starting in the twelfth century, Iranian mysticism took shape in the poetry of the Persian language; their destinies became wedded together through their

---

[35] The *Tamhīdāt* were translated into French by C. Tortel as *Les Tentations métaphysiques* (Paris, 1992).

[36] See *Le Jasmin des fidèles d'amour*, translated into French by H. Corbin (Paris, 1991) (new edition). The "Fedeli d'Amore" were the [artistic] colleagues of Dante.

[37] *Kashf al-asrār*, presented and translated into French by P. Ballanfat (Paris, 1991). (English edition: *The Unveiling of Secrets: Diary of a Sufi Master*, translated by Carl W. Ernst [Parvardigar Press, 1997].)

[38] See *L'Ennuagement du coeur*, another treatise by Rūzbihān, presented and translated into

joint and rapid rise. Poetic expression shares a similarly ineffable essence with mysticism and a similar dependence on symbols and the eternal ambiguity of language. The discursive reason is a "wooden leg," Rūmī said. Prose, which is the natural vehicle for discursive reason, cannot capture one's inner life, whereas poetry makes it possible to suggest spiritual truths that one cannot or does not want to make explicit.

Persian literature, whose central figures are 'Attār (d. 1190), Rūmī (d. 1273), 'Irāqī (d. 1289), Shabistarī (d. 1320), and Jāmī (d. 1492), would never have reached so high a degree of refinement if it had not been imbued with Sufism. Far from being just a brilliant exercise in style, this poetry became exceptionally didactic, and then illuministic.[39] Abū Sa'īd Ibn Abī l-Khayr inspired this symbiosis. He preferred to recite poetic rather than Koranic verses from the pulpit, and he considered the Koran and poetry to be on the same level.[40] Without going quite so far, Sufis such as Junayd and Ghazzālī explained that man experiences more emotion through listening to poems than to verses of scripture. They said that emotion must necessarily exist because there is so much disparity between the eternal divine Word and a person who hears it. In the late 1950s Henry Corbin said that the *Dīwān* of Hāfiz was "still being used like a Bible by Iranian Sufis."[41]

Often regarded as the greatest Iranian mystical poet after Rūmī, 'Attār was a born storyteller. His compositions were usually in rhyming couplets (*mathnawī*), a poetic genre which Rūmī would come to exemplify. 'Attār was an apothecary and perfumer, which is indicated by his surname. His master is not known to us, but 'Attār himself has always been much admired by the Sufis. For a long time it was thought that 'Attār had been killed by the Mongols in 1230 in his city of Nishapur (he would have been 114 years old at that time), but he probably died in 1190.[42] The message that shines through his famous epic poem *The Language of the Birds* (*Mantiq al-tayr*) is that the key to the mysteries of God and the universe is self-knowledge. 'Attār also

French by P. Ballanfat (Paris, 1998).

[39] Translator's Note: The term "illuministic" refers to practices and doctrines that focus on *personal* spiritual enlightenment, often through meditation or contemplation, and which are often related to gradual spiritual progress through initiatory disciplines. These practices and doctrines, therefore, are usually outside of the customary frameworks of the great religious traditions.

[40] M. Ebn E. Monawwar, *Les Étapes mystiques du shaykh Abu Sa'id*, p. 15.

[41] *L'Imagination créatrice dans le soufisme d'Ibn 'Arabī* (Paris, 1958), p. 31. (English edition: *Alone with the Alone: Creative Imagination in the Sufism of Ibn 'Arabī* [Princeton University Press, 1998].)

[42] A. Knysh, *Islamic Mysticism*, p. 152.

composed a very lively biographical collection on the early mystics, *The Memorial of the Saints* (*Tadhkirat al-auliyā'*), which highlights the extraordinary and glorifies Hallāj.[43]

Rūmī: Music and Dance

Called Mawlanā ("our master," Mevlana in Turkish) by his disciples, Jalāl al-Dīn Rūmī (d. 1273) is the best-known Muslim mystic in the West. He personifies the path of love and intoxication in Sufism, while Ibn 'Arabī represents the way of gnosis, or of metaphysical intellectuality. This distinction, we should recall, is only of relative value: the Andalusian master "is also—or, more precisely, is first and foremost—a spiritual master devoured by love."[44]

The young Jalāl al-Dīn left his native Transoxania (in northeastern Khurasan) with his family as they fled the Mongol invasion. He may have come across 'Attār along the route of his exile, but in any case, he always acknowledged a debt to 'Attār. Rūmī's family settled down in a land where there was security, in Konya (in Anatolia), which was then the capital of the Seljuk sultanate of Rūm. After becoming a noted religious scholar, Rūmī met his master in the person of Shams of Tabrīz, the "sun" (*shams*) of Rūmī. Though he was a roaming dervish, Shams was far from being illiterate, as is often asserted. He waited sixteen years before speaking with Rūmī. On his own transmutation following this experience, Rūmī said, "I was raw, I was cooked, and then I was burned to a crisp." More than just an initiatory relationship, the two men lived in an ecstatic spiritual passion that transformed them both.

Contrary to the commonly accepted opinion, it was not Rūmī who established the famous whirling dance that is characteristic of his Sufi order. It was already being practiced during sessions of spiritual music (*samā'*) along with other spontaneous gestures and movements. During these gatherings, one listened to mystical poems recited either with or without instrumental accompaniment, which would transport the listeners to ecstasy. Several sources reported that Rūmī was also seen whirling by himself, and even in the street. Afterward, when the Mevlevis, whom we call the "whirling dervishes," adopted his ritual, they kept only the circular dance. Rūmī inaugu-

---

[43] *Le Mémorial des saints*, translated into French by A. Pavet de Cour-teille (Paris, 1976). (English edition: *Muslim Saints and Mystics: Episodes from the Tadhkirat al-Auliya'* (*Memorial of the Saints*) [Routledge and Kegan Paul, 1966].) Some of 'Attār's other works which have been translated into French are: *Le Livre de l'épreuve* (Paris, 1981) (I. de Gastines); and *Le Livre des Secrets* (Paris, 1985) (C. Tortel).

[44] C. Addas, *Ibn 'Arabī et le voyage sans retour*, p. 106. (English edition: *Ibn 'Arabī: The Voyage of No Return* [Islamic Texts Society, 2000], p. 104.)

rated his *madrasa* with a memorable session of *samā'* that was attended by all of the local officials: he would always benefit from the steadfast support of the political authorities, and his order would be very influential with the Ottoman sultans. Scenes such as Rūmī dancing in the embrace of a disciple were not, of course, to the taste of certain *ulama;* however, the master, who was himself a scholar of religious sciences, knew how to respond to them, even to the point of "converting" them, and his popularity among the inhabitants of Konya—including among the Jews and Christians— protected him from any censorship.

The famous poetic summa of Rūmī, the *Mathnawī*,[45] opens with the lament of a reed (i.e. a flute) ripped from its native soil, the divine world, and aspiring to return there. Rūmī perceived this lower world as a prison—which is in accordance with a saying of the Prophet[46]—and he therefore could understand Hallāj, who sought to pre-empt his own death. In his own ecstatic way, Rūmī professed the Oneness of Being (*wahdat al-wujūd*): "[To Rūmī] God and the world, the creatures and the Creator, are but one. To believe in a God who is separated from the world is but a dualism that is opposed to *tawhīd* (divine Oneness). Multiplicity is only an appearance, an illusion. The world, the macrocosm, is similar to the human being (microcosm), the universal spirit is his soul and the material world is his body."[47] It is from this that the universalism of Rūmī derives, as well as his opening to all the forms of worship of the One, the Unique.

The *Mathnawī* of Rūmī, sometimes called the "Persian Koran," assumes the stature of a sacred text in Turkish, Iranian, and Indian environments. Unlike Ibn 'Arabī, Rūmī employed simple language and images which are comprehensible to anyone. His poetry suited peoples who did not always have access to scriptural sources or to works on Islamic sciences that were written in Arabic. His poetry strongly contributed to the development of Persian or Urdu mystical poetic expression. Its radiance is evident up to the twentieth century in, for example, the thought of Muhammad Iqbal (d. 1938) the spiritual father of Pakistan. In his poetic work, Iqbal drew upon the power of awakening and freedom found in the *Mathnawī*.[48]

---

[45] Translated by É. de Vitray-Meyerovitch and D. Mortazavi (Monaco, 1990). (English edition: The six books of Rūmī's *Mathnawī* were translated into English by Reynold A. Nicholson and presented in three volumes as *The Mathnawī of Jalālu'ddīn Rūmī* [Gibb Memorial Trust, 1990].)

[46] "This lower world is the prison of the believer. . ." (Ibn Hanbal).

[47] Introduction to Éva de Vitray, p. 16.

[48] See, for example, written in Urdu and translated into French, *Le Livre de l'Éternité (Djavid-Nama)* and *L'Aile de Gabriel (Bāl-é-Djibrīl)* (Paris, 1977).

On the other hand, the influence of Rūmī has had difficulty moving across the linguistic barrier and symbolic system of the Arab world, because many of the metaphors employed by Persian poets are not familiar to the Arab public. Moreover, Arabic religious writing favors doctrinal expositions which may be analytical or allusive, but which are primarily in prose. Arab authors are certainly fond of rhymed prose, a genre which gave rise to several collections of maxims such as the *Hikam* of Ibn ʿAtāʾAllāh. In Iran during the Sunni Mughul period and then the Safavid Shiʿite period, the tension between mystics and jurists may have been intense, but the control exerted by exoterists was more obvious in the Arab world, thus resulting in a literature that was more polemical or apologetic.

One Sufi who was consumed with love was Fakhr al-Dīn ʿIrāqī. He lived first in India but later fled to Anatolia before the Mongolian onslaught, where he met Rūmī and Qūnāwī, Ibn ʿArabī's disciple. His *Flashes* (*Lamaʿāt*) represents the exact juncture where the author of the *Mathnawī* and the Andalusian master meet, and this book inspired several generations of Persian and Indian poets.[49] ʿIrāqī was the first Persian poet influenced by Ibn ʿArabī, and he had himself buried near the latter in Damascus.

Shabistarī, originally from Azerbaijan, is known for his *Rose Garden of Mystery*,[50] a poem of almost indecipherable allusions. It has been the subject of many commentaries and has been used by many Iranian Sufis as a kind of spiritual guidebook. Very much in the spirit of Rūmī, Shabistarī proclaimed the desire of all that exists for union with God and the absolute unity of all existence. He also revisited metaphysical themes that had come from the teachings of Ibn ʿArabī.

Jāmī, who came from current-day Afghanistan, is regarded as the last great Persian poet. He also wrote a prose commentary on Ibn ʿArabī. As a good Naqshbandi (a Sufi order), Jāmī practiced a brand of militant Sunni Islam that was opposed to the various forms of Shiʿism. He left a rich biographical collection on various Sufis, the *Emanations of Divine Intimacy* (*Nafahāt al-uns*), which is, of course, indebted to earlier works of this genre.[51]

Turkish Mystical Poetry: Yūnus Emre

Throughout the medieval period, Persian was the language of letters in the

---

[49] Translator's Note: The text of this poem, along with a commentary on it and biographical notes on the author, can be found in *Fakhruddin Iraqi: Divine Flashes* (*Classics of Western Spirituality*), translated and introduced by William C. Chittick and Peter Lamborn Wilson (Paulist Press, 1982).

[50] The *Gulshan-i rāz* was translated into English by Florence Lederer as *The Secret Rose Garden* (Forgotten Books, 2008).

[51] Translated into French as *Les Voies de la vertu ou les haleines de la familiarité* (Paris, 1999).

non-Arab East; it was especially cultivated in urban areas. At the same time, there appeared other modes of expression that resulted from popular culture; these were, however, still influenced by the more "erudite" model. Yūnus Emre (d. 1321) illustrated this intersection of influences well. He was born in Anatolia but his origins were from the Turkmen tribes of Central Asia. His poetic predecessor was Ahmad Yasawī (d. 1167), a saint who is still to this day venerated in that region; he composed popular poetry which was transmitted orally and which had been influenced by the shamanism found in Turkistan while it was still not very Islamized. Yūnus adopted the rhythms of popular Turkish songs and their simple style into his poetry, but his doctrine had much in common with that of the Persian mystics: using terminology sometimes close to that of Rūmī, he sang of the desire for God and of the awakening of a consciousness of the cosmos which has the Muhammadian Reality as its reference point; from this viewpoint, the Prophet, who is the goal of all creation, is the supreme intercessor.

The Bektashi (a Sufi order) poets would claim Yūnus as the first among them; they were inspired by his humanism and his spirit of tolerance, but they would be unlike him in their syncretism.

Arabic Mystical Poetry: Ibn 'Arabī and Ibn al-Fārid

The Arabs cultivated the art of poetry to the highest degree. During the pre-Islamic period, "inspired" poets practically cast a spell over that society.

Islam has challenged this kind of influence, but not poetic activity in itself. Like Persian poetry, Arabic mystical poetry has favored the intuitive attempt to apprehend higher realities over attempts at doctrinal prose expositions, which can appear to be impotent. This poetry serves several purposes. As with the example of the famous *Burda* of Būsīrī,[52] it is sometimes widely disseminated but, because of its purposely sibylline character, it is actually targeted at a public of the already initiated.

Ibn 'Arabī, though he was particularly known for his doctrinal works in prose, left a vast body of poetic work. One collection had a special destiny: *The Interpreter of Ardent Desires* (*Tarjumān al-ashwāq*). In front of the Kaaba, in Mecca, Ibn 'Arabī met Nizām, a young Persian whose refinement of spirit and whose beauty transported him, inspiring him to write these poems. In them, the author used the symbolism of courtly love to address divine love. "The experience of human love has something in it that is fundamentally linked to mystical ardor."[53] But this use of allegory, which is very common

---

[52] See *supra*, p. 53.

[53] P. Lory, from his Foreword to *L'Interprète des désirs*, presentation and translation into

among mystics and was approved by Ghazzālī, was not something covered by the classifications understood by the jurists of Aleppo, who accused Ibn ‘Arabī of having produced an erotic work "disguised as mystical poems."[54] The Andalusian master then found himself constrained to write a commentary revealing the spiritual (and not erotic) dimension of his *Tarjumān*.

Ibn al-Fārid (d. 1235), called "the prince of lovers," led a discrete and solitary life in Cairo, but his verses continue to urge ecstatic sessions of *sama'*. He was one of the greatest poets of the Arabic language. We have only one *Dīwān* (a collection of poems) of his, from which the most famous passages are the "Wine-Song" (*Khamriyya*)[55] and the "*Tā'iyya Kubrā*" (a poem whose rhyme is always on the letter *tā'*).[56] In finely crafted verse, Ibn al-Fārid sings of universal union, which is the fruit of his immersion in the Muhammadian Reality, which existed before all creation. The opening of the *Khamriyya* refers to this:

> Rememb'ring the belovèd, wine we drink
> Which drunk had made us ere the vine's creation.

This gustatory approach to the prophetic model, which is also expressed in enigmatic language, was not comprehensible to exoterists: in the fifteenth century, Egyptian jurists brought a posthumous lawsuit against the poet, reproaching him both for his use of the image of wine, and for his call to mystical union (*ittihād*). In answer, several authors who were either Sufis or scholars having close relations with Sufism, suggested that Ibn al-Fārid was above any suspicion since he had also been a *qādī*, and also that one should not submit the words of Sufis to literal interpretation.

The Necessity of Interpreting Mystical Poetry

Following the example of scriptural sources, the speech of mystics must be subjected to interpretation (*ta'wīl*). Spiritual realities, which are subtle,

---

French of the *Tarjumān al-ashwāq* by M. Gloton, Paris, 1996, p. 11. (English edition: *The Tarjuman Al-Ashwaq: A Collection of Mystical Odes*, edited and translated by Reynold A. Nicholson [Kessinger Publishing, 2008].)

[54] C. Addas, *Ibn 'Arabī ou la quête du soufre rouge*, p. 251. (English edition: *Quest for the Red Sulphur: The Life of Ibn 'Arabi* [Islamic Texts Society, 1993].)

[55] Translator's Note: The "Wine-Song" appeared in a translation into English blank verse by Martin Lings, in *Studies in Comparative Religion*, vol. 14 (nos. 3 & 4, Summer-Autumn, 1980). The translated text, along with a concise commentary by Dr. Lings, also appears on the web site www.studiesincomparativereligion.com.

[56] Translator's Note: The entire poem is translated into English in blank verse and appears with a commentary in *Umar Ibn Al-Farid: Sufi Verse, Saintly Life* (*Classics of Western Spiritual*

can be evoked only by language, which is concrete, or through figures who share a common heritage. Thus, Sufis often identify with Majnūn, the mad lover who is lost in the contemplation of Laylā; the desire for Laylā can have no endpoint, just like the quest for God. The bacchanalian rhetoric of some Sufis, which engenders the ire of critics just as much as it engenders their own love, therefore warrants interpretation. For true Sufis, this type of allegory has a purely mystical significance: Wine (*khamr*) sometimes symbolizes the divine Essence, which intoxicates the heart of man when It shines forth within him, and at other times it symbolizes the intoxication which results from this. "Their [material] wine does not have the excellence of mine; my Wine is eternal," proclaimed Shushtarī, another poet of divine love; his approach was somewhat coarse and aimed at the common people, but his verse is still celebrated in Sufi circles of the East and the West.

Persian poets, for their part, resurrected the classical form of the *ghazal*, a short poem on non-religious love that had pre-Islamic Arab origins. They transmuted it into a prayer. However, once again, they purposely kept some ambiguity: a reader must ask himself which type of love is being addressed. This ceaseless to-and-fro between the levels of meaning fuels a tension, which is peculiar to the art of poetry, one that is never resolved. In this way one can read verses of Hāfiz (d. 1389) as either erotic or spiritual. A third interpretation is even possible: we can see in the bacchanalian poetry of 'Umar Khayyām and Hāfiz an intoxication of the intellect or a tribute to the irrational; thus, it is useful to distinguish this other level from the one that distinguishes between profane wine and mystical wine.[57]

Sufi Terminology

The debates which are provoked by mystical poetry, in Sunni and Shi'ite settings alike, raise the question of terminology. The advocates of Sufism note that each branch of knowledge has its own lexicon (*istilāh*). Why should it be any different for mysticism, which by its very nature must deal with language that is subtle? Since the period of the "manuals" (tenth century), authors have tried their hands at defining the principal Arabic terms of mystical experience. Texts then appeared which were entirely devoted to this; their formulation sometimes remained allusive, and they were addressed only to the followers of the Path.[58] At the same time, Persian poets such as

---

ity), translated and introduced by Th. Emil Homerin (Paulist Press, 2001).

[57] A.J. Arberry, *Sufism: An Account of the Mystics of Islam* (Harper & Row, 1970).

[58] See, for example, *Sufi Technical Terms* (*Istilāhāt al-sūfiyya*) of Qāshānī, an author of Ibn 'Arabī's school of thought. (English edition: *A Glossary of Sufi Technical Terms*, compiled by

Shabistarī find themselves obliged to explain to the profane the symbolism of the bodily, bacchanalian, and amorous vocabulary that they use.

Soon, this Sufi terminology figured prominently in the encyclopedias that summarized the knowledge of their time. One of the best examples is undoubtedly the *Book of Definitions* (*Kitāb al-ta'rīfāt*) of the Iranian Jurjanī (d. 1413). This linguistic, philosophical, and religious dictionary suggested taking a relevant approach to the terms of Islamic esoterism,[59] and demonstrated that Sufism was part of the Islamic culture of that period. With the aid of such resources, some Sufi *ulama* such as Nābulusī (d. 1731), who was from Damascus, would later prove the usefulness of this mystical lexicon by using it in their commentaries on the works of the earlier masters. Some Iranian spiritual figures would do the same in order to defend Persian poetry from the attacks of the Shi'ite clergy.[60]

Ibn 'Arabī and the Metaphysics of Being

Muhyī al-Dīn Ibn 'Arabī is known as the "Great Master" (*al-Shaykh al-Akbar*) of Islamic spirituality. He is known for his metaphysical doctrine on Being—or, rather, misunderstood, because this doctrine is rarely comprehended correctly. His work does not lead to indifference: it can exasperate readers with its prolixity and its hermeticism, or it can fascinate one with the universality of the gnosis which pervades it. Over the centuries, the detractors and the partisans of Ibn 'Arabī consistently engaged in pitched battles with each other; some find their *raison d'être* in this unresolved tension in Islam between exoterism and esoterism. Moreover, Ibn 'Arabī sometimes puts off even those who claim to represent Sufism. Whether or not one considers him the "seal of Muslim sanctity"—i.e. as a being who has perfected the sanctity that results from the legacy of Muhammad—, no one can dispute the decisive influence he has had on later Sufism. One example is the fact that his own detractors have not hesitated on occasion to borrow his terminology.

One of the paradoxes of Ibn 'Arabī—because every great spiritual personage lives with paradoxes—is that he declared that his ideas had to reach all Muslims, whereas most of his work is obviously reserved for a limited number of readers. Many Sufi masters—not to mention the *ulama*—have thus warned against reading his work without due attention and consideration. Some, while venerating the *Shaykh al-Akbar*, even forbade their dis-

---

'Abd al-Razzāq al-Qāshāni [Octagon Press, 1991].)

[59] This work was translated into French by M. Gloton (Teheran, 1994).

[60] A.J. Arberry, *Sufism: An Account of the Mystics of Islam*.

ciples to open the pages of his books. The interest which he arouses in the West today, thanks to the many translations of his works, leaves many Eastern shaykhs feeling dubious.

Ibn 'Arabī was born in 1165 in Murcia, in Muslim Spain (Andalusia). Settled with his family in Seville, he was intended for a military career, but, around his fifteenth year, he renounced the world and embarked on the Path. He devoted himself to asceticism and spiritual retreat, met many Andalusian Sufis, and quickly attained "illumination"—even Averroes (also known as Ibn Rushd, the famous Iberian thinker) was known to speak of his charisma. His spiritual mission on this earth was revealed to him in several visions in Córdoba, Tunis, Fes, and elsewhere. After having criss-crossed North Africa, he emigrated at the age of thirty-six to the Middle East, to the central domain of Islam—there he would be able to transmit the sacred knowledge of which he called himself the trustee. Welcomed by the temporal leaders, he first lived in Anatolia, where he was an adviser to the Seljuk prince. He then settled permanently in Damascus, where he passed away in 1240. In the East, he was surrounded by close disciples, who would spread his teaching.

More than four hundred works are attributed to Ibn 'Arabī, without taking into account various apocryphal collections. His two major works, written in the East, are the *Meccan Revelations* (*Al-futūhāt al-makkiyya*) and the *Bezels of Wisdom* (*Fusūs al-hikam*). He specified that these texts in particular were dictated to him by the divine Presence; he had no choice in the matter, which explains the unordered aspect of their contents. A summation of esoterism, theology, jurisprudence, and many other Islamic disciplines, the *Revelations* is a masterful synthesis of the legacy of Sufism, while also being energized by some very independent ideas.[61] The *Bezels of Wisdom* contains, in an extremely dense and elliptical style, the quintessence of the metaphysics and hagiology (the "science of holiness") of Ibn 'Arabī. The exoterists of Islam were not put at bay by this style, because their attacks were mainly aimed at this text. Ibn Taymiyya himself acknowledged having enjoyed *The Revelations*, before he came to *The Bezels of Wisdom*.

The work of Ibn 'Arabī has as a foundation an underlying doctrine, the essential unity of Being (*wahdat al-wujūd*): God alone is, and creation is lent its existence thanks to His theophany, which is unceasingly renewed on earth. Yet, things are not God: "The Real is the Real, the created is the created."[62] The Shaykh finally declares that the world is at the same time "Him and

---

[61] Translator's Note: Selections from the *Futūhāt* can be found in volumes 1 and 2 of *The Meccan Revelations*, edited by Michel Chodkiewicz (Pir Press, 2002 and 2004).

[62] *Futūhāt* (Beirut, n. d.), vol. II, p. 371.

not Him." The initiate must go beyond the opposition between immanence (*tashbīh*) and transcendence (*tanzīh*); he must in general unify within himself such oppositions if he wants to perceive divine realities.

Many other metaphysical and cosmological topics find their fullest development in the works of Ibn ʿArabī, such as the Muhammadian Reality and Universal Man, perpetual creation, the prophetic heritage, the "imaginal" world, and the prevalence of the divine Mercy over His Wrath, amongst others. Some of these topics had already taken shape in the works of earlier authors, while others appeared for the first time through his pen; together, they represent a "sacred repository" which the *Shaykh al-Akbar*, urged on by inspiration, simply transmitted.

Far from being a closed system, the work of Ibn ʿArabī offers, above all, a broad range of possibilities for initiates; it never ignores applications for spiritual practice. However, in the century following his death, the Master's disciples set how his teachings would be received by presenting him as a philosopher. Since the fourteenth century, critics have stigmatized what they call the "philosophical Sufism" (*al-tasawwuf al-falsafī*) of the modernists, who they claim betray the Revelation by utilizing human speculation. They have in their sites here the school of Ibn ʿArabī and, even more so, the thought of Ibn Sabʿīn. In contrast, these critics praise the "Sufism of spiritual virtues" (*al-tasawwuf al-akhlāqī*) of old, that is to say, that of the mystics before the thirteenth century, whose practices were based only on scriptural sources. Now, on the one hand, there were earlier contributions to the doctrine of the Oneness of Being before its formulation by Ibn ʿArabī and, on the other hand, the Shaykh was always faithful to the letter of the Koran and the *Hadīth*. Indeed, the hasty judgments uttered against Ibn ʿArabī demonstrate the fact that many reject any evolution of Sufism beyond its early ascetic and ethical roots, including its later initiatory and metaphysical dimensions.

The "school of Ibn ʿArabī" came into being with Sadr al-Dīn Qūnawī (d. 1273), the son-in-law and closest disciple of the Master. Well versed in philosophy, Qūnawī gave a definitely speculative tone to the legacy of the *Shaykh al-Akbar*; through his relations with Shiʿite philosophers such as Nasīr al-Dīn Tūsī, he made it possible for the doctrines of Ibn ʿArabī to feed into Iranian Shiʿite gnosis (*ʿirfān*), as well as into Indian Sufism. ʿAbd al-Razzāq Qāshānī (d. 1329) in Iran, Dāwūd Qaysarī (d. 1359) in Anatolia, and ʿAbd al-Karim Jīlī (d. 1402) in Iraq, were each eminent representatives of this school. Jīlī's book *Al-Insān al-kāmil* systematizes the teaching of Ibn ʿArabī on "Universal Man."[63] Throughout the centuries, great masters would

---

[63] Titus Burckhardt and Angela Culme-Seymour translated excerpts from Jīlī's book in *Universal Man* (Beshara Publications, 1995).

also claim to be representatives of the Andalusian master, commenting on and explaining his work.

Ibn Sab'īn, or Oneness Without Compromise

Another native of Murcia, Ibn Sab'īn, proclaimed the absolute Oneness (*al-wahda al-mutlaqa*) of God: since God alone is, the world is the result of pure illusion and lacks all substance. The inclination of Ibn Sab'īn to philosophy could be seen in his initiatory lineage, in which he had Hermes, Plato, and Aristotle appear, shocking his contemporaries. Renowned for taking doctrinal liberties, he received on behalf of the emperor Frederick II of Hohenstaufen, who was very attracted to Arabo-Islamic civilization, some questions on metaphysics, called the "Sicilian questions," which he would answer.[64] As with Suhrawardī of Aleppo, Sufism, philosophy, and hermeticism converged within him. Many critics have lumped together the doctrine of Oneness of Ibn 'Arabī with that of Ibn Sab'īn, an amalgamation which makes no sense. As proof, consider the very different destinies of their respective works: because of his inflexible metaphysics, Ibn Sab'īn will always be considered an eccentric, pursued by exoterists (in Ceuta, Bougie, and Mecca), and embarrassing Sufis who preferred to be keep silent concerning him. According to an unfounded rumor, he is said to have committed suicide in Mecca by slashing his wrists.

Bibliography

— On Sufi terminology:

Louis Massignon, *Essay on the Origins of the Technical Language of Islamic Mysticism*, translated by Benjamin Clark (University of Notre Dame Press, 1997).

Jean-Louis Michon, *Autobiography of a Moroccan Soufi: Ahmad Ibn 'Ajiba [1747-1809]*, translated by David Streight (Fons Vitae, 1999).

Paul Nwyia, *Exégèse coranique et langage mystique. Nouvel essai sur le lexique technique des mystiques musulmans* (Beirut, 1991, new edition).

— On Rūmī:

Leili Anvar-Chenderoff, *Rūmī* (Paris, 2004); A. Ambrosio, E. Feuillebois, and T. Zarcone, *Les derviches tourneurs* (Paris, 2006).

— On Ibn 'Arabī:

For a precise and synthetic exposition on the life and work of the Shaykh, refer to the book by Claude Addas, *Ibn 'Arabī: The Voyage of No Return*, translated by David Streight (Islamic Texts Society, 2000). By the same author, there is a more exhaustive spiritual biography, *Quest for the Red Sulphur: The Life of Ibn 'Arabī*, translated by Peter Kingsley (Islamic Texts Society, 1993). Two works by Chodkiewicz focus on the doctrines themselves: *The Seal of the Saints: Prophethood and Sainthood*

---

[64] Read, with some perspective, Henry Corbin's foreword to the edition of the Arabic text, in *Correspondance philosophique* (Paris, 1941).

in the Doctrine of Ibn 'Arabī, translated by Liadain Sherrard (Islamic Texts Society, 1993); and *An Ocean Without Shore: Ibn Arabi, the Book, and the Law* (State University of New York Press, 1993). There are many translations into French of the work of Ibn 'Arabī. Among them are: *Le Livre de l'extinction dans la contemplation*, by M. Vâlsan (Paris, 1984); *Traité de l'amour*, by M. Gloton (Paris, 1986); *Le Dévoilement des effets du voyage*, by D. Gril (Combas, 1994); *Le Livre des Chatons des sagesses*, by C.A. Gilis (Paris, 1997-1998); and *Le Livre des théophanies d'Ibn 'Arabī*, by S. Ruspoli (Paris, 2000).[65]

CREATING A STRUCTURE FOR SUFISM (Twelfth-Fifteenth Centuries)

In the eleventh and twelfth centuries, a time that saw the birth of most Christian monastic orders, spiritual fellowships began to appear within Sufism; they then added another dimension to that of the first fraternities. Those nostalgic for the early days of Sufism readily saw in the emergence of these initiatory paths (singular: *tarīqa*) a sign of Sufism's decline. But this rapid development of the brotherhoods stifled neither mystical inspiration nor the relation between master and disciple; nor did it affect the genuineness of individual initiatives. There was from then on a place for a variety of forms of initiation and affiliation. During the same time, Ibn 'Arabī and other authors were completing their expositions of the doctrines of Sufism. It was not necessary to oppose theosophical teachings or their circulation within society because the brotherhoods and the theosophists both had the same initiatory goal. The devotion to the Prophet, for example, which resulted in particular in the celebration of his birthday, the *mawlid*, started at the same time as Ibn 'Arabī's emphasis on the "Reality of Muhammad."

For the Sufis, the increasingly dominant role of the shaykhs and the formation of the initiatory paths fulfilled the need to compensate for the loss of spirituality which had occurred over time. As the light of prophecy was gradually dimming, it was left to the saints and to the shaykhs to take charge of the education of the believers. Thus, to compensate for that spiritual loss, a specific framework, a path marked out with "stations" and appropriate initiatory methods, was set up.[66]

The Sufi paths developed specifically in order to meet a need for both spiritual and social structures, a need which the *ulama* were unable to fulfill from then on. The "jurists" then retreated into the role of guardians or

---

[65] Translator's Note: Many important resources on Ibn 'Arabī, including references to texts in various languages, free online articles, reviews, etc., can be found on the web page of the Muhyiddin Ibn 'Arabi Society: http://www.ibnarabisociety.org/.

[66] For example, this was the determination of the Moroccan shaykh 'Abd al-'Azīz Dabbāgh. See *al-Ibrīz*, vol. II, p. 52.

administrators of the Law, leaving them hardly any influence with the believers; the study and the transmission of religious sciences were themselves undergoing ossification. As for the theologians, their words could not constitute a therapy for the human heart. Sufi shaykhs thus had the primary role of allowing people to establish closer and more personal relationships with God and with the Prophet.

In the Muslim world, the twelfth century was a troubled time. In the west, the Seljuks faced the crusaders, with whom the Fatimid Shi'ites made a pact, at least during the first crusade. In the east, the Mongolian threat took shape, while in Catholic Spain the *Reconquista* (reconquest of Muslim-held land) gained ground, pushing before it a flow of emigrants. Muslim leaders saw in Ismā'īli esoterism a major danger, and they confronted it with Sunni mysticism, a spirituality which was true to Muhammad, and which seemed to them to be the only alternative. One might refer to this as the "instrumentalization" of Sufism by the temporal power. In the Middle East, Zengids, Ayyubids, and Mamluks implemented a Sunni reaction to the danger, one which was based on the charisma of the shaykhs, who from that time on were better able to rally popular sentiment than were most of the *ulama*. Nūr al-Dīn Zengī, for example, the main architect of the *jihād* against the crusaders in Syria, venerated the figure who would become the patron saint of Damascus, Shaykh Arslān (d. about 1160).[67] His successor, Saladin the Ayyubid, who also promoted Sufism, distrusted any external spirituality which he considered to be pernicious. In 1191, the jurists of Aleppo exhorted him to condemn to death Suhrawardī Maqtūl (the "Murdered"), a young Iranian who had come to live in Syria and whose doctrine in fact combined Neoplatonism, the Mazdean tradition, and the illuminationism (*ishrāq*) of the "philosopher" Avicenna.

The Sufis also lent their support to the Abbasid caliphate, an institution which they believed guaranteed the legacy of the Prophet. In Baghdad, another Suhrawardī, 'Umar Shihāb al-Dīn (d. 1234), thus came to the aid of the caliph al-Nāsir. During his long reign (1180-1225), this caliph tried to fight against the disintegration of the caliphate, which was threatened both by external enemies and internal ideologies. Benefitting from the collapse of Seljuk Turk power, he sought to have his authority recognized in the Muslim world by relying on the *futuwwa*.[68] This was a sort of cross between the

---

[67] E. Geoffroy, *Jihād et Contemplation. Vie et enseignement d'un soufi au temps des croisades* (Paris, 2002) (new edition).

[68] Translator's Note: A *futuwwa* was a group organized around Islamic virtues such as chivalry or charity. They had close associations with Sufi orders and craft guilds. They often drew from the impoverished and disenfranchised sectors of society, but also included true aristocrats.

chivalry and the trade-guilds of our medieval West, and has many historical affinities with Sufism. Al-Nāsir gave the *futuwwa* an official and aristocratic character. Seeking to win the support of neighboring Muslim dynasties, he named Suhrawardī the "Grand Master of the Sufis" and sent him off as an ambassador. His enterprise would not come to fruition, however, because at the beginning of the thirteenth century the Mongols swept into the eastern territories.

The fall of Baghdad in 1258 put an end to the Abbasid Empire. It spelled the end of a Sunni world that was relatively homogeneous and powerful and in which Muslims lived in safety. But the collapse of the traditional religious structures would reinforce the authority of the Sufi shaykhs. The spiritual fellowships which had come into existence then offered a place for solidarity and a vision of the world which transcended the vicissitudes of history. After the fall of the caliphate, only the networks of Sufis could maintain any sort of unity in the eastern territories of Islam, and though the Persian world survived the Mongolian holocaust, it was due to the spiritual culture which inhabited it. In addition, several Mongolian princes, who reigned from then on in the Middle East and Central Asia, converted to Islam under the aegis of Sufi shaykhs.[69]

The Formation of the "Initiatory Paths" (Tarīqa)

During the first centuries of Islam, the word *tarīqa* indicated the spiritual method followed by such or such a mystic.[70] The "path," or method, prescribed by Junayd in the tenth century was still well known. According to the Master from Baghdad, the aspirant must remain in a state of purity according to the Law; he must fast, observe silence, make retreats, repeat the formula *Lā ilāha illā 'Llāh*, be inwardly connected to his shaykh, reject extrinsic thoughts, etc. Starting in the twelfth century, the word *tarīqa* also indicated a "particular initiatory path." At that time, some masters started to attract disciples who would stay with them for long periods of time; they also formed networks for initiatory transmission. Several spiritual fellowships were formed, each suggesting a specific route towards God. Little by little, the initiatory, individual "method" thus yielded its place to the

---

Some *futuwwas* developed into warrior societies, as was the case here with the Abbasid caliph al-Nāsir.

[69] *The Legacy of Medieval Persian Sufism*, edited by L. Lewisohn (London-New York, 1992), p. 34.

[70] Such as by the caliph 'Umar, for example, as mentioned by Hujwirī (*Kashf al-mahjūb*, p. 270).

spiritual community. But until the fifteenth century, and often even up to the nineteenth century, the latter did not have a fixed structure. Even today, a *tarīqa* seems more like a nebula, a cosmic cloud with hazy outlines that radiates outwards, than an institutionalized religious order.

The eponymous saints of the nascent paths were above all trustees of an initiatory heritage which they infused with their own personalities. Though they may have fashioned schools of spirituality, most of them did not intend to found a mystical order. Like the first masters, they trained beginners and formulated their own teachings, and they sometimes gave rules for living, as well. It would be their principal disciples who would set down and bring to fruition their spiritual legacies by establishing these as models. By doing this, they ensured the transmission of initiation within the different *tarīqas*. The hagiographic literature also was to contribute to the development of a spirit of camaraderie and solidarity within each path.

The "brotherhoods" do not encapsulate all that there was of Sufism, but they have been largely responsible for fashioning the initiatory landscape of the Muslim world, even to the present day.[71] Most of the great initiatory fellowships born between the twelfth and fourteenth centuries were divided into branches that later became more or less autonomous. Each branch bears the name of its founder, to which the name of the "mother-Order" is sometimes added. In present-day Tunisia, the Madaniyya Order, for example, can lay claim to the successive lineage of the Shādhiliyya (thirteenth century) Order, the Darqāwiyya (eighteenth century) Order, and the 'Alawiyya (the beginning of the twentieth century) Order, or it can simply refer to itself as the Madaniyya Order, which came into being in the twentieth century. Branches become established as Orders following problems of succession regarding spiritual masters, which has been very frequent in the world of the *tarīqas*, each branch attaching itself to one of the major disciples of a deceased shaykh. Thus, the Tunisian Madaniyya was split into several quite distinct groups.

Of the initiatory paths, some disappeared, or were merged into others, each one evolving throughout the centuries and adopting different forms. We will present here the mother-*tarīqas* and their main branches.

— *Iraq.* Until the Mongolian conquest (1258), Baghdad remained one of the major centers of Islamic life, and it continued to attract a number of Iranian Sufis. The *tarīqas* that originated there drew from the spiritual inheritance which had enriched the city since the time of Junayd.

---

[71] For a comprehensive picture of the initiatory paths, refer to the collection *Les Voies d'Allah: Les ordres mystiques dans le monde musulman des origines à aujourd'hui*, edited by A. Popovic and G. Veinstein (Paris, 1996).

The Qādiriyya Order was founded by 'Abd al-Qādir Jīlānī (d. 1166), who was originally from Jīlān, in northwestern Iran. Having come to Baghdad to study the Hanbalite school and *Hadīth*, he was initiated into Sufism there. After having withdrawn from society for about twenty years, during which time he led a life of asceticism, 'Abd al-Qādir returned to the company of men in the Abbasid capital, where his sermons attracted many listeners. A man who was both erudite and who sought spiritual realization, he taught exoteric sciences in his *madrasa* at the same time that he was closely following the spiritual progress of his disciples.[72] He was also the author of a manual, *Sufficient Provision for Seekers of the Path* (*Al-ghunya li-tālibī tarīq al-haqq*), which offers rules for all beginners. The very sober ethics that he advocated won him wide success among Hanbalites, whether they were Sufis or not, which did not prevent him from being considered the spiritual pole of his time by masters such as Ibn 'Arabī. His descendants, both by blood and by spirituality, brought about the extraordinary spread of the Qādiriyya beginning in the fifteenth century. His reputation as a saint, miracle-worker, and intercessor then spread to all Muslims. Many groups who claimed to represent him would introduce extraordinary practices, such as dances accompanied by music, gatherings during which followers would pierce their bodies, the swallowing of glass, etc.

Like the Qādiriyya, the Suhrawardiyya has Iranian origins. Abū Najīb Suhrawardī (d. 1168) also studied Islamic sciences in Baghdad. While teaching law in the Nizāmiyya *madrasa,* he trained his disciples in a *ribāt* and worked to bring about an osmosis between the Law and the Path. He is known for his manual *Rules that Disciples Must Observe* (*Ādāb al-murīdīn*). In this collection of precepts for beginners to use, he mentions in particular the dispensations (*rukhsa*) granted to those who cannot follow the strict discipline of initiates committed to the Path: his concern for these simpler associates testifies to the increasing number of participants in the Sufi congregations in society.

It was his nephew Shihāb al-Dīn 'Umar Suhrawardī (d. 1234) who founded the Suhrawardiyya Order. His stature and influence made him one of the great figures of Islam during that period. A disciple of Jīlānī, he rejected both speculative theology and philosophy. In the name of the spirituality of the first Muslims, he opposed for a while the metaphysical developments proposed by his contemporary, Ibn 'Arabī. Preaching a balanced mysticism, he had a broad audience in the Middle East, even in settings which were not specifically Sufi: the Persian poet Sa'dī and then later, in the fourteenth

---

[72] A. Demeerseman, *Nouveau Regard sur la voie spirituelle d'Abd al-Qādir al-Jīlānī et sa tradition* (Paris, 1988), p. 151.

century, the traveler Ibn Battuta were initiated into Suhrawardī's path. His work the *Gifts of Knowledge* (*'Awārif al-ma'ārif*) is different from the old manuals; he was not satisfied with collecting the sayings of the early masters, so he organized them in a way that let him express his thoughts on Sufism and to explain the initiatory rites in the light of the Koran and the *Hadīth*. Suhrawardī's exposition of the rules concerning novices contributed a great deal to the organization of the brotherhoods; his manual was also quickly translated into various Muslim languages.[73]

Suhrawardī's function as an "ambassador" to nearby Muslim powers did not diminish in any way his credibility with, or his influence on, the Sufis. The effect of his initiatory influence spread over Central Asia, India, and the Middle East, where it was characterized by sobriety, reference to the *Sunna*, and the legacy of classical Sufism. In Egypt, for example, it was presented simply under the name of the "path of Junayd": for this *tarīqa* especially, the content mattered more than the form.

Among the paths that came into being in the twelfth century, the Rifā'iyya is without question the one that most quickly established itself. Actually, Ahmad Rifā'ī (d. 1182) inherited an already established community. After being initiated by his uncle, he trained disciples in a large "convent" (*riwāq*, a kind of *zāwiya*) located in an isolated region in the south of Iraq, where he attracted thousands of followers. His teachings spread to the Middle East, where he delegated his authority to many representatives (*khulafā'*). Rifā'ī advocated a strict adherence to the *Sunna* and commended humility and compassion. Because of the love that he showed for all creation, in particular for animals, he is sometimes compared with Saint Francis of Assisi. Starting in the thirteenth century, his disciples would introduce practices which hardly conformed to his teachings: they walked on coals, swallowed snakes, pierced their bodies, and so on. These exercises, they have explained, are harmless because they are practiced under the initiatory power of the saint, and so they are protected from harm.[74]

— *Central Asia and Iran.* If most initiatory lineages of the Muslim world trace themselves back to Junayd, those of Central Asia generally rely on the heritage of Abū Yazīd Bistāmī. In the province of Khurasan in northeastern Iran, the land of pioneers in all fields of Islamic culture, spiritual commu-

---

[73] Several excerpts from Suhrawardī, translated by D. Gril into French, can be found in *Les Voies d'Allah*, pp. 547-568.

[74] The circumstances of the introduction of these practices into the Rifā'iyya Order are still controversial. The survival of pagan rites in Lower Iraq has been suggested; an alleged influence of shamanism brought by the Mongols has now been dismissed.

nities were formed, as we have seen, from the end of the tenth century. Further east, in Transoxania (present-day Turkmenistan), Yūsuf Hamadhānī (d. 1140) was at the starting point of several paths, especially the Yasawiyya and later the Naqshbandiyya; the former would evolve in Turkish settings, and the latter in Iranian settings. This Hanafite scholar, who was connected to the current of Kharaqānī and Bistāmī, revivified *malāmatī* spirituality for its strict requirements and inwardness, and he played a major role in the Islamicization of the Turks of Khwarezm, in the south of the Aral Sea. His disciple Ahmad Yasawī (Yesevi, according to the Turkish pronunciation; d. 1166) also contributed to the conversion of the nomadic Turks, but the wandering *babas*[75] who claimed to be linked to him were still strongly influenced by shamanism and their practice of Islam was rather flexible. They shared the destiny of the Turkish peoples, who emigrated towards Anatolia during the eleventh and twelfth centuries. Yasawī did not actually found an initiatory order, but rather he exerted a broad circle of influence upon dervishes bound together by their Turkish origins.

The Qalandar dervishes, who came from Central Asia, formed a disparate movement and practiced religious syncretism. Some became established in India, where they came into contact with Hindu-Buddhist asceticism. Under the aegis of the Persian Jamāl al-Dīn Sāwī (d. circa 1232), the Qalandars moved bit by bit towards the west, into Anatolia and the Middle East, where they were hated because they did not comply with the Koranic regulations; they consumed hashish and their physical appearance was unusual: they shaved their heads, beards, moustaches, and eyebrows; and they wore iron rings on their wrists and in their ears, and even on their sexual organs, to preserve their chastity.

The Kubrāwiyya presents a very different profile. The eponymous master, Najm al-Dīn Kubrā (d. 1221), was originally from Khwarezm. The epithet "Kubrā," which recalls the Koranic expression *al-tāmma al-kubrā*, "the great cataclysm,"[76] was given to him because of his great talent for persuading his adversaries during controversies. Having left his home to study Islamic sciences in the Middle East, Najm al-Dīn was initiated there by several shaykhs, including two disciples of Abū Najīb Suhrawardī. Upon his return to his native land, he built a *khānqāh* where, taking the rules of Junayd as his

---

[75] Translator's Note: *Bābā* is a title once given to members of some Sufi Orders primarily in Persia and Turkey. In the Bektashi Order, it referred specifically to that person, below the head of the Order, who had the function of teaching and doing pastoral work in the provinces. They were located all over the Ottoman world. The term is used more loosely here, applying to wandering preachers who claimed to have Sufi affiliations.

[76] Koran 79:34.

inspiration, he created an environment for developing his disciples, which is why he would be called "the fashioner of saints." Although he was connected to the Iraqi tradition, he founded an original initiatory school: its method is based on perceiving the subtle centers of the human body (*latā'if*) and is aimed at the progressive illumination of the inner being. He was unambiguously Sunni, but several of his spiritual successors would turn towards Shi'ism. He died as a martyr during the Mongolian invasions. He left behind several small treatises in Arabic, mostly having to do with his visionary experiences, especially the *Blossomings of Beauty* (*Fawā'ih al-jamāl*).[77]

'Alā al-Dawla Simnānī (d. 1336) is one of the major figures of the Kubrāwiyya. He was born into a family of eminent administrators from Khurasan working for the Ilkhānate Mongols, and he entered their service while still very young. At twenty-four, he renounced the world following an inner crisis and devoted himself to the spiritual life. Initiated into the path of Kubrā, he soon founded a *khānqāh*. He stayed connected to Sunni Sufism, but also maintained relations with representatives of other religions—in particular with nearby Buddhist monks. Simnānī was influenced by Ibn 'Arabī, although he refuted certain formulations that were in use by the school of the Andalusian master. In several works, he further developed the doctrines of Kubrā on the "inner centers" of man. Because of his intellectual and spiritual scope, Simnānī seems more like a great master of Central Asian Sufism than a founder of a particular path, even if a *tarīqa* claims a connection to him.

In Iran, the initiatory paths, which were originally Sunni, gradually moved towards Shi'ism. Shi'ism only truly imposed itself on the Sufi brotherhoods at the beginning of the sixteenth century, but the land was imbued with it for centuries before. In the fifteenth century, a Shi'ite branch of the Kubrāwiyya, the Nūrbakhshiyya, thus was tempted by a political messianism: it proclaimed Muhammad Nūrbakhsh (d. 1464) to be the *Mahdī* (a figure who must come at the end of time to fight against the Antichrist), and promoted him as the Imam of the Islamic community. But the movement was severely repressed by the Timurids, Tamerlane's successors. In Shiraz there still exists a schismatic branch of the Nūrbakhshiyya, the Dhahabiyya; it is called this because its followers, rejecting the mahdist claims, left the Nūrbakhshiyya (in Arabic, *dhahaba* means to leave).

One sees the same progressive slip of Sunnism into Shi'ism in the Ni'matullāhiyya. Born in Aleppo, Shāh Ni'matullāh Walī (d. 1431) studied Islamic sciences in Shiraz, then a bastion of Iranian Sunnis. When he made

---

[77] *Les Éclosions de la beauté et les parfums de la majesté* (Nîmes, 2001). This translation into French by P. Ballanfat begins with an excellent introduction (pp. 8-127).

a pilgrimage to Mecca he became a disciple of the Yemeni scholar and Sufi 'Abd Allāh Yāfi'ī (d. 1367).[78] Ni'matullāh parted from his master to go to Transoxania, near Samarkand, where he attracted many disciples thanks to his spiritual prestige. But some Sufis took umbrage at his success and slandered him before Tamerlane. The Shaykh then kept close to Kerman, in Persia, where the center of his Order still is today. At the beginning of the sixteenth century, certain followers of the Ni'matullāhiyya were persecuted by the Safavids and fled Iran, but most became Shi'ites. This path is very much alive today in Iran and in the Iranian diaspora.

Let us return to Central Asia where the Naqshbandiyya remained fundamentally Sunni, and even hostile to Shi'ism. Being the direct heir to the spirituality of Khurasan and the *malāmatī* school which was connected to it, the Naqshbandiyya also favored sobriety and inwardness. The path was constituted as an Order under the auspices of Bahā' al-Dīn Naqshband (d. 1389), but the Naqshbandis regard 'Abd al-Khāliq Ghujduwānī as its true originator. The latter introduced the assiduous practice of the inner *dhikr* or "*dhikr* of the heart*," which came from Abū Bakr, the close Companion of the Prophet, and which would become characteristic of the Order. This path, which is the Persian version of the heritage of Yūsuf Hamadānī, received the name of *tarīqat al-khawājagān*, "the path of the masters." According to Naqshbandi tradition, Bahā' al-Dīn Naqshband had been initiated and inspired directly by "the spiritual body" (*rūhāniyya*) of Ghujduwānī, who had been dead since 1220.

The Naqshbandis established in principle some practices which one sometimes finds in Sufism, such as "watching over one's steps," the "awareness of breathing," "the constant review of one's actions," the "retreat (solitude) in the middle of the crowd," the "journeying towards the spiritual homeland," etc.[79] Several initiatory methods, in particular "orientation of the master towards the disciple" (*tawajjuh*) and "attachment to the master" (*rābitat al-shaykh*), have been substantiated since the time of Bahā' al-Dīn, but they would take on different meanings with the passage of time. The Order, which holds to the immutable principle of creating harmony between the Law and the Path, would manage to maintain its Sunni orthodoxy among the populations of Central Asia.

The Naqshbandiyya initially spread throughout Transoxania, the homeland of Bahā' al-Dīn. In the fifteenth century, it prevailed over the other

[78] A prolific author and an "historian" of Sufism, Yāfi'ī greatly contributed to the spread of the doctrine of Ibn 'Arabī. A Yāfi'iyya branch in Yemen still claims a connection to him.

[79] One can find a presentation on this which is, to say the least, adapted for Westerners, in the French book by O. Ali-Shah, *Un apprentissage du soufisme* (Paris, 2001).

initiatory paths in the region thanks to the ascendancy of Khwādja Ahrār (d. 1490). Maintaining that a spiritual man must involve himself in temporal affairs in order to better serve created beings, this shaykh urged the Timurids to act more in accordance with the regulations of Islam. At the same time, he created a vast economic network that made protecting peasants from the tax levies of the Mongols possible. The Naqshbandiyya spread as far as the Caucasus region, Kurdistan, and Anatolia, where its orthodoxy earned the favor of the Ottomans. It then expanded into the Arab Middle East and into India, where Ahmad Sirhindī (d. 1624) would be regarded as the "renewer of Islam (*mujaddid*) for the second millennium of the Hijra."[80] In his *Letters* (*Maktūbāt*), which has been a source of much meditation for Naqshbandis up to this day, this master referred even more than his predecessors to the Law and the prophetic model. He also ordered the Mughals to be firmer in their application of the *Sharī'a*. Like many, he distanced himself from Ibn 'Arabī's doctrine of "the oneness of Being," although he was subject to its influence. Starting in the seventeenth century, the Mujaddidiyya branch, which stemmed from Sirhindī, spread from China to Arabia, and into Indonesia. The Naqshbandiyya is currently the major Sufi path in Asia (i.e. the Near and Middle East).

— *India*. The expansion of Sufism into India can be measured by the adoption in this country of the Arabic term *faqīr* ("poor in God"), which designates all those who have given up the world. The meaning of the French and English word "fakir" retains a distant echo of the Arabic term. Sufis arrived in the sub-continent starting in the eleventh century (Hallāj stayed there for a while around 900 C.E.), first in the company of merchants, and then with the conquerors. Coming into contact with Hindu *yogis*, many dervishes in the circle of influence of the Qalandars adopted a wandering and ascetic way of life, practicing celibacy and vegetarianism. Of a very different style, a mysticism using the medium of the Persian language flourished in the Punjab under the Ghaznavid dynasty of the eleventh century; Hujwirī, the patron saint of Lahore, exemplified this mysticism. The first great initiatory paths from the Middle East followed the founding of the Sultanate of Delhi in the thirteenth century. This was the time during which the Suhrawardiyya was becoming established in India, while the work of 'Umar Suhrawardī, the *Gifts of Knowledge* (*'Awārif al-ma'ārif*), was being used as a reference in the other nascent paths, especially the Chishtiyya.

---

[80] Translator's Note: The "Hijra" refers to Muhammad's emigration from Mecca to Medina in 622 C.E., which officially started the Muslim era. Thus, the second millennium of the Hijra refers to the second thousand (lunar) years after that watershed event in Muslim history.

Mu'īn al-Dīn Chishtī (d. 1236) was one of the stream of dervishes who came from Central Asia. Like Kubrā, he traveled to Iraq, and then settled in Ajmer (Rajasthan). The Chishtiyya was organized and spread throughout all of Muslim India under the aegis of the third successor of Chishtī, Nizām al-Dīn Awliyā' (d. 1325), who had as his own disciple the great poet Amīr Khusrau. The latter two men were at the root of a Sufi Indo-Persian culture which was characterized by its openness towards Hinduism. The Chishtis were the ones who made the *malfuzat* (collections of sentences or "sayings" of the masters compiled by their disciples) fashionable; this literary genre was not new in Sufism, but it took on its own special character in India.

In the fourteenth and fifteenth centuries, major branches of the earlier paths appeared, such as the Shattāriyya. Stemming from the Suhrawardiyya, it considered itself independent from and superior to the other paths. In fact, it adopted some positions which were foreign to those of the mother-Order: 'Abdallāh Shattārī (d. 1485) moved about accompanied by disciples wearing black military dress and beating drums.

— *Muslim Spain and the Maghreb.* In Maghrebian-Andalusian settings, Sufism was structured later than in the east due to the combined hostility of Malikite clerics and Almoravid sultans. The jurists, wanting to prevent the inescapable wakening of mysticism, went so far as to burn the *Revival of the Religious Sciences* (*Ihyā' 'ulūm al-dīn*) of Ghazzālī in Córdova. In Andalusia, the course of the Path was still left to the individual and was not very formalized for initiates. However, Ibn 'Arabī's *Epistle on the Spirit of Saintliness* (*Risālat rūh al-quds*), a collection of biographical notes on his masters from the Muslim west, testifies to the richness of the Andalusian spiritual landscape in the twelfth century.[81]

The school of Almeria, in Andalusia, was suffused with Neoplatonism and heralded the doctrines of Ibn 'Arabī. It had as a key figure Ibn al-'Arif (d. 1141), whose *Beauties of the Spiritual Gatherings* (*Mahāsin al-majālis*) was clearly influenced by eastern Sufism and whose teachings spread to the Middle East in a kind of backwash. As for Ibn Barrajān (d. 1141), he proposed a daring metaphysical interpretation of the Koran. Almoravid jurists and sultans were annoyed at the popularity of these shaykhs, and soon eliminated them. Ibn Qasī (d. 1151) suffered the same fate after having led an armed rebellion against the Almohads in Algarve, in southern Portugal.

The Andalusian Abū Madyan Shu'ayb (d. 1198) was trained by several

---

[81] Translated into French under the title *Les Soufis d'Andalousie* (Paris, 1995) (new edition). (English edition: *Sufis of Andalusia: The Ruh Al-Quds and Al-Durrat al-Fakhirah of Ibn 'Arabī* [University of California Press, 1971].)

Moroccan shaykhs. These included: Abū Ya'zā, called Yalannūr, "the possessor of light," an illiterate Berber who was strictly vegetarian and who lived
among the wild beasts, but who taught in simple language what the eastern
mystics expressed in more sophisticated ways; and Ibn Hirzihim (venerated
nowadays in Morocco under the name of Sīdī Harazem), who was a pro-
ponent of the thought of Ghazzālī, which he introduced to Abū Madyan.
After an initiatory journey to the east and after years of spiritual retreat, Abū
Madyan settled in Bougie (Bijāya, in Algeria), one of the major stops along
the road connecting Spain to the east. There his unprecedented spiritual radiance spread throughout the Maghreb. Some of his disciples stayed in the
Muslim west, founding autonomous groups; others spread the path to the
Middle East. Called to Morocco by the Almohad sultan Ya'qūb al-Mansūr,
Abū Madyan died on the way and is buried near Tlemcen.

The censorship exerted by the Malikite school of law explains the pi-
etistic character of Abū Madyan's teachings, which hardly venture into the
metaphysical developments underway in the east.[82] Through the cross-fertilization of men and doctrines which he stimulated, Abū Madyan brought
about a kind of synthesis between Moroccan, Andalusian, and Eastern Sufism. Ibn 'Arabī never met the Saint of Bougie, but he quoted him in his work
more than any other master. Abū Madyan was a major initiatory source for
Maghrebian Sufism. Although he did not found an Order, he is like a tree
whose branches have enveloped the Maghreb and part of the Middle East;
some Sufis call themselves Madyaniyya, as is still the case in Ifriqiya (present-
day Tunisia) and Egypt, but most have taken other names.

Starting in the fourteenth century, Maghrebian-Andalusian Sufism first
assumed a communal aspect. Located mainly in Morocco and derived for the
most part from the school of Abū Madyan, large *zāwiyas* (establishments
for Sufis) acted autocratically and played a substantial role in politics and
society. Whole tribes and villages lent their allegiance to their shaykhs. In the
fifteenth century, the power of the Marinid dynasty was failing, and on their
own initiative these shaykhs led a *jihād* against the Portuguese who caught
up with them on the Moroccan coasts.

Maghrebi-Andalusian Sufism was characterized by an individual, and
essentially urban approach. Muslim Spain was familiar with this modality
which favors intellectual or philosophical development over the social formation of the mystic. Ibn al-Khatīb (d. 1375) had a very eclectic intellectual
personality. He wrote a treatise on mysticism which was imbued with Ibn
Sab'īn's doctrine of "absolute Oneness," which seems to dissolve the dis-

---

[82]   V. J. Cornell, *The Way of Abū Madyan* (Cambridge, 1996).

tance between God and man; those who plotted against this grand vizier of the Nasrid dynasty in Granada took advantage of his daring and called him a heretic, for which he was condemned to death. In the Maghreb, urban Sufism took the form of a school which was reluctant to give itself a name, but which we might call Shādhilism. This term comes from the Shādhiliyya path which, we will see, spread through Egypt starting in the middle of the thirteenth century. It was the Andalusian Ibn 'Abbād (d. 1390) who introduced the writings of the Shādhili Egyptian masters such as Ibn 'Atā' Allāh into the Maghreb. After having studied exoteric sciences, Ibn 'Abbād turned to the spiritual life while still fulfilling the function of imam and preacher at the famous Qarawiyyin mosque and university in Fes. A theorist and commentator of Shādhili doctrines, he advocated a demanding spiritual education and so limited the number of his disciples: he himself only directed a few.

In the fifteenth century, a great quest for the blessings (*baraka*) of both shaykhs and the descendants of the Prophet (the *shorfa*) energized all of Moroccan society. Jazūlī (d. between 1465 and 1470) combined within himself the double charisma of a spiritual person and a *sharīf*. This Shādhili shaykh was responsible for a movement of devotion to the Prophet which aimed to bestow the Muhammadian grace on as many people as possible. This transmission of *baraka* on a grand scale obviously dispensed with the highly focused relationship between master and disciple which had been advocated by Ibn 'Abbād. Jazūlī left behind a collection of prayers on the Prophet which is very famous in the Muslim world, the *Guide to Good Works* (*Dalā'il al-khayrāt*). Through the cosmic dimension which it attributes to the Prophet, the book reflects the doctrine of the "Universal Man" (*Al-insān al-kāmil*). Jazūlī's spiritual prestige led to concern on the part of the Marinid officials and to the resentment of other shaykhs. Less sought after following this, the shaykh died, apparently poisoned, in his *zāwiya* in Marrakesh.

Ahmad Zarrūq (d. 1494), a native of Fes, was another important figure of the Shādhiliyya *tarīqa*. He emphasized the necessity for inwardness and sobriety. Called "the critic of the Sufis," he was situated at the junction between the law and mysticism. One can see the influence of the discipline of jurisprudence upon his book *Rules of Sufism* (*Qawā'id al-tasawwuf*). After numerous stays in Egypt, he rooted the Shādhiliyya initiatory tree in Morocco. He settled down and died in Tripolitania (in present-day Libya), a region between Egypt and Morocco, but it was from Fes that his rejuvenated path, the Zarrūqiyya, would contribute to the North African Shādhiliyya until our own times.

— *Egypt and Syria.* Until the middle of the thirteenth century, the initiatory impulse in the Near East came for the most part from the Muslim west. Many western Muslims settled in Egypt in particular after accomplishing the pilgrimage to Mecca. To this traditional factor was added, from then on, the Catholic *Reconquista* that hunted down the Muslims of Spain. The warm welcome reserved by the Ayyubid dynasty officials for the foreign *ulama* and Sufis encouraged the emergence of a very rich Islamic culture in both Egypt and in Syria. The beachhead for western Sufis in the east was Alexandria. From there a disciple of Abū Madyan, 'Abd-al Razzāq Jazūlī (d. 1198), spread the path along the length of the Nile Valley on the route of the pilgrimage. Two of his successors are still revered there as patron saints, the Moroccan 'Abd al-Rahīm (d. 1196) in Qena, and the Egyptian Abū l-Hajjāj (d. 1244) in Luxor.

Ibn 'Arabī himself joined this flow of western emigrants to the east. Although he was not the founder of any particular path, he passed on an initiatory influence that was linked to his work and which has survived throughout the centuries. Simultaneously, the doctrine of Ibn 'Arabī penetrated deep into most Orders from the end of the thirteenth century, but not always in an explicit way. Ibn Sab'īn, the other Andalusian whose spiritual career was fulfilled in the Near East, was not only the misunderstood metaphysician mentioned above: he founded a path whose rules advocated detachment and a peripatetic life. The Andalusian Shushtarī (d. 1269) was Ibn Sab'īn's successor in Egypt, but he was also affiliated with the Shādhiliyya, and is especially known for his mystical poems.

Having its source in Morocco, the Shādhiliyya rooted itself deeply in Egypt before spreading to a large portion of the Muslim world. It remains to this day, in its various branches, one of the major paths of Sufism. After having searched for the spiritual Center of his time in the east, Abū l-Hasan Shādhilī (d. 1258) found him close to his own part of the world, in the Rif Mountains of Morocco, in the person of 'Abd al-Salām Ibn Mashīsh (d. 1228). This hermit, whose sanctuary on the summit of a mountain is still a place of pilgrimage, was in the lineage of Abū Madyan. In addition, he is considered by some to be the true source of the Shādhiliyya, which quickly overtook the Madyaniyya in Egypt and in the Maghreb.

Ibn Mashīsh predicted that his disciple would fulfill a great destiny in the east. The first stage of this would take place in Ifriqiya (present-day Tunisia): Abū l-Hasan took a spiritual retreat in the mountains between Tunis and Kairouan, close to Shādhila. The name later given to Shādhilī would come from the name of this village, but the saint gave a spiritual meaning to the name: "The one who has turned aside from this world (*shādhdh*) to devote himself to Me (*lī*)." The popularity of Abū l-Hasan in Tunis drew the condemnation of the jurists upon him. Leaving behind him a spiritual center that has been active to this day in that city, he settled in Alexandria in 1244. Traveling almost every year to the holy places of Islam, he would traverse all of Egypt and then cross the Red Sea. This put him in contact with many who became his disciples and he thus spiritually "irrigated" the valley of the Nile. He died during one of these trips, in the desert that lies along the Red Sea.

Shādhilī taught inner sobriety and the concentration on God alone through the *dhikr*. Condemning all ostentation (in dress, spiritual states, miracles, etc.), he wanted his disciples to blend into society. Adherence to the Law and to the *Sunna* was for him a precondition for initiatory progress. These *malāmatī* traits reveal the affinities that unite the Shādhiliyya and the Naqshbandiyya, as well as why they both have connections to the world of the *ulama*. Anxious to get to the essential, Shādhilī offered few intellectual interpretations of his own experience of sanctity, yet the influence of the doctrine of Ibn 'Arabī would grow within his Order.

Neither he nor his successor, the Andalusian Abū l-'Abbās Mursī (d. 1287), left any written works, but the spiritual efficacy of their litanies (*hizb;* pl. *ahzāb*) is recognized within the Order. The third master, the Egyptian Ibn 'Atā' Allāh (d. 1309), transmitted and developed their teachings in a book that is known throughout the Muslim world. His book of *Wisdom* (*Hikam*) offers in the form of pithy sentences an initiatory pedagogy that addresses itself directly to the very human soul of the disciple, which explains the numerous commentaries on the work.[83] As for *The Subtleties of Grace* (*Latā'if al-minan*), they represent the spiritual testament of Ibn 'Atā' Allāh, and the reference text for Shādhiliyya doctrine.[84]

Two twin branches of the Shādhiliyya, the Hanafiyya and the Wafā'iyya, each exerted a major influence in Egypt until the Ottoman era, but the presence of the path spread well beyond, into the vast environment of the *ulama*. After returning to Morocco in the fourteenth century, the Shādhiliyya had several major renewers in the Maghreb, especially beginning in the eighteenth century. In our own times, its branches have reached as far as Indonesia. It has played a pioneering role in the transmission of Sufi doctrine to the West, through such intellectual converts as René Guénon, Frithjof Schuon, Titus Burckhardt, Martin Lings, etc.

The Ahmadiyya, a typically Egyptian Sufi order, took its name from Ahmad Badawī (d. 1276). Since his childhood, this Moroccan-born saint veiled

---

[83]   P. Nwyia, *Ibn 'Atā' Allāh et la naissance de la confrérie shādhilite* (Beirut, 1990) (new edition); A. Buret, *Hikam. Paroles de sagesse* (Milan, 1999). (English edition: *Ibn 'Ata' Illah: The Book of Wisdom/Kwaja Abdullah Ansari: Intimate Conversations* [Paulist Press, 1978].) Other works of Ibn 'Atā' Allāh which have been translated into French are: *Traité sur le nom ALLĀH*, by M. Gloton (Paris, 1981); and *De l'abandon de la volonté propre*, by A. Penot (Lyon, 1997).

[84]   This book was translated into French by É. Geoffroy, under the title *La Sagesse des maîtres soufis* (Paris, 1998).

with two pieces of fabric "the blinding brilliance which the divine light had caused to shine from his face."[85] In 1237, he settled in Tanta, in the Nile delta, and there habituated a terrace until the end of his days. His disciples would be called "the Companions of the Terrace" (*al-sutūhiyyūn*). The selection of such a place for his life reflects the ecstatic character of this personage: Badawī was one of the "enraptured in God" (*majdhūb*) who concerns himself very little with human codes of conduct. His mysterious appearance and the vague details of his life account for the fact that a golden but rather belated legend set him up as the patron saint of Egypt. Unlike the Shādhiliyya, which is a more urban Order, the Ahmadiyya is more popular in rural environments and among the common folk.

Of Egyptian stock, Burhān al-Dīn Disūqī (d. 1288) was affiliated with several Orders before receiving permission to found his own *tarīqa*. We know few details of his life, but he left, unlike Badawī, some written teachings. Around the fifteenth century, this saint became part of the "four (spiritual) Poles" that popular Egyptian tradition assigns to this lower world: he took a place next to the Iraqis Jīlānī and Rifā'ī and the Egyptian Badawī. His Order, the Burhāniyya, is today flourishing in Egypt and the Sudan.

In the twelfth and thirteenth centuries, Syria was essentially under Iraqi influence. Several descendants of 'Abd al-Qādir Jīlānī emigrated to Syria, and his Order spread widely among the Hanbalite *ulama*. Damascus was always a Sunni bastion facing various Shi'ite communities within Syria: Twelvers, Ismā'īlis, Druzes, and Nusayris.[86] This became, therefore, a rather temperate kind of Sufism because it was under the control of the *ulama* who were predominant in the region. Starting in the fifteenth century, Syrian Sufism would be renewed equally through the Maghreb (the Madyaniyya and Shādhiliyya), the Caucasus, and Central Asia. Though it was established late, the Naqshbandiyya is today the most widespread Sufi brotherhood in Syria.

— *Anatolia.* The universalism and the message of love that Rūmī brought spilled over into all aspects of the brotherhoods. It was his son Sultan Walad (d. 1312) who founded the Mevlevi Order (the *Mawlawiyya* in Arabic) and who standardized the famous whirling dance. The *Pirkhāne* of Konya, where the small rooms of the followers were arranged around the mausoleum of Mevlāna, became the center of the Order. In the fifteenth century, the triumphant Ottomans began to look with favor on the Mevlevis, these

---

[85] C. Mayeur-Jaouen, *Al-Sayyid al-Badawi, un grand saint de l'islam égyptien* (Cairo, IFAO, 1994), p. 192.

[86] The latter were called Alawis ("partisans of 'Alī") by the French during the time of their mandate in Syria (1922-1945).

orthodox Sufis who they saw as a possible rampart against the rebellious dervishes of the Anatolian lands. The Mawlāwiyya followed the tracks of the conquering Ottomans into the Balkans and Arab countries.

Like Rūmī, Hajjī Bektāsh (d. 1337) was pushed by the Mongolian invasion towards Anatolia. At the confluence of the Turkish current of Ahmad Yasawī and the Iranian Qalandars, this saint became an emblematic figure for dervishes and, more broadly, for the Turkmen tribes established in Anatolia. He seems to have harbored the seed of the syncretism that the Bektashis would come to practice. Anatolian Christianity, in particular, had an apparent influence on the rituals that he established, even if that influence has sometimes been exaggerated by the detractors of the Order. However that may be, religious formalism was not accepted in this region where, according to the Bektashi formula, "a saint belongs to everyone." The dogmatic flexibility of the Bektashis paradoxically allowed them to be active agents in the Islamicization of Asia Minor and the Balkans. Around 1500, Balim Sultan introduced some innovations into the Order—for example, he encouraged the dervishes to be celibate—and he gave it its definitive rules.

At the beginning of the fifteenth century, a movement stemming from extremist Shi'ism taught a Kabbalistic system that relied on the numerical value of letters, from which is derived the name of the sect, *al-Hurūfiyya* (*hurūf* means "letters" in Arabic). Its founder, Fadlullāh, who advocated supra-confessionalism (i.e., looking beyond, or "above" religious differences) and who claimed divinity for himself, was executed for heresy by the Timurids in 1394. This hurūfism contaminated the Bektashis, whose leaders nevertheless tried to minimize its influence.

On the plateaus of Asia there were still remnants of ancient religions, and these would be partially Islamicized. In regard to the Bektashis, it may be necessary to speak not of "Sufism" but rather of spirituality that was partially inspired by Islam. Obviously, there exists a gap between urban and rural mysticism. One can thus see how much distance separates the Turco-Persian dervishes' lack of a distinct form from the debonair "syncretism" of a Rūmī, for example. The latter became the apostle of ecstasy and of openness to other religions, and the recollection of ancient Iran showed through in his work, but all of this was integrated into a properly Islamic perspective.

— **The Caucusus**. The last of the major Sufi brotherhoods to appear in the medieval era was the Khalwatiyya (known as the Helvetiyya in Turkey). It took its name from the Arabic term *khalwa*, the "spiritual retreat," which is the practice that characterizes this Order. The master who bore this name, 'Umar Khalwati (d. 1397), was called this because he liked to withdraw from the world, into the hollow trunk of a tree. The Khalwatis have also maintained a taste for asceticism. This shaykh was not an organizer, and it was left to Yahyā Shirwānī (d. about 1463), a native of the Caucusus, to establish the Order. As we have seen, a great deal of time can pass between when someone begins an Order and when someone else provides it with real momentum. Established in Baku, on the Caspian Sea, Shirwānī gave the Khalwatiyya a hierarchic structure. Because of the large number of followers who were attracted to him, he had to send representatives to the various regions of the Caucasus. He was probably the first shaykh to adopt this pyramid-shaped delegation of authority. After moving into Anatolia at the end of the fifteenth century, the Khalwatiyya obtained support from the Ottoman rulers and then swarmed into all the territories under Ottoman domination, particularly into Egypt. A brotherhood that was primarily of the city and was clearly Sunni, it had the same reverence for Ibn 'Arabī as the Ottomans. The sultan Mehmet, who conquered Constantinople in 1453, had a Khalwati shaykh for his spiritual guide. The Order follows a progressive initiation through the invocation of seven divine Names. In the past, Khalwatis would often practice occult sciences (divination, alchemy, the interpretation of dreams, etc.).

The fate of certain brotherhoods can often be surprising. For example, the Safawiyya was formed in fourteenth century Azerbaijan. The geographic and initiatory origins of this Order are similar to those of the Khalwatiyya. Initiated by Safi al-Dīn Ardabīlī (d. 1334) in Ardabil, between Tabriz and the Caspian Sea, he seemed at first Sunni. At the end of the fifteenth century, the masters of the Order directed it towards Shi'ism and, for the good of the cause, proclaimed themselves descendants of 'Alī. Their successor, Shah Ismā'īl (d. 1524), then founded the Safavid dynasty, imposing Twelver Shi'ism on an Iran that had till then considered this as the dogma of a minority. Some fanatical partisans, the Qizilbash ("red heads"), assisted him in this effort and went so far as to divinize him.[87] Shah Ismā'īl and the Safavid rulers who followed then chased the Sunni Sufis out of Iran.

Bibliography

On the initiatory paths, "Orders," or "brotherhoods," refer to the collection in French: *Les Voies d'Allah. Les ordres mystiques dans le monde musulman des origines à aujourd'hui*, edited by Alexandre Popovic and Gilles Veinstein (Paris, 1996).[88]

---

[87] The Qizilbash earned their name due to their red head-coverings, whose twelve folds symbolized the twelve Imams of Twelver Shi'ism.

[88] Translator's Note: A standard English reference that covers the history of the development of Sufi brotherhoods is *The Sufi Orders in Islam* by J. Spencer Trimingham (Oxford University Press, 1998); a good online resource can be found at www.uga.edu/islam/sufismorders.html,

INTEGRATION AND EXPANSION: "SUFISM, THE HEART OF ISLAM"

At the height of the geopolitical upheavals and the transformations which these brought about, Sufism flourished in its various dimensions. In the thirteenth century, while Sufi literature was reaching its peak, Sufism entered the mainstream of Islamic culture; it alone was a force of revitalization of Islamic intellectual life. Attracting more and more of the faithful, Sufism changed the tenor of popular piety and the religious life which would be used to express it. Its ubiquitousness on the Islamic scene revealed itself in many aspects; we will pause to examine the most significant ones.

Recognition of Sufism by the Ulama

Sufism permeated the circles of the educated and the *ulama* very early on. As early as the eleventh century in Baghdad, the exoteric sciences and Sufism developed intimate relations. Pious scholars led lives of saints, and did not hesitate to call themselves "Sufis"; the *madrasas* welcomed as many shaykhs as jurists, and Sufi masters came to play an increasingly important role in the cities.[89] The alliance, which we have mentioned above, sealed by Qushayrī and Ghazzālī between the disciplines of Sufism, Ash'arite theology, and the Shafi'ite school of law, was corroborated in the thirteenth century; it was responsible for a remarkably long line of Sufi scholars. Among the famous Shafi'ite doctors of the law who admired the Sufis, let us quote the "sultan of the *ulama*," 'Izz al-Dīn Ibn 'Abd al-Salām (d. 1261), to whom the following admission has been attributed: "I did not know true Islam until after my encounter with Shaykh Abū 1-Hasan Shādhilī." These scholars often took a spiritual master and affiliated themselves with a *tarīqa*. Imam Nawawī (d. 1277), for example, the author of the *Gardens Reserved for the Pious* (*Riyād al-Sālihīn*), was known as an expert of *Hadīth*. It is less well known that he was involved in mysticism and took up his pen to defend Sufi terminology; posterity also attributes to him many spiritual "unveilings" and miracles.

In Mamluk Egypt, the Shādhiliyya wove itself into the fabric of the elite of the *ulama*. The grand *qādī* Ibn Daqīq al-'Īd (d. 1351), considered to be the "renewer of Islam for the seventh century of the Hijra," gave his allegiance

---

a web site under the aegis of the University of Georgia.

[89] D. Ephrat, *A Learned Society in a Period of Transition: The Sunni 'Ulama' of Eleventh-Century Baghdad* (New York, 2000).

to Shaykh Ibn 'Atā' Allāh, the author of the *Hikam*, and had himself buried near him. His biographers attributed various spiritual favors to him. Tāj al-Dīn Subkī (d. 1370), another famous Shafi'ite scholar, for his part considered the Sufis as the "elect."[90] In the same era, in Andalusia, the Malikite jurist Abū Ishāq Shātibī (d. 1388) advocated a Sufism which was faithful to the Law, while in the Maghreb his contemporary Ibn Qunfudh, a jurist and *qādī* of Constantine (in Algeria), became the champion of "the glory of the saints."[91]

Here and there, theologians and lawyers recognized that innate knowledge, granted by divine grace (*al-'ilm al-wahbī*) is superior to the speculative knowledge that they themselves practiced. On various occasions, they confirmed that this spiritual knowledge is the true foundation of prophecy. As early as the eleventh century, in Nishapur, the philosopher Avicenna had already declared to his students after coming from his meeting with Shaykh Ibn Abī 1-Khayr: "All that I know, he sees."[92] In the following century, the aged Averroes, in Córdova, received a lesson from the young Ibn 'Arabī: "What have you found through 'unveiling' and divine inspiration?" inquired the old man. "Is it identical to what we obtain from speculative reflection?" "Yes and no," replied Ibn 'Arabī, "It is between the 'yes' and the 'no' that spirits take flight, and heads are separated from their bodies."[93]

The Iranian theologian Fakhr al-Dīn Rāzī (d. 1209), was at first sanctimonious and hostile to Sufism; by the end of his life, he repented of this and recognized that "the Sufis are the best of men."[94] He then tried to comply with the spiritual discipline of a master, who asked him to withdraw into a cell; once he was there, the master, thanks to his psychic powers, began to strip away from him all of his book-learned knowledge. But Rāzī, giving in to his panic, quit his retreat.[95] Many jurists regretted having discovered Sufism too late, as was the case for an important Hanbalite *qādī* from Cairo for whom

---

[90] See his *Mu'īd al-ni'am* (Beirut, 1986), p. 94.

[91] N. Amri, "La gloire des saints. Temps du repentir, temps de l'espérance au Maghreb 'medieval'", in *Studia Islamica* 93, 2001.

[92] M. Ebn E. Monawwar, *Les Étapes mystiques du shaykh Abu Sa'id*, p. 200.

[93] C. Addas, *Ibn 'Arabī et le voyage sans retour*, p. 20. According to the Shaykh al-'Alawī, Averroes had affirmed that "the revealed Law encourages us to follow the path of the Sufis" (*Risālat al-nāsir ma'rūf*, p. 62).

[94] See his work *I'tiqādāt firaq al-muslimīn wa l-mushrikīn* (Cairo, 1937), pp. 72-73.

[95] This episode is cited by M. Chodkiewicz in *Un océan sans rivage*, pp. 52-53. (English edition: *An Ocean Without Shore* [Islamic Texts Society, 1993].) See also the introduction by P. Ballanfat to Najm al-Dīn Kubrā's *Les Éclosions de la beauté et les parfums de la majesté*, pp. 44-47.

"that which touches the heart" could not be found in exoteric knowledge, but in the invocation of God (*dhikr*).[96]

Although he was not himself initiated, the thinker and historian Ibn Khaldūn (d. 1406) had a rather refined knowledge of Sufism. He dedicated a treatise to it as well as the sixth chapter of his *Prolegomenon* (*Muqaddima*).[97] He said, in substance, that through their ascetic discipline Sufis achieve an unveiling of spiritual realities to which others do not have access. In accord with other scholars, he revered the earliest Sufis and dismissed the followers of "philosophical Sufism," namely Ibn Sab'īn and, to a lesser extent, Ibn 'Arabī.

In the fifteenth and sixteenth centuries, some illustrious *ulama* finally managed to obtain for Sufism its "certification of nobility." Generally affiliated with it themselves, they regarded the knowledge of the Sufis as infallible. So it was that Zakariyyā Ansārī (d. 1520) played an essential role in the transmission of the initiatory Orders that were present in Egypt. This grand *qādī*, who would, despite his objections, receive the honorific title of *shaykh al-islām*, taught Shafi'ite law and Sufism jointly, an example which would be followed by several generations of Sufi *ulama*. More importantly for posterity, Suyūtī (d. 1505) took advantage of his celebrity in the Muslim world to conduct a shrewd apology for Sufism. He was the first to include *tasawwuf* in a collection of *fatwas*.[98] He saw in the *dhikr* the highest form of worship, even higher than canonical prayer—demonstrating to us that it is necessary to interpret the words of Sufis and not to stop at their literal meanings. Suyūtī maintained that saints have the gift of being everywhere at once, replaced the esoteric hierarchy of the saints from the Sunni point of view, defended the orthodoxy of Ibn al-Fārid and Ibn 'Arabī, and affirmed that gnostics ranked above jurists. He himself chose to enter the Shādhilī Order, to which he devoted a piece. Suyūtī, to whom a thousand pieces in the various fields of knowledge have been attributed, is still one of the most widely read authors in the Muslim world. Following in his footsteps, Ibn Hajar Haytamī (d. 1566) stressed the place of Sufism in *fatwas*.[99] History has conferred on him a special importance: Since his lifetime in the Ottoman-era, he has up to the present day continued to be, for the opponents of Wahhabism, an essential reference.

---

[96] Sha'rānī, *al-Tabaqāt al-sughrā* (Cairo, 1970), p. 80.

[97] The treatise was translated into French by R. Pérez (*La Voie et la Loi*) and the *Muqaddima* by V. Monteil (*Discours sur l'Histoire universelle* [Beirut, 1968]; see p. 1004 *et seq.*).

[98] A *fatwa* is an opinion given by a scholar in response to an issue submitted by some authority or by a private person or entity. It usually concerns a legal point touching on religious life or on human relations.

[99] See his *Fatāwā hadīthiyya*, "*Fatwas* concerning *hadīth*."

During the same period, Sha'rānī (d. 1565) hinted at the thin border separating the Sufi master from the scholar-jurist. The successor to Suyūtī, he maintained the need for a Sufi *ijtihād* (effort of interpreting the Law) which would be the result of spiritual intuition. Transcending the divisions between the representatives of the various theological or legal schools, he thought that only an inward approach could retrieve the true source of the Law. In his eyes, Sufism must reign over all disciplines that are based on rational deduction. A key figure in mystical thought, he was an important influence on the Sufi reformers of the eighteenth and nineteenth centuries.

Because of his colorful hagiographic writing, his initiatory position at the junction of several Orders, the precise rules that he assigned to beginners, and his function as a shaykh of a *zāwiya*, Sha'rānī was both an actor in, and a privileged witness to, the Sufi experiment. The fact that illiterate mystics and the "enraptured in God" (*majdhūb*) were attracted to him, along with his condemnation of a certain popular Sufism, highlights the paradox of a Sufi culture which becomes dominant but which easily engenders counterfeits, thus becoming the victim of its own success.

Sufism is Prominent as the Spirituality of Sunni Islam

All the scholars whom we have just mentioned worked to present Sufism as the heart of the Islamic religion. From this point on, Sunni *tasawwuf* denied any affinity with Shi'ite esoterism when it refused to comply with the standards of the Law; it also rejected Hellenistic philosophy (*falsafa*) because it competed with Revelation, and thus with inspiration which is its heir. Ancient philosophy, beyond its speculative aspects, had indeed an initiatory aspect that was ignored in the West, and the presumed relations between Avicenna and the Sufis left the appearance of a certain rivalry between philosophers and mystics. The shaykhs had been warning against this influence since the eleventh century, and they sought to marginalize those whom they considered "philosophical Sufis." Even today, the philosophical character attributed to part of Ibn 'Arabī's work continues to be the source of similar polemics.

At the end of the medieval period, Sufism no longer needed to seek acceptance by orthodoxy, because it was itself the living source. It was from then on incorporated into the body of the sciences taught wherever Islam was to be found. The Sufi manuals of the tenth and eleventh centuries, as well as the spiritual texts of Ghazzālī and Suhrawardī, were read and commented upon just as were treatises on *Hadīth* or law. Mysticism figured prominently in the encyclopedic works which were so favored by the period. The central themes of Sufi doctrine, such as the "Muhammadian Reality," touched many minds and appeared in books which were not directly related to Sufism. Similarly, well-read men and *ulama* would refer to the esoteric hierarchy of the saints, mentioning its "pole" (*qutb*), its "pillars" (*awtād*), its "substitutes" (*abdāl*), etc.

The making of an initiatory pact (*'ahd*) with a master did not pose any problem for the *ulama*, since they were the masters of the art of the "contract" (*'aqd*), which is a recurring principle of Muslim law: the former represents the esoteric aspect of the latter. Usually, these scholars were affiliated with several brotherhoods, which promoted the penetration of Sufism into society. For all that, the mystical dimension did not entirely penetrate the circle of the clerics: the "minor jurists," in particular, remained outsiders to the spiritual adventure which the Sufis proposed.

Hanbalism and Sufism

The legal school founded by Ibn Hanbal has often been criticized for its narrow and literalistic fideism. Wrongly so, because this school does not attack Sufism in itself more than any other school, and it has in the end even shown itself to be open to a great extent to this dimension of Islam. As we have seen, during the first centuries some major Sufis (Ibn 'Atā', Hallāj, Ansārī Harawī) followed the Hanbalite school of law and, as of the eleventh century, Baghdad housed many Hanbalites who were both jurists and Sufis. The *madrasa* of the Hanbalite 'Abd al-Qādir Jīlānī thus sought to harmonize the law with spirituality. Many Hanbalite scholars and Sufis defended the memory of the controversial Hallāj more or less openly. In his piece *The Confusion of Iblīs* (*Talbīs Iblīs*), Ibn al-Jawzī (d. 1200), a Hanbalite, did indeed denounce excesses in which, as he saw it, Sufis indulged, but his indictment spared no one (philosophers, theologians, preachers). Yielding to the established hagiographic tradition that was then in place, he also composed pieces on the lives of saints.

The polemist Ibn Taymiyya (d. 1328), on the other hand, is often portrayed as the most savage adversary of the Sufis. This Syrian scholar, who promoted "Neo-Hanbalism," fought against all that seemed to him to contravene the scriptural sources and the example of the first Muslims (*salaf*). Regarding the domain of mysticism, he condemned the worship of saints and pleas for intercession (he approved the intercession of the Prophet for believers on the Day of Judgment, but not in this world), and stigmatized the metaphysical "monism" of Ibn 'Arabī, Ibn Sab'īn, and their respective schools. Yet he deserves credit for having read the texts of these authors, and for making a distinction between Ibn 'Arabī and those that claimed to represent his ideas. That would not be the case with his later imitators, the Saudi Wahhabites and those who allied themselves with them, both of whom abridged the ideas of Ibn Taymiyya.

Ibn Taymiyya took up many Sufi themes and used a great deal of Sufi terminology, but he emptied these of all esoteric content: he gave his approval to the spiritual "stations" and "states" that mark out the Path, such as the love between God and man; he accepted the miracles of the saints, excused the intoxication of ecstatic mystics, recognized the role of "inspiration" and "unveiling" as long as they do not contradict the Koran and the *Sunna*, etc. He praised the early masters such as Junayd or Tustarī and considered Bistāmī to have been an "authentic" spiritual personage. Having received initiation into the Qādiriyya, he noted that there had been only two generations between himself and 'Abd al-Qādir Jīlānī. Finally, he fulfilled the role of a true spiritual master in Damascus.[100] But his refusal of any Sufism other than an ethical one and his rejection of any esoteric mediation between God and man would earn him a reputation for hostility towards Sufism. His terms in prison, let us note, were due more to his theological positions, which opposed the dominant Ash'arism of the time, than they were to his rampant conflicts with various kinds of mysticism.

His main disciple, Ibn Qayyim al-Jawziyya (d. 1350), broadened the Hanbalite openness to Sufism. He was initiated by his master into the Qādiriyya. Among the main works which he left behind was a commentary on Ansārī's *The Stages of the Travelers Towards God*,[101] in which he wrote that "the most eminent jurists and theologians have recognized the superiority (or 'excellence') of Sufis." Ibn Taymiyya also influenced several Shafi'ite scholars. Among them was Ibn Kathīr (d. 1373), who was known for his commentary on the Koran; in some of his other writings he recognized the esoteric hierarchy of the saints, and he used Sufi terminology. As for Ibn Hajar 'Asqalānī (d. 1449), a specialist in *Hadīth* and a grand *qādī*, he defended the allusive language of the Sufis and commented on the mystical verses of Ibn al-Fārid. Afterward, Hanbalites would continue to open themselves to the inner dimension of Islam, and some would prove themselves to be open to the doctrines of Ibn 'Arabī.

Places of Sufi Social Interactions

Beginning in the thirteenth century, establishments devoted to the mystical life flourished in all the territories of Islam. The *ribāt*, as we have seen, were first situated on the frontiers of Islamic domains, facing non-Muslims. Little

---

[100]   E. Geoffroy, "Le traité de soufisme d'un disciple d'Ibn Taymiyya: Ahmad 'Imād al-dīn al-Wāsitī (m. 711/1311)," *Studia Islamica*. n° 82, 1995, pp. 83-101.

[101]   Part of which was translated into French as *Les Sentiers des itinérants* (Paris, 1999). (English edition: *The Stations of the Wayfarer* [Fons Vitae, forthcoming].)

by little, they lost their military role and only remained in Arab territory; then they only welcomed the soldiers of the internal *jihād*, the Sufis: in the twelfth century, Baghdad had several *ribāts*, and the "grand shaykh" (*shaykh al-shuyūkh*) of the Sufis, who had been approved in this position by the caliph, was the head of one of them.

Present in Iran since the tenth century, *khānqāhs* welcomed people affiliated with their own congregations, but also all passersby and visitors. They proved to be a major source of social integration. Saladin imported this institution to the Near East, and the first *khānqāh* that he constructed accommodated three hundred eastern Sufis. *Khānqāhs* then became public establishments, in other words, financed by the Ayyubid and then the Mamluk regimes, which were able in that way to exert some control. The residents of the *khānqāhs* were so prosperous that the traveler Ibn Jubayr, while visiting Damascus in the twelfth century, described them as "the kings of this country." Many masters proved to be reluctant in the face of this institutionalization of Sufism. It seemed to them paradoxical because the occupants of the *khānqāhs* collected a sort of salary, even though the "poor in God," the Sufis, were supposed to rely on divine providence, or to earn their livings. Many of the *ulama* lavished instruction in religious sciences on the *khānqāhs*, a process which contributed to the integration of Sufism into Islamic life.

Unlike the *khānqāhs*, which would disappear when the public monies could no longer finance them, the *zāwiyas* were places of spontaneous and private initiative, from which the spiritual impulse sprang. Known only in the Arab world by this name (its equivalent in the Turkish world was the *tekke*, and in India the *takya*), the *zāwiya* is the "corner" into which one withdraws to practice the inner life. In the beginning, the residence or the shop of a shaykh was able to act as a *zāwiya*; but towards the thirteenth century the institution of the *zāwiya* experienced a major expansion and reinforced the Sufis' vocation for hospitality: whether they were important *ulama*, emirs, or people of modest means, the disciples made the personality of their shaykhs radiate into society. In the Maghreb, large *zāwiyas* were established in rural areas. Usually self-sufficient, they provided instruction in Islamic sciences and contributed greatly to social cohesion.

The spread of Sufism quickly moved beyond those specific places. Since the eleventh century, let us recall, the *madrasas* of Iraq had welcomed Sufism. Towards the thirteenth century, the same thing spread, for example, to Egypt, where the *madrasas* and the institutions dedicated to the science of *Hadīth* (*dār al-hadīth*) included Sufism in their programs. At the al-Azhar University in Cairo, Ibn 'Atā' Allāh taught both law and Sufism, and this practice would continue with others. At the same time, Sufis financed mosques, where both instruction and invocation (*dhikr*) were held.

The sessions of prayers on the Prophet (*majlis salāt 'alā l-nabī*), which were nights dedicated to litanies on the Prophet, appeared at al-Azhar at the end of the fifteenth century, then in the Umayyad Mosque in Damascus; they soon spread to other areas of the Muslim world.

Ribāts, khānqāhs, and *zāwiyas* were sometimes monumental complexes. A large *zāwiya* generally included a private mosque, a *madrasa*, a place for lodging people, and some private areas. The most important blocks were concentrated around the tomb (*mazār, maqām*) of the founding saint or one of his successors. These sanctuaries were used as gathering places for Sufis and began to attract larger and larger crowds.

The "Cult of Saints"

Rising rapidly during the Fatimid era, the worship of the saints had as a tangible indication the "visit" (*ziyāra*) to their sanctuaries. Though it directed the course of popular piety starting in the thirteenth century, it also inspired the "erudite" teachings of the masters and their doctrines of holiness. From the *dargah* (tomb of a Sufi saint) of Chishtī in Ajmer, India, to the mausoleum of Jīlānī in Baghdad, or while passing through Humaytharā, Egypt, where the presence of Shaykh Shādhilī gave life to the desert, the places where the saints lived and died were considered to be full of *baraka*, and they still to this day exert their extraordinary faculty of attraction.[102] Each person is there to seek what will fulfill his needs: the Sufis go there to ask for the "illumination" of the heart, while the average believers have more material requests, related to marriage, sterility, exams, etc. In both cases, it is the intercession of the saint that is sought. In spite of the opposition of Ibn Taymiyya to this type of practice, scholars have been able to ascertain its orthodoxy. For impoverished believers, the visit to the sanctuary of a saint often takes the place of the pilgrimage to Mecca.

In Egypt, the birthday festivals of saints (*mawlid*) expanded in scale starting in the fifteenth century. Through the imitation of the *mawlid* of the Prophet, these festivals dedicated to the many saints of the country mark out both the Egyptian year and space. The most important *mawlid* is still that of Ahmad Badawī, in Tanta, which can strike one like a crazy carnival. Through the various aspects of the devotion to the Prophet which they manifested,

---

[102]   By way of example, the tomb of Shādhilī "was at the beginning of the 20th century still a modest cubic building of dry stones, a simple stage on the roads to the Hajj; since the paving of the desert road, it is today a city in training, with lodgings for the pilgrims, mosques, and parking lots where buses stream in and out during the annual pilgrimage to the tomb of the saint"; see C. Mayeur-Jaouen, "Tombeau, mosquée et zāwiya: la polarité des lieux saints musulmans," in *Lieux sacrés, lieux de culte, sanctuaires* (École française de Rome, 2000), p. 139.

and through the veneration that they themselves arouse after their deaths, Sufi masters have helped to enrich the calendar of Muslim festivals, which some would soon come to regard as "blameworthy innovations" (*bid'a*).

The Esoteric Governance of the World

Numerous Koranic verses point out that power belongs only to God. Consequently, who are the real representatives (*khalīfa*) of God on earth: those who hold temporal authority, or the prophets and their heirs, namely, the *ulama* and saints? Medieval Islamic society was clearly in favor of the second choice. We have highlighted the fidelity of Sunni Muslims to the caliphate, the institution inherited from the Prophet, which represented to them a protection against any attempt of usurpation. However, with the notable exception of al-Nāsir, the caliphs became pawns in the hands of the emirs who actually held the power. It was not due to chance that the initiatory paths developed into structured networks just when the Abbasid caliphate had collapsed: it was at that time that one started to refer to the successor or the representative of a master using the term *khalīfa* (from which the word "caliph" also comes). A master would delegate the authority with which he had been invested by God to others, and these competed more and more with the temporal powers: this is when a time of the "caliphate of the saints" came to be.[103]

The idea that "the esoteric State of saints" (*dawla bātiniyya*) is superimposed on the government of the here-below undoubtedly has scriptural supports. In a long *fatwa*, Suyūtī made an inventory of *hadīths* mentioning the cosmic role that various categories of saints (*qutb, awtād, abdāl*, etc.) are supposed to play in the unseen organization of the world. For most authors, every temporal age has a hundred and twenty-four thousand saints, meaning the number of prophets known to humanity. The doctrine according to which the saints govern the world, each one in a given territorial jurisdiction, spread through society around the thirteenth century. It had been formulated by Ibn 'Arabī, but it also appeared in the writings of other Sufi authors. In Muslim social life, the effect was seen in the titles which some saints received, titles which were usually reserved for the temporal authorities. In Cairo, for example, Shaykh Muhammad Hanafī (d. 1443) was called "the sultan" or "the king."

In many cases, sultans and emirs seemed to accept this invisible government. In any event, they had an interest in it because the shaykhs had such an influence on society that it was difficult for the rulers to oppose them. The charisma of a saint or the influence of a strongly established *tarīqa* constitut-

---

[103] See D. Gril in *États, sociétés et cultures du monde musulman médiéval*, p. 444.

ed a potential threat to the temporal powers. In general, the leaders listened to the counsels or the reproaches that the shaykhs addressed to them. It is reported that the caliph Hārūn al-Rashīd (d. 809) cried with remorse after being admonished by a saint. The Sufis thus managed to intercede for the people, and even to modify the policies of the princes. In the sixteenth century, Ahmad Sirhindī convinced the Mughal rulers to give up the syncretic religion adopted earlier by the emperor Akbar. Sirhindī was a Sufi affiliated with the Naqshbandiyya, an Order which always advocated that its followers get involved with the princes. Other Sufis, however, refused to have any contact with the leaders, whom they considered to be impure.

Sultans and emirs tried to deal carefully with the supernatural power of the saints, because it could be turned against them. Obviously, their concern was to legitimate their own power in a society which had a thirst for sanctity. Some, however, really did seek the spiritual assistance of the shaykhs and, like the Mamluk sultan Baybars, to vow allegiance to a spiritual master. After the sack of Baghdad in 1258, the Mamluks, who were former Turkish or Circassian slaves, accommodated the Abbasid caliph in Cairo so that he could provide the moral approval for their rule. Although they controlled the mysticism in the *khānqāhs*, they attended the *zāwiyas* on a purely individual basis and defended the Sufis against the jurists. The marriage between the temporal dynasty and Sufism was consummated with the Ottoman sultans, who imposed the theses of Ibn ʿArabī as the doctrine of the state, and all of these sultans were affiliated with one or more of the *tarīqas*.

Bibliography

Éric Geoffroy, *Le Sufism en Égypte et en Syrie sous les derniers Mamelouks et les premiers Ottomans: orientations spirituelles et enjeux culturels*, IFEAD (Damascus, 1995).

Ibn Khaldūn, *La Voie et la Loi*, edited and translated by R. Pérez (Paris, 1991).

Catherine Mayeur-Jaouen, *Al-Sayyid al-Badawī un grand saint de l'islam égyptien*, IFAO (Cairo, 1994).

SUFISM AND REFORMISM (Eighteenth-Twentieth Centuries)[104]

A Decline of Sufism?

The Ottoman centuries are often viewed as a time when Islamic culture

---

[104] We have written some chapters that deal more or less with late Sufism. So we want to react against the now outdated view of a "classical" Sufism, a zenith of Muslim mysticism, which stopped, according to some, in the tenth century and which lasted no longer than the thirteenth century; this golden age was then supposed to be followed by a long period of decline. This view, in our opinion, is too dependent on Western historiographical editing.

was no longer vibrant. The thinking is as follows: Muslim scholars were satisfied to comment on or summarize the works of old, and the control exercised by the Ottoman empire over the religious hierarchy blocked any vitality of thought. Sufism itself degenerated into a popular religion where superstition and charlatanism got along well together, and pseudo-mystics, taking advantage of the credulity of the public, flourished. The first petty saint to come along would be designated as the "pole of the saints," and the "madman of God" who acted eccentrically could attract more people than a Sufi who behaved normally. Now, it is true that since the fifteenth century Sufism and Islamic culture in general experienced a downturn, and masters consequently were pressed by a wind of reform. Shaykh 'Alī Ibn Maymūn al-Fāsī (d. 1511), for example, considered himself a strict Muslim, and he railed against the corruption of the *ulama* and the degeneration of Sufism. However, it should be noted that this type of charge had been leveled by masters for centuries, undoubtedly with the aim of reinvigorating the aspiration of beginners.

The Ottoman period did, in fact, include some positive aspects. The worlds of the *ulama* and the Sufis became more and more intertwined and mystical thought was from then on part of Islamic culture. The figure of 'Abd al-Ghanī Nābulusī (d. 1731) testifies to this. An independent spirit, although he was attached to two initiatory Orders, he wrote on the various branches of Islamic knowledge, and he distinguished himself in poetry, accounts of journeys, and writings on Sufism; in the latter he appeared to be an authorized interpreter of Ibn 'Arabī.

The Search for Original Purity (Eighteenth-Nineteenth Centuries): Sufism and Wahhabism

At the turn of the eighteenth and nineteenth centuries, the world of Sufism experienced a period of ferment comparable to that of the twelfth and thirteenth centuries. This "renewal," which accompanied an awakening within Islam and the third wave of its expansion, was primarily a reaction. Many Muslim leaders attributed the following curses to the decline of religious purity: the weakening of the great Muslim empires (Ottoman, Safavid, Mughal), the increasingly more marked domination of Europe, the wearing down of Muslim societies, and the deviations which would sully those societies.

Since its beginnings in the Arabian Desert, the Wahhabite movement, founded by Ibn 'Abd al-Wahhāb (d. 1792), imposed a return to an Islam that was presumably as it had originally been, delivering it from later innovations and superstitions. The Sufism of the reformists underwent changes during the same period, and it experienced at first the same surge of purification.

The Sufism of the reformists and Wahhabism both demanded that Muslim societies return to the example of the first community of Medina so that they would live in conformity with the principles of Islam. They proved themselves to be intransigent concerning the practice of religion and they identified with Ibn Taymiyya, who wanted to restrict Sufism to his solely ethical approach. They also condemned slavish imitation in matters concerning the Law (*taqlīd*) and claimed that they were reopening the "doors of *ijtihād*," which supposedly had closed around the tenth century. Like the Wahhabites, the Sufi reformists vigorously condemned some extravagant practices within certain brotherhoods, as well as the popular religion which thrived around the tombs of the saints; they also wanted to react against the relaxation of the initiatory discipline.

The comparison, however, stops there, because affinities between Wahhabism and Sufism can only be provisional. Fundamentally, the two movements are completely opposed to each other, and their differences would be accentuated with time. We understand this better today: Sufism is the natural enemy of the rough and dry Islam preached by the Wahhabites, and the Saudi state did not hesitate to support or to promote an armed struggle against the circles of mystics. The Wahhabites are rigid in their opposition to any inner dimension of Islam and to any symbolical value within the rites. Refusing to admit that Sufi masters are able to give valid spiritual direction to the believers, they always find fault with the veneration which disciples have for their shaykh. The Wahhabites believe that the very special place in which the Sufis hold the Prophet leads to *shirk*, the act of "associating" others in the worship of God.

The Muhammadian Path

In their search for a return to the sources, Sufi reformists referred more than ever to the Prophet. They rediscovered the discipline of *Hadīth* and advocated a "Muhammadian Path" (*tarīqa muhammadiyya*) that transcended the various initiatory paths. This expression, which was implicit in earlier Sufism, appeared around the sixteenth century and became recurrent in reformed Sufism. Readily identifying themselves as Muhammadians rather than as Qādiris or Naqshbandis, and although they were still affiliated to one or more initiatory Orders, the Sufi reformists linked themselves directly to the spiritual entity of the Prophet, so much so that some claimed to encounter him "in-the-flesh-and-blood." According to Muhammad Sanūsī, the follower of the Muhammadian Path must think constantly of the Prophet, he must imitate him in everything, and he must constantly recite formulas of blessings on him; his heart, while being absorbed in the contemplation of the "Muhammadian essence," will be able to see the Prophet in his physical appearance. This direct relationship with the Prophet made many "jurists" shudder because it placed the mystic at the source of the Law, upstream of the schools of jurisprudence (*madhāhib*), of their quarrels and their pettiness. Such a relationship had as a result Sufi *ijtihād*, which Suyūtī and Sha'rānī had encouraged, and it also minimized any intermediaries who might block the relationship between believers and the Prophet.

Renewed Paths and New Paths

The signs of the Sufi revival were almost identical in India as in the Maghreb: they were characterized by: a purification of the mystical life, basing it on the *Sharī'a* and the example of Muhammad; a militant socio-political reformism, which was a response to Western influence; and an increase in the number of *tarīqas* and their relatively centralized organization. It was by no means a question of a concerted pan-Islamic movement: the actions varied according to the individuals involved and to circumstances.[105] This movement was described a few decades ago as Neo-Sufism, which supposes a rupture with the teachings of the "medieval" (i.e. up to the fifteenth century) masters. It was nothing like this, since the Sufi reformists drew their inner doctrines from Ibn 'Arabī and their external rigor from Ibn Taymiyya. For example, the precursor of the Indian Muslim reformists, Shāh Walī Allāh (d. 1762), resorted to *ijtihād* as had Ibn Taymiyya before him, and he rejected the worship of the saints; however, he continued to venerate Ibn 'Arabī, calling for a more precise interpretation of the doctrine of the "oneness of Being." Another kind of example is that of Sayyid Ahmad Barelwī (d. 1831), who led large-scale missionary activities in the north of India and who sought to free the country from the British by founding a sort of Islamic state; yet, he was still a traditional Naqshbandi shaykh.

For many Sufi masters, reform was, above all, inward. This kind of reform was aimed at centering the candidates on the essential principles of the Path by removing any dross from their practice. The Moroccan shaykh 'Arabī Darqāwī (d. 1823) put the accent on spiritual practice and not on the theory of Sufism. His teachings recalled those of past masters: in this domain, originality has no significance because the greatest saints have the sole mission of revivifying the spiritual tradition of their initiatory line.[106] Having the temperament of an ecstatic, Darqāwī preached a path of detachment, and his disciples, the Darqāwa, often led lives of wanderers, carrying walking-

---

[105] M. Gaborieau and N. Grandin, "Le renouveau confrérique," in *Les Voies d'Allah*, p. 83.

[106] *Darqāwī, Lettres d'un maître soufi*, edited and translated by T. Burckhardt, Milan, 1978. (English edition: *Letters of a Sufi Master* [Fons Vitae; 2nd edition, 1998].)

sticks and wearing large rosaries around their necks. There were many of them in Morocco and western Algeria, where they resisted the French presence until the beginning of the twentieth century. But beyond this, Shaykh Darqāwī gave a fresh energy to the Shādhiliyya, whose various branches (the Darqāwiyya, Madaniyya, Yashrūtiyya, 'Alawiyya, etc.) are still very much alive today, and have spread as far as Indonesia.

A Syrian shaykh, Mustafā Bakrī (d. 1749), was responsible for substantial reform within the Khalwatiyya; this resulted in a surge of expansion within the Order, which also saw its initiatory extensions spread as far as Southeast Asia. The direct disciples of Bakrī in Egypt, the shaykhs Hifnī and Dardīr (second half of the eighteenth century), were celebrated al-Azhar *ulama*; they challenged some of the practices of the brotherhood and intervened directly in political and social life. This spirit of reform still motivates the current representatives of the Khalwatiyya.[107]

For the Naqshbandis, their renewal came from Mawlānā Khālid (d. 1827). Trained in exoteric branches of knowledge, this Kurdish shaykh settled in Damascus where he adopted the reformist stance of another great Naqshbandī, Sirhindī. He contributed new initiatory methods to the *tarīqa*; for example, he required disciples to orient themselves internally towards his own person, and not towards his representatives in the provinces. Like Sirhindī, he put pressure on the temporal leaders so that they might return Muslims to a more strict observance of the *Sharī'a*, which he saw as the only way to reinforce Islam against the upsurge of Christian power. He rallied the *ulama* of Syria to his cause, who sensed that he would be the "renewer of the thirteenth century of the Hijra." One of his disciples, the great Hanafite scholar Ibn 'Abidīn (d. 1836) accepted, contrary to nascent Wahhabism, visits to the tombs of shaykhs and the esoteric hierarchy of the saints. The Naqshbandiyya-Khālidiyya Order quickly made headway into the Caucasus (Dagestan, Chechnya), where it organized the fight against the Russian invader. Imām Shāmil (d. 1859), one of the most important opponents of this occupation, held to the key principles of Shaykh Khālid. In competition with the Qādiriyya, the Khālidiyya made it possible for Sufism to play a major role in that region starting in the middle of the nineteenth century.

The greatest figure of the Sufi revival is without question Ahmad Ibn Idrīs (d. 1837). After having studied Islamic sciences in Fes, he affiliated himself with several branches of the Shādhiliyya, which had deep roots in that great city of Islam. Then he settled in Mecca, which was then, along with Medina, the hub for reformist Sufis. He advocated direct affiliation with the

---

[107] R. Chih, *Le Soufisme au quotidien. Confréries d'Égypte au xxe siècle* (Paris, 2000).

Prophet and the practice of spiritual *ijtihād*. He thought that the believer has no need of intermediaries in order for him to have access to the Koran and the *Sunna*. His rejection of the four Sunni schools of jurisprudence earned him the wrath of the Meccan jurists, which compelled him to flee to the 'Asīr region of Yemen. The importance of Ibn Idrīs does not lie in his written work, which was modest, as much as it does in the enigmatic radiance of his personality. Through his scholarship and his concern with inward reform, he held the Wahhabites who confronted him at bay. The Pan-Islamicism to which he ascribed would later be used as a final political weapon by the Ottoman sultan 'Abd al-Hamīd (d. 1909). It presaged the urgent appeal of the reformist *ulama* to overcome divisions between Muslims.

Several disciples of Ibn Idrīs created *tarīqas* which were to transform the initiatory landscape in parts of the Muslim world, from the Maghreb to Southeast Asia. The closest disciple to Ibn Idrīs was undoubtedly Muhammad Sanūsī (d. 1859). Born in Algeria, he, too, received his training in Islamic sciences in Fes, and then, in Arabia, took Ibn Idrīs as his master. With the death of the latter, Sanūsī established the Sanūsiyya in Libya and in neighboring Saharan areas, where he occupied himself with "peacefully re-Islamicizing, without any political motives, the disinherited populations of the region."[108] Sanūsī's doctrine was centered on the Muhammadian Reality. At the beginning of the twentieth century, Sanūsis carried out armed *jihād* against the Italian invaders in Libya, the English in Egypt, and the French in Algeria and in Niger; it is from this that the "black legend" of Sanūsi militancy, so called by the colonial powers, sprang.[109] The Sanūsiyya gradually faded away as an initiatory Order and kept only one institutional role: in 1950, a shaykh of the brotherhood was promoted to be the king of Libya; he would be overthrown by Gaddafi in 1969.

Rather than forming a small elite, the new Sufi paths sought to spiritualize the practice of Islam on a broad scale. The proselytism of the Tijāniyya is the best illustration. Originating in the region of Tlemcen, Algeria, Ahmad Tijānī (d. 1815) studied religious sciences in Fes, like so many others. He was initiated into several brotherhoods. Then, in 1782, while in a waking state, he saw the Prophet, who enjoined him to found his own *tarīqa*. Claiming for himself the function of the "seal of the saints" (*khatm al-awliyā'*), he presented the Tijāniyya as the culmination of the former initiatory paths.[110] This

---

[108]   J.-L. Triaud, "La Libye," in *Les Voies d'Allah*, p. 411.

[109]   J.-L. Triaud, *La Légende noire de la Sanūsiyya. Une confrérie musulmane saharienne sous le regard français* (Paris, 1995).

[110]   According to A. Hampaté Bâ, this path "plays, in Islām, the role that Islām plays among the religions," i.e. it synthesizes and completes the former initiatory paths (*Vie et enseignement*

brotherhood forces followers to give up any other affiliations and claims that disciples who renounce their affiliation with the Tijāni Order incur punishment from heaven which can lead to death. Such requirements led to criticisms from many Sufis and, of course, from exoteric scholars.

Since his time in Fes, where he was protected by the Sharīfian monarch, Ahmad Tijānī succeeded in establishing his Order throughout the Maghreb by creating a vast network of delegates (*muqaddams*). Like the Shādhili masters, he did not recommend the giving up of worldly goods (*zuhd*), but, instead, he advocated the practice of giving thanks (*shukr*); he himself lived well. After his death, the Tijāniyya spread throughout West Africa (Senegal, Guinea, Mali) by means of such followers as Hajj 'Umar Tal (d. 1864). The number of affiliations with the Tijāni *tarīqa* was so enormous there that Tal founded an Islamic state tied to the Tijāniyya, a state which was dismantled by the French in 1893. A dissenting branch, whose way has been called Hamallism and which came into being in Mauritania, owed its celebrity to some of its representatives: Shaykh Hamallah (d. 1943) differentiated himself from the mother-Order through some particular practices and then was persecuted by the French; Tierno Bokar (d. 1940), "the sage of Bandiagara," in Mali; and his disciple Amadou Hampaté Bâ (d. 1991), who was better known in France. To date, the Tijāniyya is the major initiatory brotherhood in sub-Saharan Africa.[111]

Lesser Jihād *and Greater* Jihād

After he had returned from a military expedition, the Prophet said to his Companions: "We have returned from the lesser *jihād* to devote ourselves here to the greater *jihād*." To those who asked him what the greater *jihād* is, he answered, "That of the heart!" or, according to another account, "the struggle of the human being against his passions" (Bayhaqī). For Sufis, this *hadīth* establishes the superiority of the inward, spiritual battle over outward combat. Indeed, although an opposing army only attacks sporadically, the ego harasses a human being incessantly.[112]

In the nineteenth century, the presence of the colonial powers caused many Sufis to find a calling to armed resistance, since projects of reform and re-Islamicization ran head on into the European desire for hegemony. In

---

de Tierno Bokar, le Sage de Bandiagara, [Paris, 1980], p. 230). (English edition: *A Spirit of Tolerance: The Inspiring Life of Tierno Bokar* [World Wisdom, 2008].)

[111] One can refer to the collection edited by J.-L. Triaud and D. Robinson, *La Tijāniyya, une confrérie musulmane à la conquête de l'Afrique* (Paris, 2000).

[112] See É. Geoffroy, *Jihād et Contemplation. Vie et enseignement d'un soufi au temps des croisades* (Paris, 2002) (new edition).

practice, positions often diverged within the same brotherhood on how to behave towards Westerners. Although some Tijāni or Qādiri groups maintained good relations with the French, others were fundamentally hostile to them. We will next cover two different attitudes concerning the practice of *jihād*: that of the Sudanese Mahdī, and that of the Emir 'Abd al-Qādir.

— **The Sudanese Mahdī.** Born in Dongola, the young Muhammad Ahmad affiliated himself with the Sammāniyya brotherhood in 1861. His reputation for piety quickly grew; perceived by his fellow-members as puritanical, he broke with some of them. In 1821, Muhammad 'Alī, the governor of Egypt, conquered Sudan; the country then underwent economic oppression and a process of modernization by force. All of that aroused a vast movement of revolt, amplified by the fact that Cairo appointed for Sudan some senior Christian officials who came from Europe. It is in this context that Muhammad Ahmad went through a spiritual crisis in 1881, following which he proclaimed himself the long-awaited *Mahdī*, an eschatological function that several spiritual figures had already claimed.[113] Muhammad al-Mahdī demanded from his followers that they revive the ideal of the first community of Medina and that they scrupulously respect the Koran and the *Sunna*. Presenting himself as the "successor to the Messenger of God," he rejected the concerns of the brotherhoods and declared *jihād* against the Turco-Egyptians, whom he considered infidels. After taking Khartoum, he died in 1885, but his disciples continued his work. As would often happen with Sufi reformist movements, this work would be taken up again by the nationalists of the twentieth century.

— **Emir 'Abd al-Qādir.** The life of the Emir 'Abd al-Qādir (d. 1883) moved to some extent in the opposite direction from that of the Sudanese Mahdī. In the case of the Emir, there was no claim, either spiritual or temporal, but an investiture which he received in spite of his objections. Defending his country from the French between 1832 and 1847, he decided to stop the lesser *jihād* in order to transmute it into a greater *jihād*, into a mystical conquest, because he saw in each a result of the divine Will, which one must honor under any circumstance. His enemies were not mistaken in one thing: behind the "brave and magnanimous warrior," Bugeaud (the French Governor-General of Algeria at the time) had distinguished "a sort of prophet."[114] During the Emir's captivity in France, which lasted until

---

[113] See *supra*, p. 24.

[114] M. Chodkiewicz, introduction to *Écrits spirituels* of the Emir (Paris, 1982), pp. 15-16.

1852, he became aware that he had been charged with a mission, that of "enriching France with his spirituality so that France might enrich the East with its technical prowess."[115] This explains the great curiosity of the Emir in respect to technological progress, but also the interest that he has aroused until today in France, which was to become a "Muslim power."

In 1853, 'Abd al-Qādir emigrated to the east, where, in 1855, he settled in Damascus, the city where Ibn 'Arabī lies at rest. In fact, although he was attached to several initiatory Orders, he was firstly a disciple, across the centuries, of the *Shaykh al-Akbar*, with whom he communicated, it is said, in the spiritual world. The Emir experienced frequent states of "rapture" (*jadhb*), observed by several witnesses. He proved, in his *Book of Halts* (*Kitāb al-mawāqif*) to be an authoritative interpreter of the work of Ibn 'Arabī. In this book, he adapted the doctrines of the Master to a new context. Assailing the practice of imitation (*taqlīd*) in matters of jurisprudence, the refined theologian in him redefined the relationship between rationalism and mysticism in Islam. He had a great influence on the reformist *ulama* of Damascus, but he addressed himself primarily to the elite of the future who would be able to restore Islam to its universalist dimension.

Sufi Reformism at the Beginning of the Twentieth Century: Amadou Bamba and the Shaykh al-'Alawī

The wave of reformist or reformed Sufism continued up to the beginning of the twentieth century. The Murīdiyya, whose followers are known in France as "Mourides," is very typical of Senegalese Islam. Following the earlier reformist Sufis, the founder of the Order, Amadou Bamba (d. 1927), took the title of "servant of the Messenger of God," and exalted the Prophet, with whom his disciples would virtually identify him after his death. He refused to be part of any armed resistance against France—which did not stop the occupiers of Senegal from exiling him for about fifteen years—and he put a positive face on the situation by preaching the motto "to work is to pray": strong in numbers, the brotherhood put thousands of hectares on plantations into production,[116] organized the culture of groundnuts in Senegal, and ran various industries, all of which led to considerable economic power. Did this involvement in the world work against the initiatory substance of Amadou

---

(English edition: *The Spiritual Writings of Amir Abd Al-Kader* [State University of New York Press, 1995].)

[115]   B. Étienne, *Abdelkader* (Paris, 1994), cover.

[116]   Which a French disciple called the "green *jihād*"; see D. Hamoneau, *Vie et enseignement du cheikh Ahmadou Bamba* (Beirut, 1998), p. 296.

Bamba's path? The Murīdiyya is estimated at the present time to number more than two million. Those who emigrated to the West are often itinerant salesmen.

It is at first sight surprising that Shaykh Ahmad 'Alawī (d. 1934) should appear among the "Sufi reformists," he whose Western disciples compared him to a "saint of the Middle Ages" or to a "Semitic patriarch."[117] Although he was certainly a man of tradition, those who came into contact with him also viewed him as a "modern mystic."[118] Seen by many as the "renewer of the fourteenth century of the Hijra," this Algerian shaykh, who was born in Mostaganem, first reformed the Sufism of his time. He did this by condemning some practices of the brotherhoods while focusing on what is essential, namely, the *dhikr*, the invocation of the Name of God. The Shaykh personally supervised the effect of this invocation on his disciples during their periodic retreats. His personal charisma and his initiatory methods led him, around 1914, to unfasten himself from the Shādhiliyya-Darqāwiyya in order to found his own branch, the 'Alawiyya.

To reform Algerian Islam, which had been weakened by French colonialism and Christian missionaries, Shaykh 'Alawī began in 1923 to publish a weekly journal which was aimed at reinvigorating Islamic culture in the region. He then founded the first "association of Algerian *ulama*" with *salafī* reformists such as Ibn Bādīs. But the latter soon pulled out to create their own association and their own newspaper, in which they took on "maraboutism," which they were not able—or did not want—to distinguish from true Sufism. In response to them, Shaykh 'Alawī defended a spiritual and open vision of Islam. Ibn Bādīs would eventually change his attitude towards Sufism before he died. The radiance of spirituality must shine upon society so, under the aegis of the Shaykh, many educational and charitable organizations were created.

Following the example of Emir 'Abd al-Qādir, with whom he shared many points of view, the Shaykh showed great openness towards other religions and to the West. He did, however, oppose the naturalization suggested by colonial France, and he campaigned for stronger Arabic language instruction. As with the Emir, Ibn 'Arabī's doctrine of the "oneness of Being" was a strong influence in shaping the universalism of the Shaykh. His initiatory influence was felt in several countries of the Middle East, but he influenced the West in particular beginning in 1920.

---

[117] J. Cartigny, *Cheikh Al Alawi. Documents et témoignages* (Paris, 1984), p. 51.

[118] A. Berque, "La Revue africaine" (Algiers, 1936), pp. 691-776.

Many other figures, less well known or more remote, could be mentioned to show that Sufis have not lived in a snug kind of quietism. Many reformist *ulama* could testify to this, since most of them have recognized a debt to Sufism.

Sufism: A Fertile Ground for "Salafī" Reformism

Contemporary Muslim "reformers" who speak out against Sufism suffer from a lapse in memory. Their leading thinkers have all come from the school of Sufism, which they criticized on this or that point, but to which most never ceased to belong. Ibn 'Abd al-Wahhāb, the founder of Wahhabism, was one of the only ones to reject this heritage, and his family publicly disowned him when he urged his followers to desecrate the tombs of the Companions and the saints buried in Arabia. His doctrines, moreover, do not constitute a "reform" of Islam; dictated by the rough-and-ready mentality of the Bedouins of Najd (central Arabia), they represent, at best, a literalistic view of the religion.

Around 1890, the movement of *islāh*, "reform," appeared in Egypt. The *ulama* in favor of this reform were also called *salafī* because they wanted to return to the pure Islam of the "pious predecessors" (*al-salaf al-sālih*), meaning the first generations of Muslims, in order to regenerate the religion and to adapt it to the ethics of the century. However, at the end of the nineteenth century it was difficult to distinguish between the domain of the *ulama* and that of the Sufis, or between "erudite" Islam and "popular" Islam. Indeed, it could easily be said that Sufism was the "fertile ground" from which the reformists sprang,[119] and that the proponents of reform were seeking to free *tasawwuf* from some customs and superstitions which, in their eyes, were suffocating it.

The initiator of *salafī* reformism in the Near East, Jamāl al-Dīn Afghānī (d. 1897), had a strong penchant for Sufism. His desire to regenerate Islam was largely inspired by the spiritual texts of the Sufi masters, on whom he commented during his teaching. His disciple Muhammad 'Abduh (d. 1905) was won over at the time of their first meeting by Afghānī's spiritual interpretation of the Koran. 'Abduh had been previously attached to the Shādhiliyya *tarīqa*, in which his great-uncle had had the function of shaykh. He gave in to the initiatory discipline, and in 1874 he wrote the *Epistle on Mystical Inspirations* (*Risālat al-wāridāt*) in which he took up Ibn 'Arabī's theses on the oneness of Being once more. This text would later embarrass the *salafis*, so much so that 'Abduh's leading student, Rashīd Ridā, would not include it in the

---

[119] G. Delanoue, *Moralistes et politiques musulmans dans l'Égypte du xixe siècle*, IFAO, Cairo, 1982, vol. I, p. 243.

posthumous edition of his master's works! Challenged by the political and social reality of Egypt, 'Abduh thereafter proved to be more combative than contemplative; though he criticized some Sufi practices, he never ascribed the decline of Muslim countries to the influence of *tasawwuf,* unlike many of his less-notable successors, and remained affiliated with the Shādhiliyya.

His successor at the head of the movement, Rashīd Ridā (d. 1935), was subject to the influence of Wahhabite doctrines and he demonstrated that he was less open to spirituality. He did, however, pay tribute to strictly Sunni Sufism for its dedication to education and purification of the heart, and ac-knowledged this saying of a shaykh of the tenth century: "Sufism consists of realizing noble manners (*akhlāq*) within yourself; the more you acquire them, the more you progress in Sufism."[120]

As for Hasan al-Bannā' (d. 1949), the founder of the Muslim Brother-hood, he was a very active member in his youth of the Husāfiyya *tarīqa,* which is in the Shādhilī line. The shaykh of this path was a fastidious Sunni and he imprinted upon the young man a preoccupation with the comple-mentarity of spirituality and action.[121] The charter of the association of the Muslim Brotherhood, created in 1928, stipulates that the new *salafī* move-ment would have as its base "a Sufi reality." At its origin, the movement did indeed invite many analogies with a *tarīqa*: the Brothers vowed alle-giance through a pact (*bay'a*) to their leader, called the "General Guide" (*al-murshid al-'āmm*); moreover, they recited a kind of daily litany (*wazīfa*) composed by Bannā'.

The movement was quickly politicized, and adopted an overall hostile position towards the brotherhoods. Its attacks are mainly attributable to the competition that existed from then on between *salafī* groups and Sufis. The Muslim Brotherhood served as a model for almost all Islamist groups, but not all of these condemned Sufism. Thus the Syrian Sa'īd Hawwā (d. 1989), a Brother who was in favor of the armed struggle against the regime of Hafez al-Asad, was nonetheless a Sufi. After long years spent in prison or exile, he continued to advocate a "*salafī* Sufism." He was the author of several works intended to promote a rather moderate mysticism among pro-Wahhabite *salafīs,* whom he reproached for closing off the spiritual dimension of Islam.

The Indian Muhammad Iqbal (d. 1938), the father of Pakistan, who considered himself a disciple of Rūmī, was obviously more universalist in his thinking. Iqbal had as a spiritual ideal "the Universal Man" (*al-insān al-kāmil*), who is the representative of God on earth; he found the substance

---

[120] Cited by Shaykh 'Alawī, in his *Risālat al-Nāsir Ma'ruf,* p. 92.

[121] T. Ramadan, *Aux sources du renouveau musulman* (Paris, 1998), p. 182.

of this doctrine in his study of the writings of 'Abd al-Karīm Jīlī (fourteenth century). Having studied in Europe, he also was influenced by the suprarational philosophy of Schopenhauer, Nietzsche (on the "superman"), and of Bergson. Iqbal also criticized the deviations of popular Sufism, but he did not stop his affiliation with the Qādiriyya for the rest of his life.[122]

The Indian theologian Abū l-'Alā' Mawdūdī (d. 1979) was one of the leading intellectuals of fundamentalist Islam in the twentieth century. He studied mysticism with reformist Sufis and he was even interested in the theosophist Shi'ite Mullā Sadrā (d. 1641). For him, Sufism is part of the *Sharī'a*; it is indissociable from Muslim law, whose inner dimension it represents.[123] Although he may have recognized this spirituality within Islam, he wanted to eradicate all esoterism within it. After having worked on the Islamic Constitution of the new Pakistani state, he returned at the end of his life to his early association with the Chishtiyya *tarīqa*, into which he initiated aspirants.[124]

One could mention many other reformers of the twentieth century who sometimes produced further fruit from their initiatory heritage by developing a parallel Sufism within the groups to which they held allegiance. Sa'īd Nursī (d. 1960), for example, a Turk of Kurdish origin, urged his supporters of the Nurdju movement, a group that was close to the Naqshbandis, to practice the *dhikr*. A contemporary, 'Abd al-Salām Yāsīn, an Islamist Moroccan with roots in the Bushīshiyya Order, continues to identify with the spirituality of Sufism. Can one still speak here of *tasawwuf*? There are objective criteria such as the regular affiliation with an authentic line, the practice of the *dhikr* and litanies, etc. But doctrines and behaviors vary considerably within Sufism, and the appropriation of a mystical group by a political or Messianic ideology is always possible. Such ideologies may even find Sufism to be fertile ground since a spiritual circle, if it does not hold to a strong sense of duties and rights of the Path, tends to become dry or radicalized.

Be that as it may, Sufis reformists and *salafī* reformists generally agree on several points: they condemn the westernization of minds but do not reject technology; they refuse to be prisoners of the schools of Islamic law; finally, they appeal to people to spread the message of Islam throughout the world, which involves a certain sociopolitical activism. On this point, it goes without saying, their strategies vary considerably.

---

[122] E. Sirriyeh, *Sufis and Anti-Sufis* (Leeds, 1999), p. 133.

[123] 'Abd al-Qādir 'Isā, *Haqā'iq 'an al-tasawwuf* (Aleppo, 1970), pp. 607-609.

[124] E. Sirriyeh, *Sufis and Anti-Sufis*, p. 164.

Sufism and Islamicism in the Twentieth Century: Politicization

The nationalists of the twentieth century—Arabs, Turks, or others—as much as the *salafī* reformists—often regarded Sufism in its form of organized brotherhoods as the symbol of the decline. Most new countries which appeared in the Muslim world thought the "*zāwiya* mentality" was antiquated, fearing the impact of the brotherhoods in society. In many respects, when they took over control from the colonial powers, they also took over their contempt or fear for the Sufi circles. Little by little, the brotherhoods disintegrated under the effect of the secularization of society, which was sometimes bolstered by the declared hostility of the authorities. The most extreme example is the official prohibition of the Turkish brotherhoods by Atatürk in 1925, but one could also cite the USSR under Stalin or Khrushchev, Algeria under Boumédiène, or Tunisia under Bourguiba. Although other more realistic countries tried to regulate Sufi life rather than control it, Egypt is to date the only country to be endowed with a "Supreme Council of Sufi Orders," gathering together the *tarīqas* recognized by the state. One is certainly entitled to think that mysticism cannot deal well with bureaucracy. For their part, Sufis have sometimes reacted as violently to the rapid secularization of authority as to foreign imperialism. In 1970 and 1980 in Syria, they stood side by side with the Muslim Brotherhood in opposing the "infidel regime" of Hafez al-Asad.

Starting in the 1980s, the politicization of the Islamic scene could not but involve the Sufi community. Faced with the rise of Islamicism, some countries understood it might be very helpful to utilize Sufi communities. This is the line adopted in Egypt by Sadat and then by Mubarak, and even by Gaddafi who seeks to develop closer relations with the shaykhs of the brotherhoods; the Algeria of Chadli became aware of this too late. The brotherhoods which had been forced to go into hiding resurfaced in one form or another. The Islam of peace and openness that is preached by most shaykhs is undoubtedly the best antidote to the narrow ideas that fuel Islamicism. But even if governments here and there have given some support to the brotherhoods, this has not gone without some harmful side effects, such as the subjugation of spirituality to politics.

In the fight for influence that they must carry out against Islamicist movements, Sufis have created foundations, schools, holding companies, newspapers, television channels, etc. They create their own special interest groups, by means of "Islamic associations" or of "associations of *ulama*," for example, by negotiating for their electoral support and investing in their political parties. It is like this especially in Indonesia, Pakistan, and Sudan. In Turkey, the *Refah* party of Erbakan, which was in office in the 1990s, was under the influence of the Naqshbandiyya; in addition, the former president of the Republic, Turgut Özal (d. 1993), was affiliated with this Order. Heads of state have hardly hidden their affiliations with Sufi movements: examples include Abdurrahman Wahid, former president of Indonesia, or Hasan II of Morocco, who was affiliated with the Tijāniyya. Sincerity in the spiritual quest and political opportunism are not necessarily mutually exclusive. At the end of the 1990s, Chechen freedom fighters, who are primarily Naqshbandis, sought to adopt a "Sufi Constitution" in view of statehood, but the deterioration of the situation has made it possible for the pro-Wahhabites to gain ground.

Sufis and Islamicists are sometimes at loggerheads. In Afghanistan, for example, the "Islamic Association" of former president Rabbani and the late Commander Massoud, firmly rooted in the Naqshbandiyya, was the principal obstacle to the expansion of the Taliban. Certain Sufis groups, however, imperceptibly align themselves with the discourse of Islamicists or adopt behaviors similar to theirs. The *Refah* party was presented, in Turkey as in the West, as a party of moderate Islamicism. In Lebanon, the Ahbāsh, disciples of Shaykh 'Abdallah Habashī, have fought against the Islamicists while borrowing from them an unbridled activism and overtly political tactics, to which is added a distinct sectarianism.[125] In Senegal in the 1980s, Mustafa Sy, a Tijānī, created an Islamic movement that was very involved in the social and educational spheres. In the 1990s, he led a bloody revolt against the current rulers before allying himself with President Abdoulaye Wade. Fundamentalists and Sufis sometimes also make peace in order to fight against foreign imperialism; this is the case in the Caucasus, which must deal with Russian designs.

During the twentieth century, the brotherhoods, formerly relegated to rural areas, learned to adapt to the world of the cities where they created new networks of solidarity. They also benefited from various movements of emigration to the West or between Muslim countries, which led to their expansion. Some disappeared, while others drew renewed vigor from the challenges thrown their way by fashionable ideologies. Their increased involvement in social and political life was undoubtedly a necessary passage, but should not mortgage their future. Should some descend into the arena to take a stand against other currents within Islam, or even to yield to activism, the shaykhs are still able to combine the inwardness that the spiritual life requires, with maintaining a presence in the world. Except in duly documented cases, it is risky to declare that such and such a shaykh or that such and such a brotherhood has steeped itself in exoterism while emptying itself of any initiatory substance.

---

[125] M. Yared, "Habachi et les islamistes: le duel à mort," in *Les Cahiers de l'Orient*, n° 50, 1998, pp. 83-97.

"Sufi Scholars" in Contemporary Times

We would not know how to set an "orthodox," learned, Islam against a Sufi Islam any more today than in the medieval period. Sufi scholars have not disappeared, especially in two ancient and central seats of Islam, Egypt and Syria. Al-Azhar University of Cairo has stayed very much open to Sufism and, during the twentieth century, several high officials of this institution (called *Shaykh al-Azhar*) were also Sufis. The better known Shādhilī Sufi 'Abd al-Halīm Mahmūd (d. 1978), who studied in France and knew René Guénon in Cairo, wrote some works in which he engaged in a "defense and illustration" of Sufism, while assailing the laxity of some practices in the brotherhoods. The current Shaykh al-Azhar has joined the Sufi movement, but so have, in particular, the Rector of al-Azhar University, and the grand *mufti* of Egypt.

In Damascus, the former grand *mufti* of the Syrian Republic, Ahmad Kuftārū (d. 2004), was also a celebrated Naqshbandi shaykh. A strong supporter of a Koranic Sufism, who was engaged in social issues and in serving the cause of Islam, he suggested replacing the term *tasawwuf* with that of *ihsān*, that is, "excellence" or "the quest for perfection."[126] As for Shaykh al-Būtī, he is one of the most listened to *ulama* in the Muslim world. This academic, who is an observer of the various tendencies within Islam, reproaches the *salafīs* for their intolerance with regard to other Muslims and their incomplete interpretation of Ibn Taymiyya. He also agitates for an effort of interpretation (*ijtihād*) of Sufi texts.[127] Initiated into Sufism by his father, Būtī perfectly illustrates the model of the scholar who is imbued with the values of Sufism.

Bibliography

Les Cahiers de l'Orient, n° 50, "Les Sufis à l'assaut de l'islam" (Paris, 1998).

Johan Cartigny, *Cheikh al-Alawi. Documents et témoignages* (Paris, 1984).

Émir Abd el-Kader, *Écrits spirituels*, edited and translated by M. Chodkiewicz (Paris, 1982).

Bruno Étienne, *Abdelkader* (Paris, 1994).

Marc Gaborieau et Nicole Grandin, "Le renouveau confrérique," in *Les Voies d'Allah* (Paris, 1996), pp. 68-83.

Tariq Ramadan, *Aux sources du renouveau musulman* (Paris, 1998).

---

[126] E. Geoffroy, "Soufisme, réformisme et pouvoir en Syrie contemporaine," in the journal *Égypte/Monde arabe* (CEDEJ. Cairo), n° 29, 1997, p. 14.

[127] *Al-Salafiyya* (Damascus, 1988).

Chapter 4

SUFISM AS IT IS LIVED

MASTER AND DISCIPLE

A Necessary Relationship

"It is through God that one knows masters, and through masters that one knows God."[1] This statement by Ibn ʿArabī does not exempt the novice from undertaking a quest for a master. The course of the Path, that is, the long inward journey leading a man who is the captive of his ego to the potential state of "Universal Man," certainly includes too many tribulations and dangers to be accomplished alone. Very early on, shaykhs recommended that aspirants place themselves under the direction of a spiritual guide (*murshid*).[2] Bistāmī said in a similar vein: "He who does not have a guide, has Satan for his guide." "I would not have known my Lord without my teacher," states a famous proverb (*law lā al-murabbī ma ʿaraftu rabbī*). The outer master is only the *mirror* of the "inner master," of the Self toward which the lower self must evolve. The enlightened disciple can find learning material everywhere in creation. Even so, he cannot do without a shaykh. A shaykh is essential due to the situation of man's exile in the here-below. Throughout the history of Sufism, even "inspired" or ecstatic saints have had a terrestrial guide. The beginner who claims to follow the Path without a master is like a patient who wants to take care of himself without a doctor. The shaykh is a doctor of souls, a mediator between God and men, and a support for his disciple's contemplation, all at the same time.

"Attaching oneself to this master or that master serves no purpose"; "It is necessary to seek only in oneself": We should not be misled by these blunt formulations from Bahāʾ al-Dīn Naqshband since they were aimed only at undermining the conformism which prevailed in the Sufism of his time.[3] And even though some disciples of Ibn ʿArabī may have considered a single reading of his works as a sufficient support for realization, the *Shaykh al-Akbar* himself mentioned on several occasions the need for the average aspirant to have a master. During the first centuries of Islam, noted a shaykh, the func-

---

[1] Ibn ʿArabī, *Futūhāt makkiyya*, vol. II, p. 366.

[2] A Sufi master is usually called a shaykh; in Iran and the Indian sub-continent, he carries the title of *murshid* or *pīr*.

[3] Kharaqānī, *Paroles d'un soufi*, p. 65.

tion of educator-master was not necessary because Muslims were still immersed in the prophetic presence. Thereafter, this calling became necessary.[4]

The Koran itself invites believers to question those who are "experts"
in God (25:59), and more precisely the "people of *dhikr*" (16:43). Sufis often refer to this verse: "Those are they whom God has guided; so follow
their guidance" (6:90). "A shaykh has the same rank among his people as a
prophet has in his community," the Prophet stated (Ibn al-Najjār). The term
shaykh here means both "chief" and "elder," but neither meaning excludes
the other. Shaykhs thus take on the spiritual direction that prophets carried
out in their communities, but they are no more than the surrogates of the
Prophet. As Ghazzālī and Suhrawardī in particular set forth, the relationship
that links the shaykh to his disciple is in the image of that which the Prophet
maintained with his Companions. The Muslim spiritual seeker can hope for
no more an accomplished mediator than the Prophet, who said: "It is my
Lord who educated me, and He has perfected my education" (Ibn Sam'ānī).

The relationship between master and disciple finds another prototype in
the encounter of Moses and Khadir. In the account given in the Koran, Moses
showed so much impatience in grasping the meaning of Khadir's behavior
that the latter decided to take leave of him.[5] This message serves as a lesson
to any beginner: the initiatory relationship is founded on the total submission
of the disciple to the master.[6] The goal is not to control the disciple, but to
make him "transparent" so that he can be invested with the spiritual state of
his master. The ego of the novice is perpetually questioning—"Why this?"
"How is that so?"—, posing an obstacle to the divine light and love which
flow from his master. "The aspirant must be in the hands of his shaykh like
a corpse in the hands of the washer of the dead": this formula, attributed to
Sahl Tustarī, is found in all the books of Sufism. Ghazzālī employed a different image: the disciple must attach himself to his master "like a blind man
who walks along the bank of a river."[7]

An Excessive Veneration?

In order for this submission to the shaykh to be effective, the disciple must
know that his master has achieved spiritual perfection. He must regard him

---

[4] Ibn al-Mubārak, *Kitāb al-Ibrīz*, vol. I, p. 52.

[5] See *supra*, p. 61.

[6] Suhrawardī, *'Awārif*, p. 409; 'Abd al-Qādir Jazā'irī, *Le Livre des haltes*, translated into
French by M. Lagarde, vol. I, pp. 562-565.

[7] *Ihyā' 'ulūm al-dīn*, vol. III, p. 65.

as a pole, a magnet around which he is, as it were, in orbit. It is in this sense that many shaykhs let it be understood that the master is a veritable *qibla* (the direction of Mecca). Some Orders have developed additional techniques regarding a disciple's "orientation" towards his shaykh. For Naqshbandis, the *rābita* (attachment to the master) establishes a "bond" of love, which creates a kind of "telepathic" communication between the two: the disciple concentrates mentally on the image of his shaykh to get to a state of ecstatic rapture (*jadhba*) that pulls him away from this world. Exoterists, and even some Sufis, condemn this method as bordering on idolatry, for when a disciple inwardly visualizes his shaykh while invoking God, is this not "associating" (*shirk*) a human being with the Divinity? The defenders of *rābita* cite some Koranic verses: "O you who believe! Fear God and seek the means of going towards Him!" (Koran 5:35) or, "O you who believe! Fear God and stay among truthful beings!" (Koran 9:119). They also rely on this *hadīth*: "The best among you are those who cannot see without immediately remembering God" (Tirmidhī).

The veneration of the Sufi for his shaykh is only a support, which reminds him of his veneration for the Prophet, and of his worship which is dedicated to God. Even so, exoterists find it easy to launch such criticisms when they see disciples prostrating themselves before their shaykh, which has indeed occurred. Authentic masters also condemn this type of behavior, even if they are able to justify its symbolical value; they recall that the spiritual guide is only "protected" (*mahfūz*) against sins whereas the Prophet enjoys freedom from sin (*'isma*). Exoterists have criticized another attitude which leads to ambiguity, which appeared only around the seventeenth century: "the extinction of the disciple in the master" (*al-fanā' fī l-shaykh*). Sufis see in this a precursor to the extinction of the human being in the Prophet (*al-fanā' fī l-rasūl*) and, beyond, in God (*al-fanā' fī Llāh*). Through the love that he holds for him, the disciple is able to annihilate himself in his master. This is the goal of the initiatory relationship, which must allow an osmosis between master and disciple to occur, or, the transfer of the spiritual state of the former to the latter. "I took you as my disciple only so that you would be me, and I you."[8] That explains why, according to an apparent paradox, the "servant" (*khadim*) of a shaykh sometimes becomes his successor. In practice, the master is at the service of his disciples. He is seen as a being who has been "sacrificed," because his spiritual function is weighty and demands that he always be available.

---

[8]   Ibn 'Atā' Allāh, *La Sagesse des maîtres soufis*, p. 113.

A Reciprocal Code of Conduct

The candidate must observe a code of spiritual courtesy (*adab*) towards his master, on which all of Sufism's treatises insist. This *adab* is primarily an inner attitude. The disciple, for example, should not lightly attach himself to an instructor-master, because it would be likely that he would later come to disparage him; he should hide nothing from him; he should not scrutinize his spiritual state or raise indiscreet questions about him or his family. This *adab* also implies an outer behavior, which returns to the rules that the Koran had stipulated for the Companions: "O you who believe! Do not be forward in your behavior before God and His Messenger!" (49:1); "O you who believe! Do not raise your voice above that of the Prophet!" (49:2). Among these outer conventions, let us point out that the disciple should not turn his back on his shaykh, nor should he look at him insistently: some disciples, it has been said, never saw the face of their master. The disciple should also avoid speaking in a loud voice in the presence of his shaykh, laughing excessively, making remarks about him, and *a fortiori* contradicting him (unless the master invites him to do so), etc.[9]

The master, on the other hand, also follows a code of ethics in his relationship to the disciple. This code is less formal, less explicit than that which is incumbent upon the disciple, and the treatises of Sufism only mention it infrequently. But, a shaykh should not seek to increase the number of his novices through any influence he may have upon people nor any attraction he may have for them; thus, he will deliberately avoid attracting the disciples of another shaykh to him under the pretext that the latter has a spiritual rank lower than his. The disciple is not his possession, but a "deposit," as it were, that God places in his hands. He must keep secret what he perceives in his disciple, as well as anything the latter says in confidence to him. Lastly, his guardianship of a disciple is a responsibility that he has to God and must bring about a great humility in him. "Approach masters who say: 'I know that I do not know,'" confided Shaykh Bentounes.[10]

The true teacher knows the aptitude of each one of his disciples and thus treats him accordingly. He must place himself at the disciple's level and, following the example of the Prophet, speak to him according to his degree of understanding. For this reason, it is not advised that a novice follow a master who is "enraptured in God" (*majdhūb*), no matter how obvious his sanctity.

---

[9] One can find an account of the key conventions to respect regarding this point in *Les Voies d'Allah*, pp. 548-557 (a translation of the *'Awārif* of Suhrawardī by D. Gril); see also *Le Soufisme au quotidien*, by R. Chih, pp. 231-233.

[10] *Le Soufisme cœur de l'islam*, p. 223.

In principle, a shaykh does not receive any material remuneration because his function is a service, a kind of "alms," as several Koranic verses suggest.[11] Today, a master who has responsibilities for various souls generally does not have time to hold a job; his disciples would then provide for his needs.

A Single Master

The disciple can associate with several masters before attaching himself to one of them. Very subtle affinities seem to determine his choice, although in reality the aspirant does not choose anything: "I had waited for you for ten years," said a master to a novice when they met for the first time. A patient who is following a course of treatment from several doctors has little chance for a cure. Similarly, a disciple who is motivated by real spiritual aspiration (*himma*) will follow only one master. Just as with ordinary paternity, spiritual paternity is exclusive. "The disciple who has two masters is like a woman who is between two men," states a proverb. A shaykh made this bold comparison: "Just as God does not forgive when another is worshiped instead of Him, the love which one holds for his master does not permit one to associate another with his master."[12] A Sufi can be affiliated with several brotherhoods, but he will have a true initiatory bond only with one master.

For some, it is not acceptable for a disciple to go see masters other than his own without his master's permission; however, other masters may encourage their disciples to meet a given shaykh. The rule, in this respect, varies according to the historical period and particular Sufi environments. Also, a master sometimes sends one of his disciples to another shaykh because he thinks that the latter is especially likely to help that disciple's progress. If the shaykh dies before his disciple has reached spiritual "realization," the disciple must find another guide. But the first master is often irreplaceable and, after his death, his "spiritual being" (*rūhāniyya*) can continue to instruct an advanced disciple.

A Second Birth

As in any initiation, the follower passes through the dual process of death and rebirth. This protocol can be observed only under the control of a shaykh who "educates" the disciple from the beginning to the end. After the disciple's "childhood" will come his maturity, spiritual "virility" (*rujuliyya*):

---

[11] See especially Koran 57:36-37, and 76:9.

[12] Sha'rānī, *Anwār qudsiyya*, vol. I, p. 187.

women, of course, have access to this degree of realization, too.[13] All novices, however, do not reach the goal of initiation. Even before agreeing to direct someone, a shaykh therefore evaluates whether that person has the necessary tendencies and if he is ready to pay the price of initiation. According to Sha'rānī, there is a necessary condition for this: the Path should not be "sold off" cheaply, even in the interest of the disciple. Certain shaykhs turn aspirants away, or make them wait. In the past, a probationary period was obligatory, lasting between forty days to three years, with the master as the sole judge of this.

After having accepted the beginner, the shaykh puts his sincerity and will to the test. Shiblī, whose father was the caliph's chamberlain, was ordered by Junayd to beg for a year in the marketplace. More recently, the young 'Arabī Darqāwī, who also came from a noble family, had to walk back and forth across the city of Fes loaded with baskets of prunes. For such distinguished well-educated men, such tasks were humiliating.[14] In the same way, masters often made beginners give up their books because all that knowledge was likely to block their direct contact with the world of the spirit. It was by no means a matter of renouncing exoteric knowledge, but one of illuminating it through inward knowledge.

For those who really commit themselves to the Path, this period of waiting for initiation can be long. For the Mevlevis, a new person must first serve the community for a thousand and one days, during which time he devotes himself to all kinds of tasks (cleaning living quarters, cooking, etc.). Some masters have themselves been the first to do this kind of thing. Many Sufi texts report that aspirants saw the shaykh for the first time while he was sweeping buildings or washing the latrines of the *zāwiya*. Ghazzālī, the "proof of Islam," would have carried out these humble tasks himself.[15]

In the past, education (*tarbiya*) was sometimes rigorous. It is reported that some master struck his disciples with a stick, to the point of breaking their bones, or kept them thirsty until they achieved "illumination" (*fath*); or, some other master sent his young disciple to a far-away shaykh who gave him a saving slap in the face. These tests are only one means, since the purpose of spiritual education is not to exhaust the disciple, but to lead him to God. It is love which determines the initiatory relationship; "the disciple must be able to enjoy the words addressed to him by his shaykh as much as

---

[13]   Ibn 'Atā' Allāh, *La Sagesse des maîtres soufis*, pp. 294-295.

[14]   Hujwirī, *Somme spirituelle*, p. 408; Shaykh 'Arabī Darqāwī, *Lettres d'un maître soufi* (Milan, 1978), p. 19.

[15]   Sha'rānī, *Anwār*, vol. II, p. 160.

he enjoys the act of sex."[16]

As the spiritual father of his disciple, the shaykh sometimes asks him to consider that he no longer has a biological father. It is frequent that an advanced disciple physically resembles his master. However, the images employed by shaykhs seem rather more maternal than paternal, and masters manifest a mercy and a leniency toward their entourages that is well and truly maternal. Abū l-Hasan Shādhilī was compared to a tortoise, which raises its young by means of its glances. The term *tarbiya* ("education") means "to nourish a child." The master is often described as a "foster-mother" who offers the child her breast, and the accomplished disciple is described as one who has been "weaned."[17] A shaykh of the twentieth century literally fed his disciples from his own hand. It can be said that a master "hatches" his disciples; he often worries even about the practical details of their lives.

Spiritual education takes various routes. Only certain shaykhs deliver explicit doctrinal teaching because the spiritual state of the master is more efficacious than his word or his pen. Initiation is sometimes done without the knowledge of the disciple, through the power of silence, since "he who does not benefit from the silence of the masters cannot benefit from their words." The glance of the master is to a certain degree an extension of that of the Prophet looking upon his Companions, which has as its source the glance of God upon His creation: "Happy are they who have seen me, and happy are they who have seen those who saw me" (Tabarānī). It is said that the great saints of the past could by their simple glance bring a person to sainthood: "By God," said Abu l-ʿAbbās Mursī, "it is enough for me to direct my glance only once on a being to grant him spiritual plenitude."[18] Unlike a simple "spiritual adviser," a shaykh transmits to his disciples, and then through them to all creation, the spiritual powers (*baraka*) of which he is the trustee.

Although a Sufi master may not feel a calling to teach the exoteric law, he often does so anyway because, in many cases, he belongs to the world of the *ulama*. A shaykh of the sixteenth century stated that a spiritual guide must know all the statutes of Islamic law, but he meant by this that the guide was to know them through spiritual "unveiling."[19] According to the typical rules, a master can have only a rudimentary knowledge of the *Sharīʿa*; his qualification is of another order.

---

[16] Ibid., vol. I, p. 173.

[17] See, for example, M. Chodkiewicz, "Les maîtres spirituels en Islam," in *Connaissance des religions*, nos. 53-54, 1998, pp. 39-41.

[18] *La Sagesse des maîtres soufis*, p. 113.

[19] Shaʿrānī, *Durar al-ghawwās* (Cairo, 1985), p. 94.

Sufi Psychology, or the "Science of the Soul"

The initiatory relationship presupposes two principles: thanks to the divine influx (*baraka*) which is bestowed on him, the shaykh lends his "spiritual support" (*madad*) to the disciple; on the other hand, thanks to the knowledge of the human soul that he acquires through his own experiences, the master can understand each disciple in an individual way. Sufis have developed a science of the soul (*nafs*) and have used this knowledge, which is both inspired and empirical, in an initiatory instructional methodology. Although the jurists set down laws and the theologians set down dogmas, the Sufi masters developed a method focused on carrying out spiritual "work" on the ego. This knowledge has usually been transmitted orally, but we can find traces of it in texts which, since the ninth century, have dealt with "diseases of the soul and their remedies."[20]

Sufism, like any mysticism, tends to purify the human soul. This process of purification presupposes a transformation of the soul which, according to the Koran, moves through three degrees. "The soul which incites to evil," i.e., to the lower instincts and passions, must gradually give way to "the soul which does not cease blaming" its owner for these inclinations and which aspires to the Light. At the end of this inner combat, it will become "the soul at peace," which is purified, transparent, and no longer an obstacle to the Presence.[21] This is one of the goals envisioned by the following wisdom, which is sometimes attributed to the Prophet: "He who knows himself [or knows his soul] knows his Lord." This saying has been interpreted differently by many commentators, according to their spiritual degree.

Those who were most severe with regard to the human soul were the Malāmatis, who thought it necessary to struggle unflinchingly against the dark soul, to practice the *jihād* against that which "takes his passion for a divinity" (Koran 25:43). Other Sufis considered that one did not have to slay the soul, but rather to overcome it or tame it, because each man, whether he wants it to be so or not, is a mixture of higher and lower states. Some, finally, see the soul as an effect of illusion, which one should not dwell on, since only the divine *nafs*, the Self, can be said to truly exist. In the fight against the defects of the soul, the prescriptions varied a great deal from one master to the next. Those who have had ascetic tendencies have recommended starving the carnal soul so that it will let go, but Sufis have usually insisted on the power of the invocation (*dhikr*).

---

[20] This is the title of a piece by Sulamī, translated into French by A. Zein (Milan, 1990).

[21] The Koranic references which refer to the three degrees of the soul are, respectively: 12:53, 75:2, and 89:27-30.

The ambivalence which is characteristic of the soul is willed by God since, according to Islam, He is the origin of good as well as evil. The Sufis thus have raised the delicate question of the role of Satan—or Iblīs—in human consciousness. The Koran relates how the angels, who were initially surprised by this effect of the divine Will, agreed to prostrate themselves in front of Adam, this man who would go on "to spread evil and to spill blood." Iblīs, who worshiped only God and knew what would become of humanity, refused to prostrate.[22] Deposed by God for his insubordination, he vowed to tempt man from that time forward. Seeing in him a gnostic angel, some Sufis have felt sorry for his tragic destiny and have thought of him, along with the Prophet, as the most perfect of monotheists; in this plan, Satan is the instrument of the divine anger in humanity, while the Prophet is the instrument of the divine Mercy.

For most masters, however, such a rehabilitation of Satan and his promotion to martyr is accessible only to those who have gone beyond the duality of good and evil and who have comprehended the essence of all oppositions. It is perilous for the average spiritual seeker, and *a fortiori* for the faithful, because Satan is the enemy of man, as is often recalled in the Koran. His blind pride—"I am better than him [man]" (Koran 7:12)—goes against the submission required of believers, but also against the "extinction" of the mystic in God. If *walāya* ("sainthood") is proximity to God, the Arabic term *shaytān* (Satan) carries within it the idea of separation and remoteness. "Neither My earth nor My heavens contain Me; only the heart of My believing servant contains Me": this single *hadīth qudsī* is enough to contradict the contempt that Iblīs has for man.

Although God did not grant any real power to Iblīs (Koran 15:42 and 17:65), the heart of man is the arena in which a perpetual combat between God, assisted by the angels, and Iblīs, assisted by the carnal soul, takes place. The weapons used on both sides are the extrinsic thoughts (*khawātir*) which besiege man. One usually assigns four origins to them: divine, angelic, egotistic, or satanic. In general, a disciple does not have enough discernment to glimpse their source. And if the bad suggestions coming from Satan may be legion for things regarding everyday life, they are of an even more perverse nature in the spiritual life. "The satisfaction of the ego with disobedience is clear and evident," said Ibn 'Atā' Allāh, "but it is hidden and sly with obedience [i.e. works of worship]. Now, the cure of what is hidden is difficult."[23] Iblīs, it is said, can manifest himself in a pious believer, an informed mystic,

---

[22] Koran 2:30-34.

[23] *Hikam*, Aphorism no. 151.

an appealing shaykh, etc. For this reason, certain brotherhoods have required that disciples divulge all their thoughts and visions to their master. Contrary to most current therapies, this "analysis" is aimed at restructuring the personality of the disciple "upward" and relies on a spiritual alchemy between master and disciple.

In several places, the Koran mentions the importance of dreams (*manām*) and visions (*ru'yā*). The Prophet himself paid close attention to them and interpreted the dreams of his Companions. It is always a major sign for an initiate when he experiences a vision through his spiritual "body," whether during sleep or in the waking state. For Sufis, dreams and visions represent a mode of participation in prophecy, since, according to a *hadīth*, a vision is a forty-sixth part of prophecy (Bukhārī). These occur in the "imaginal world" (*'ālam al-khayāl*), also called the "world of symbols" (*'alam al-mithāl*), which is intermediate between our perceivable world and that of divine realities. They make it possible for initiates to have access to the invisible world, to be instructed by the prophets, Khadir, or by dead or living saints. Before committing himself to initiating someone, the shaykh sometimes analyzes the dreams of the person who wishes to become attached to him. Among the Khalwatis, disciples are initiated into the invocation of the seven divine Names according to their experiences related to dreams. Whether it is a question of extrinsic thoughts or dreams, the purpose of the analysis is always to release the mind of the aspirant so that he can proceed, through a proven maieutic method, to his proper "birth."

Succession and Delegation of Authority

The Prophet, at the hour of his death, placed Abū Bakr at the head of the community only in a very allusive way. It is rare that a shaykh designates his successor explicitly, as if he preferred to let heaven decide: the Path is not his possession; it comes from God and returns to Him. The absence of this designation can also mean that the master did not find anybody among his disciples who was ready to succeed him, or that the person whom he would choose would not be accepted by the other disciples after his death. Disciples are usually dazed when it happens that a shaykh invests his function upon a newcomer, a very self-effacing disciple, a servant, etc. This person will then have difficulty in establishing himself in the function, and is even sometimes outright rejected. If a deceased shaykh has not nominated anyone, or if nobody claims succession, that path will die out or it may become dormant, possibly to reappear later; more often, several aspirants who were close disciples or representatives of the master will put themselves forward. This competition can be harsh, because each applicant chooses words or gestures of the late shaykh that would favor his claim, and he asserts that his inheritance from the master is unique. "Every man tastes jealousy," said Sha'rānī in this regard.

Even when the shaykh has stipulated the name of his successor in a written document, or has spoken it in front of his disciples, there are often dissidents who dispute this choice and who cause a split. These conflicts concerning authority, which sometimes bring about the creation of other branches of an initiatory path, allow, however, a diversification of the temperaments and methods within the Path.

The hereditary devolution of the function of shaykh coexisted very early on with a succession that was purely spiritual; it especially helped in preventing any competition between disciples. Since the eleventh century, a master might designate his son or his nephew: this was the case with Ibn Abī l-Khayr, then with Jīlānī, Rifā'ī, Ni'matullāh, and with others. Real family dynasties thus appeared which sometimes lasted for centuries. This was the case, for example, with the Jīlānīs of Baghdad, and the Wafās or Bakrīs in Cairo. Indeed, it is usually accepted that this hereditary transmission conveys the *baraka* of Muhammad, and the founding saints of the Sufi Orders are often descendants of the Prophet. This principle makes it possible to limit the quarrels of succession and to avoid the division of inherited property acquired by a brotherhood. On the other hand, it presents the danger of instituting routine and of weakening initiatory content. It always presents a challenge for the successor of a master who was particularly charismatic. In some other brotherhoods, the shaykhs are elected by a kind of "council of the sages" made up of the most advanced or oldest disciples: their choice will be determined by what each one will have learned through their dreams. The disciples of the late shaykh will then have to renew their pact of allegiance.

Among the initiatory paths created in the twelfth and thirteenth centuries, some developed quickly and so their expansion required the delegation of spiritual authority. This authority was at first abstract: a master sent some close disciples to areas which to him seemed favorable for the blossoming of his path; at other times, a master's fame attracted disciples from various regions who, after having stayed near him for a while, set out again for their country of origin, where they spread the teaching of the shaykh and, possibly, initiated novices. The process was institutionalized starting in the fifteenth century, when Sufism became a "mass phenomenon." The masters then appointed representatives (*khalīfa; muqaddam* in the Maghreb) either to stay near and assist them if their disciples were numerous, or to go to the various provinces where their paths had been established. The representatives regularly visited these communities which were spread out all over. Nowadays, it is not rare for a shaykh to have disciples on several continents. If a master regards a representative highly enough to let him initiate and educate others, he gives him an authorization (*idhn*), which sometimes takes the form of a "diploma" of investiture. It sometimes happens that a master will allow some of his representatives to become independent; these then acquire the function of shaykh.

Bibliography

Cheikh Khaled Bentounès, *Le Soufisme coeur de l'islam* (Paris, 1996). (English edition: *Sufism: The Heart of Islam* [Hohm Press, 2002].)

Rachida Chih, *Le Soufisme au quotidien. Confreries d'Egypte au xxᵉ siècle* (Paris, 2000).

Michel Chodkiewicz, "Les maîtres spirituels en Islam," in *Connaissance des religions*, nos. 53-54, 1998, pp. 33-48.

METHODS AND RITES OF AFFILIATION

René Guénon said that initiation has three preconditions: first of all the "qualification" of the individual, that is, his ability to follow the Path; then, the unbroken transmission of a spiritual influence by means of attaching oneself to an initiatory organization; finally, application to inward work. Among these conditions, the second requires more stringency than the others.[24] Sufism, as we have seen, is characterized by the transmission of the Muhammadian spiritual influx (*baraka*), which comes from God via the Archangel Gabriel. Various initiatory lineages which criss-cross each other in time and space have no other function than to authenticate this transmission which has been granted to every living shaykh. The Sufi master is therefore before all else an "heir" who, according to his own qualities, makes the spiritual inheritance which he has received bear fruit for the benefit of his disciples, but also for all humanity.

Initiatory Rites

— *The "Investiture of the Cloak"* (Khirqa). At the time of this initiatory rite, which was practiced primarily in the Middle East but which is no longer done, the master covered the disciple with a "cloak" (*khirqa*) or some other piece of cloth, transferring to him his own spiritual realization. Beyond the bond linking the two of them, the initiate was thus attached to

---

[24] *Aperçus sur l'initiation* (Paris, 1983), pp. 34-35. (English edition: *Perspectives on Initiation* [Sophia Perennis, 2004].)

a lineage (*silsila*) going back to the Prophet. Several shaykhs or *ulama* gave the status of *Sunna* to this rite because the Prophet covered a woman named Umm Khālid with a cloth, saying to her: "Cover yourself and acquire noble conduct."[25]

When receiving the *khirqa*, the initiate placed himself under the authority of the master: This is the *khirqat al-irāda*, at the end of which the aspirant (*murīd*) accepted the spiritual discipline that was incumbent upon him. The other mode of initiation, the *khirqat al-tabarruk*, transmitted a simple "blessing," a protective spiritual influx. This less demanding rite prevailed during the medieval period, but it gradually lost its authenticity and contributed to the conventions of clothing adopted by some "Sufis," who would deck themselves out in carpets, cloaks, canes, and various caps. The early masters had already criticized certain dervishes for sheltering charlatanism under their patched-up robes (*muraqqa'a*).

— *Making "the Pact"* (*'Ahd, Bay'a*). This rite, which has undeniable scriptural support, is today the common form of attaching oneself to a master and his path. It reactualizes the pact made at the beginning of time between God and humanity (Koran 7:172). In a more tangible way, this rite renews the commitment contracted by the Companions with the Prophet at Hudaybiyya: "Those who make the pact with you [Muhammad] make it with God: the hand of God is on their hands. He who breaks it is perjured to his own detriment. God will grant a reward without limits to he who is faithful to his commitment" (Koran 48:10). "God was satisfied with the believers when they swore allegiance to you [Muhammad] under the tree" (Koran 48:18).

As the first verse specifies, the pact is sealed with a "handshake" (*musāfaha*). The ritual proceeds in the following way: The master and disciple are in a state of ritual purity, the latter having made a prayer of repentance. Then the aspirant places his right hand under that of the shaykh; in that way, it is God Himself who, beyond the Prophet, puts his "hand" on that of the novice. This conversion, or "return to God" (*tawba*) is regarded as the first stage of the Path. After he takes the hand of the disciple, the master recites several formulas in a low voice—among which are the above-mentioned verses—affirming that he takes the disciple as a "son" or "brother," and that he agrees to guide him on the Path. The aspirant promises to respect the pact, to obey his shaykh and, through him, God. Sometimes, the agreement is tacit. Sometimes other disciples who are present also place their hands on those of the master and the aspirant. The master or one of his close

---

[25] See, for example, Suhrawardī, *'Awārif*, p. 97.

disciples then teaches the novice the prayers that he will have to recite. So far, the initiation is only virtual. For it to be truly effectuated, it is up to the novice, connected from then on to the Muhammadian influx, to accomplish his spiritual work.

This commitment is built upon a solemn act of allegiance to the shaykh. In theory, the initiatory pact cannot be broken, even if the individual no longer has any connection with his organization. "To break the pact returns one to apostasy," stated Sha'rani,[26] but the Egyptian master was referring here to the pact made with God to follow the Path, not to a commitment to a specific master. If it is proven that a shaykh is not attached to an authentic lineage or that he has clearly contravened the Law, the disciple has the right to leave him. It may also happen that a shaykh proves to be "sterile" on the initiatory level and so his disciple cannot make any progress. If the shaykh refuses to let his disciple leave, the latter can ignore him, according to the most widespread opinion. When a disciple no longer has faith in his master, it is advised that he change guides, because his companionship consequently loses any efficacy.

— *"The Secret Teaching of Formulas of Invocation"* (Talqīn). This practice, which seems to be disappearing today, is based on a prophetic practice. It is reported that after having been assured that there were no non-Muslims left in his house, the Prophet would lock up himself with his Companions and would have them repeat the formula *Lā ilāha illā Llāh* ("There is no divinity but God"), explaining to them the spiritual benefit which they would derive from this repetition (Ibn Hanbal). He also used to teach 'Alī the invocation of God, having him close his eyes and pronounce *Lā ilāha illā Llāh* three times.

"He who does not have any spiritual ancestry," says a Sufi proverb, "is like a child who is a bastard." The *talqīn* has the precise effect of connecting an initiate to his spiritual lineage, thus making him a link in the initiatory chain. The Sufis compared the *talqīn* with a seed planted in soil: for this teaching to bear fruit, it is necessary to "water" it through the regular practice of the *dhikr*. This rite, which has often lost its initiatory substance, can prove itself so powerful that the initiate, according to Sha'rānī, is able to understand the language of all creatures, including that of inanimate objects.

From True Aspirant to Simple Associate

The true initiatory relationship requires that the master follow the evolution of the disciple in order to perfect his education, but there are parallel

---

[26] *Anwār qudsiyya*, vol. I, p. 80.

forms of attachment that are more flexible than those summarized by the term *tabarruk*. In this type of affiliation, the initiate simply seeks to benefit from the protection of the master and his path without, however, committing himself as would a true disciple; he will perform the rites, more or less. Thus, there are several concentric circles around a master, starting with the nearest circle of the most faithful disciples up to the outer circles of sympathizers who represent—to compare this to the Catholic world—a kind of "Third Order."[27] Obviously, within the Sufi Orders there are many who are called but few who are of the elect, and the masters, often asked for help on worldly matters, complain that the aspirants to full spiritual realization are rare.

A Fluid World: Multiple Affiliations

A person who is attached to this or that brotherhood simply to profit from the *baraka* can multiply his affiliations and thus his access to the blessings, since all *tarīqas* have their origin in the person of the Prophet. A little-known fact is that multiple affiliation has been widely practiced for centuries. In primitive Sufism, the aspirants on the Path moved about a great deal, coming to know several masters at the same time, and seeking "the freshest source," according to an expression of Shaykh Shādhilī.

The procedures of affiliation were formalized with the appearance of the different spiritual brotherhoods. Even so, Sufism remained a fluid world, where the various initiatory influences interpenetrated and enriched each other. Doctrines and rituals often show similarities, and a member of one *tarīqa* can generally take part in the sessions of *dhikr* of other Orders, or can seek the intercession of deceased saints coming from a spiritual brotherhood other that his own. Most Sufis are aware that all are following the same Path of Muhammad, which can only relativize their membership in such and such a particular path. Initiates thus pass from one *tarīqa* to another or, as was recommended by Ibn 'Arabī himself, they have multiple attachments. Sha'rānī mentioned having twenty-six affiliations, while another was known to have made the pact with sixty shaykhs!

The fact remains that a Sufi can vow allegiance to only one master at the same time and, according to some, only the first pact is valid. In fact, the two modes of affiliation coexist because they are complementary: a disciple has

---

[27] Translator's Note: In Catholicism, lay people can affiliate themselves with the religious orders (e.g. the Benedictines, the Carmelites, etc.), while still remaining in the world. They may take various kinds of vows, and live thus between the two worlds, so to speak. These "tertiaries" are said to belong to the "Third Order," with the first two orders designating the monastic communities of men and women.

an official master, but he may seek the company of other shaykhs who can be like initiatory way stations for him. The quasi-rule of multiple affiliation is unlike what is practiced in the Christian, Hindu, and Buddhist worlds.[28] It has permitted a broad initiatory coverage of the Muslim world, and the spread of Sufi culture throughout society.

Uwaysi Initiation

Sufis were careful to surround the transmission of the Muhammadian "secret" with safeguards; the initiatory chain must thus reach back in an unbroken line to the Prophet. The purpose of these spiritual genealogies was, firstly, to ensure the consistency and thus the efficaciousness of initiation, but also to avoid the criticisms of the exoterists. Concerning these criticisms, renowned scholars have had to authenticate the main initiatory chains of Sufism, which were transmitted by 'Alī to Hasan Basrī. The common rule demands that the novice or the aspirant to initiation be in physical contact with the master; he must be able at least to be in the company of the shaykh in order to imbue himself with his example. For the advanced disciple, on the other hand, the master is always present, even if he is thousands of kilometers away.

At the same time, there is also an initiation of a subtle nature which is not necessary under normal circumstances: this is the *uwaysī* initiation, by which a spiritual seeker is instructed either by a living master, but one who is never actually seen, or, more often, by a master who has been dead for a long time. Only confirmed Sufis can receive this type of initiation. The term *uwaysī* comes from Uways Qaranī, a Yemeni whose aura of holiness had reached the Prophet. Although they were contemporaries, the two men never met physically, but the Prophet suggested that 'Umar and 'Alī seek him out. The mysterious relationship which linked Uways and the Prophet is the source for the initiation in spirit which certain spiritual seekers have received. The initiator can be a prophet, the enigmatic Khadir, the Mahdī, or more simply a deceased saint. The Khadiriyya brotherhood, for example, founded by 'Abd al-'Azīz Dabbāgh, owes its name to the fact that the saint was instructed directly by Khadir.[29]

Among the most celebrated *uwaysis*, let us mention Abū Yazīd Bistāmī (d. 875), who was instructed in spirit by Imam Ja'far Sādiq (d. 765), and Kharaqānī (d. 1029), who was initiated in turn by Bistāmī. This manner of initiation has a place in particular within the Naqshbandiyya, which includes

[28] M. Gaborieau, in *Les Voies d'Allah*, p. 211.

[29] *Kitab al-Ibrīz*, vol. I, pp. 51-52.

these masters in its lineage. Thus the eponymous master of the Order, Bahā' al-Dīn Naqshband (d. 1389), was in contact with Shaykh Ghujduwānī (d. 1220). In that brotherhood, disciples communicate with their initiator via his "spiritual being" (*rūhāniyya*), which can take the shape of a subtle body. This mode of initiation is often associated with an attachment to a living master, which makes it possible for formal initiation to be maintained.

Bibliography

Michel Chodkiewicz, "Note complémentaire sur les rites d'initiation dans les turuq," in *'Ayn al-hayāt—Quaderno di Studi della Tarīqa naqshbandiyya*, no. 5, 1999, pp. 45-64.

Éric Geoffroy, *Le Sufism en Égypte et en Syrie* (Damascus, 1995), pp. 194-203.

CODES OF CONDUCT

Correct Inner Attitudes

In traditional Sufism, the aspirant must observe a code of conduct which gives spiritual cohesion to his life. All his thoughts, all his gestures thus tend towards God, and his life becomes an act of worship that is perpetually renewed. He realizes within himself the divine Oneness (*tawhīd*), instead of just affirming it. This taking charge of all aspects of everyday life is very characteristic of Islam, which does not encourage a separation between matter and spirit. For Sufi masters, the respect for these conventions takes on such importance that it can be said to summarize by itself the substance of Sufism.[30]

Since the tenth century, masters have written treatises on "rules of conduct" (*ādāb*) for the use of novices. These rules strive to shape the correct inner attitude which aspirants must acquire. The outer behavior, say the masters, reveals what a disciple is experiencing inwardly, and each action must be regarded as a step on the Path. Watching a man performing the ritual prayer while showing signs of distraction, the Prophet made this remark: "If his heart were immersed in meditation, this would be translated into his limbs" (Suyūtī). The rules concerning the spiritual life are said to be "inner" and those dealing with social life "outer," but there is no split within this or that attitude. For Sufis, the model in this domain is the Prophet, who embodies all the virtues, both inner as well as outer.

Particular rules of conduct correspond to each of the five senses (hearing, sight, sense of smell, touch, taste). In any circumstance, a disciple should

---

[30] See, for example, Suhrawardī, *'Awārif*, p. 54.

actuate his senses only while also seeking God's approval for this. The rules typically mentioned in the manuals dealt with food, clothing, sleep, travel, and, more generally, with the "spiritual etiquette" which it is advisable to observe in society. They define an ideal towards which the aspirant must strive unceasingly. Let us give some examples:

— *Food.* The aspirant must limit as much as possible his consumption of food and drink. He feeds himself not to satisfy his carnal desires, but to strengthen himself for worship. "If Pharaoh had been hungry," noted Bistāmī, "he would not have said 'I am your supreme Lord!'"[31] After having washed his hands, the aspirant begins his meal by saying, "In the name of God," takes a little salt, and puts only what he needs in his bowl. He swallows only small mouthfuls, which he chews carefully. He does not speak and does not look at what others eat. He finishes his meal by saying, "God be praised," takes a little salt, and then washes his hands and rinses his mouth.

— *Clothing.* The novice should pay only minimal attention to his outer appearance. His robe or his djellaba should not go down below the ankle; it must be clean, and of only one color. He will dress in white only on Friday, because this color requires more maintenance.

— *Sleep.* It is recommended to go to bed in a state of ritual purity. The aspirant should go to sleep only if he has been overcome by sleep. Because night is reputedly more favorable than day for worship, some Sufis began the practice, starting in the fifteenth century, of drinking coffee in order to stay awake. But sleep is also blessed for it is then that visions occur, which are gifts from God. These visions make it possible for man to become aware of his physiological dependence, and for the submission which must result from this.

— *Travel.* The aspirant leaves on a peregrination or a journey only after having obtained the approval of his parents and/or his master. With each step he maintains his consciousness of God: "And the servants of the All-merciful, those who walk humbly upon the earth. . ." (Koran 25:63). He must carry with him a small container of water with which to make his ablutions. When he arrives in a locality where there is a *zāwiya*, he must pay a visit to its shaykh. When entering, he removes his right shoe first (when he

---

31   See Koran 79:24.

leaves, he will first put on the left), washes his feet, and performs a prayer of greeting.

Within the establishment where "the poor in God" live, the aspirant observes silence as much as possible, and in no circumstance does he raise his voice. When he studies or meditates, he must sit with his legs crossed, if possible while facing Mecca, and his robe or djellaba must cover his legs. He must remain motionless as much as he can, without extending his legs (especially if he is in front of one of the brothers, or the *qibla*). Some of these rules are common to all Muslims who have received even minimal education because they are based on the example of Muhammad, but there are other rules which are particular to Sufis, such as the handshake.[32]

The domain to which the Sufi rules for living apply is so broad that it includes the rites prescribed by the five pillars of Islam. Where the jurists cite legal statutes (*ahkām*) in connection with the ablution, the prayer, or the fast, the Sufis speak of *ādāb*, adding to the strictly prescriptive framework a moral and spiritual requirement, an effort toward interiorization.[33] Suhrawardī said that it is because of this meaning that is given to "spiritual conventions" that true Sufis are able to respect the equilibrium between the exoteric and the esoteric in all things and in all circumstances.[34] When Sufism became well integrated within Islamic culture, these spiritual codes were partly adopted by the believers.

Between Brothers

The spiritual courtesy which prevails in the relationship between master and disciple also applies to the relations between disciples: to improve the ego, there is nothing better than improving one's behavior towards the "brothers" on the Path. Since masters cannot always be available for each of their disciples, it falls to their representatives or experienced disciples to train the novices. As in all initiatory relationships, the follower must strive for sincerity, so that his brothers would be like a mirror for him,[35] and reveal to him the exact image of his spiritual state.

Disciples must show leniency, self-sacrifice, and kindness. When one of

---

[32] For a descripton of the rules intended for aspirants, see Hujwirī, *Somme spirituelle*, pp. 382-410; Sha'rānī, *al-Anwār al-qudsiyya* ("The Holy Lights on the Knowledge of the Rules of Sufism"), in Arabic; *Les Voies d'Allah*, pp. 145-148, among other occurrences in that book.

[33] See, for example, Sarraj, *Luma'*, p. 141 *et seq.*; the entire section of Ghazzālī's *Ihyā'* on the pillars; and Suhrawardī, *'Awārif*, p. 275 *et seq.*

[34] *'Awārif*, p. 275.

[35] As is suggested in this *hadīth*: "The believer is the mirror of his fellow believer" (Tirmidhī).

them sees a fault in another, he must hide this and not expose it; if he does not like one of his brothers, he must question himself, and find in himself the source of this discord. Of course, he can feel affinities for one person rather than for another, but he will see to it that this preference is not too obvious. The giving of assistance to one another is applicable in all areas of life: the experienced disciple advises the beginner and is indulgent with him. In exchange, the beginner is quick to serve the community, because that is part of his initiation.

There is no place for individualism within the community. "We did not accept as companions those who said, 'my sandal,'" recalled one master.[36] The Sufi "does not lend nor does he borrow":[37] he no longer possesses anything of his own. Seeking to abandon the attributes of the ego, how could he become attached to personal effects? A member of an Algerian brotherhood confided in us that the brothers in the *zāwiya* would grab the first jacket that came to hand, they would use any money that they found in the pockets, and then would put the jacket back where they had found it. Such a symbiosis is not always easy within a community and, nowadays, individualism is not exempt from Sufi circles any more than is jealousy or pettiness. A *tarīqa* does not bring only saints together; it accommodates individuals such as they are. The initiatory paths would be useless if they accepted only beings who were spiritually advanced.

A Rule for Community Life

As soon as a community is established around a master, some rules become necessary. One of the first shaykhs to establish a rule for his disciples was Abu Sa'īd Ibn Abī l-Khayr (eleventh century). The precepts enacted by this shaykh were all based on Koranic passages. Most Sufi Orders accept these:

1. Disciples must keep their clothing clean (Koran 74:4) and must stay in a state of ritual purity (Koran 9:108).
2. They must not chatter in places of prayer (Koran 24:36).
3. They perform the ritual prayer communally (Koran 23:9).
4. It is recommended that they pray during the night (Koran 17:79).
5. At dawn, they invoke God through a request for forgiveness (*istighfār*, Koran 51:18).
6. Then they read the Koran until the rising of the sun (Koran 17:78).

---

[36] Abū Najīb Suhrawardī, *Ādāb al-murīdīn* (Cairo, n. d.), p. 76.
[37] Ibid.

7. Between the evening prayer and the night prayer, they invoke God (*dhikr*) and recite litanies (Koran 52:49).
8. They welcome the poor and all those who ask for asylum (Koran 6:52).
9. They never eat alone (Koran 2:172).
10. They do not leave the company of others without getting their permission (Koran 24:62).[38]

These rules, which were usually transmitted orally, expressed the spiritual method of the founding saint. They were common while traditional Islamic society and the establishments intended for Sufis (*khānqāh, zāwiya, tekke,* etc.) continued to exist.

In many respects, parallels are evident between these and the rules governing the lives of Christian monks. According to the words of a *hadīth* whose authenticity is not certain, "There is no monasticism in Islam." Nevertheless, for centuries many Sufis lived under conditions similar to those of monks. Although they did not take vows of celibacy and could leave their place of retreat more easily than could monks, they sometimes resided there for good, seeking spiritual realization in that spot. Others chose the itinerant life and became beggars, just like the brothers of the mendicant orders of the medieval West. "The poor in God," especially during the period when they were novices, considered "peregrination" (*siyāha*) to be its own spiritual method. The *siyāha* was to some extent a kind of spiritual retreat while walking, a pilgrimage without end, an earthly projection of the initiatory Path.

INITIATORY METHODS

The Invocation (Dhikr)

"Increase your invocation of the Name of God so much so that it is said of you all: 'They are insane!'"

—*hadīth* (Bayhaqī)

— **The Highest Form of Worship**. The Arabic term *dhikr* has the multiple meanings of "remembrance," "reminder," and "invocation." Applied to the domain of religion, it summarizes everything that is related to the spiritual practice in Islam. Indeed, only the *dhikr* makes it possible to combat the amnesia that affects man, making him forget his divine origins and the Pact

---

[38] For further details, see M. Monawwar, *Les Étapes mystiques du shaykh Abu Sa'id*, pp. 324-325.

(*mīthāq*) sealed with God in pre-eternity, as well as the repeated lessons of human history. The Koran continually warns us about this amnesia: "Invoke your Lord when you forget" (18:24); "Remember Me, and I will remember you" (2:152), etc. In the *sūra*, "The Moon," a question is repeated again and again to an insistent rhythm: "Yes, We facilitated the comprehension of the Koran so that it may be a Reminder. But are there any who will remember?" The warnings are not given for nothing, and only love, the ultimate goal of creation, can motivate man to invoke God.

In many places in the Koran, the term *dhikr* means the remembrance or the invocation of God, and the Koran itself is called *dhikr* (Koran 15:9). This generic term delineates all modes of the presence of God in human beings, whatever the situation or the activity. ". . . Those who invoke God standing, sitting, or reclining" (Koran 3:191). The practice of the *dhikr* is thus superior to any other form of worship: as is stressed by the Sufis, only the *dhikr* is prescribed for every moment, whereas the rites such as the prayer or the fast have set times and can be the object of exemptions. The Koran is explicit on this point: "The invocation of God is that which is greater!" (29:45); "O you who believe! Invoke God often!" (33:41). The practice of the *dhikr* is the key to inner peace: "Do not hearts find peace in the remembrance of God?" (13:28), and to fulfillment in this world: "Whoever turns away from the invocation of Me will lead a wretched life" (20:124).

In a tone of confidentiality, this *hadīth qudsī* evokes the proximity to God to which the *dhikr* leads: "I am the Intimate of he who invokes Me" (Daylamī); "I am near the idea that My servant forms of Me, and I am with him when he invokes Me; if he calls upon Me within himself, I will mention him in Myself. . ." (Bukhārī). The Prophet himself recognized the excellence of the *dhikr* compared to the ritual of the five pillars (Ibn Hanbal). He encouraged believers to devote themselves to the *dhikr*. "Hearts become rusty as does iron," he said to his Companions. "And what makes them shine?" asked one of them. "The invocation of God and the reading of the Koran," he answered. He also said: "He who invokes his Lord and he who does not are like one who lives and one who is dead" (Bukhārī), and further: "This lower-world is cursed, as all that exists in it, except for the invocation of God and that which accompanies it. . ." (Nawawī).

If the scriptural sources of Islam go on at such great length on the benefits of the *dhikr*, it is because the repetition of formulae of short incantory prayers is of universal value. Like the *dhikr*, the methods of the Hesychasts (e.g., the monks of the Sinai and Mount Athos), or the "prayer of Jesus" in the Russian Churches, or the Japanese *nembutsu*, or the Hindu *japa-yoga*, these all have the same goal: producing rhythmic vibrations which are reflected throughout the various levels of one's being; they all lead man to be absorbed in the Named, whether He be called God, Jesus, Brahman, or Buddha. In Sufism, spiritual concentration is divided into invocation (*dhikr*) and meditation (*fikr*). "The invocation is a light," said a master, "and meditation is its ray." In Islam, one does not meditate on the divine Essence, but on the Names, the Attributes, or on "signs" (*āyāt*) within the universe, which are the tangible presence of God in His creation.

The Prophet, we have seen, initiated his Companions into the invocation of *Lā ilāha illā Llāh* ("There is no divinity but God alone"), the formula of the Islamic testimony of faith. Starting with the Companions, the method of *dhikr* was transmitted from generation to generation, from master to disciple. The first Sufis regarded it as the key pillar of the Path and the preface to sanctity, because it can banish the state of distraction that is typical of ordinary human consciousness. Although the *Sharī'a* is aimed at purifying the body and the carnal soul, only the *dhikr* can purify the heart. The ultimate goal sometimes assigned to the *dhikr* is that he who dedicates himself to it becomes so completely imbued with the Named to the point of being extinguished in Him (*al-fana' fī 'l-madhkūr*). The created being is then returned to the state of non-differentiation with God which he had known in the spiritual world.[39] Motivated by their taste for hyperbole and paradox, the Sufis of the early period, however, denounced the *dhikr* as a veil which hid the divinity. Since the eleventh century, many masters have given detailed explanations of the methods of *dhikr*, its effects, its dangers, and the necessity for a master's guidance.

To maximize the effectiveness of the *dhikr*, the disciple must be in a state of ritual purity and must wear clean clothing, and should invoke at night or in a darkened place (the Prophet, it is said, practiced the invocation between dawn and sunrise). This place will be scented. Keeping the eyes closed or half-closed and turned towards the *qibla*, the disciple sits cross-legged, arms resting on the thighs; in late Sufism, he might sometimes be asked to create a mental image of his shaykh. Before starting, he directs his heart towards God, requesting forgiveness for his state of distraction, and strives to drive away his wandering thoughts.

— Formulas of the Invocation. The *dhikr* is the subject of specific protocols in the treatises of Sufism, but these instructions vary a great deal with time and place. The major formulas are *Lā ilāha illā Llāh* ("There is no divinity but God alone") and *Allāh* ("God"). Both have been used throughout the

---

[39] See, for example, Kalābādhī, *Traité de soufisme*, p. 116 (English edition: *The Doctrine of the Sufis*, translated by A. J. Arberry [Cambridge University Press, 1977]); Qushayrī, *Risāla*, p. 224.

centuries. The first formula initially entails the negation of all that is not God (*lā ilāha*: "there is no divinity"), then the affirmation of God's absoluteness (*illā Llāh*: "if it is not God"). This invocation is appropriate for beginners and for all those who are still prisoners of duality, for the "Name of Majesty," *Allāh*, can in principle be invoked only by a person immersed in Oneness. Ibn 'Arabī practiced the invocation of *Allāh* for a long time before favoring *Lā ilāha illā Llāh* in the end.[40]

The treatises especially dwell on the methods of the invocation of *Lā ilāha illā Llāh*. The disciple must accentuate the contrast between the initial *negation* and the final *assertion* by reinforcing the phonetic attack at the beginning of each segment of the phrase: *Lā ilāha . . . illā Llāh*. Sometimes, he pronounces *Lā ilāha* while inwardly moving from the navel towards the right shoulder, then *illā Llāh* while moving towards the heart, the center of one's spiritual "secret." The breath thus moves in a kind of a circle. The head follows this movement or remains motionless; it can also move from side to side. While pronouncing *Lā ilāha* ("there is no divinity"), the disciple dispels base thoughts, the phenomenal world, and the consciousness of self, so that nothing remains but God when he comes to *illā Llāh* ("if it is not God"). "The invocation," wrote Najm al-Dīn Kubrā, ". . . is a truth which dissipates illusory desires and establishes true realities."[41] The rhythms can differ within the same school. Kubrāwīs, for example, practice the *dhikr* using rhythms with two, three, or four beats per measure.[42] The Name *Allāh* is often invoked while visualizing the luminous writing of each one of its letters. Here, too, the manner of pronouncing the Name will produce various effects.

With time, the methods of invocation became increasingly sophisticated. Starting in the thirteenth century, the initiatory paths began to record them in detail. In the Sufism of Central Asia and India, undoubtedly due to the influence of Hindu-Buddhist techniques, the pronunciation of the formulas of *dhikr* is accompanied by increased control of the breath. "Retention of the breath" (*habs-i dam*, in Persian), which consists of blocking breathing below the navel, aims at purifying the mind; it has been systematized by the Naqshbandis. Let us also point out the "*dhikr* of the saw," so called because a hoarse and powerful sound accompanies each inhalation and each exhalation. Introduced by Ahmad Yasawī in Central Asia, this *dhikr* has spread as far as the Maghreb.

---

[40] C. Addas, *Ibn 'Arabī ou la quête du soufre rouge*, pp. 200-201. (English edition: *Quest for the Red Sulphur: The Life of Ibn Arabi* [Islamic Texts Society, 1993].)

[41] *Fawā'ih al-jamāl*, edited by F. Meier (Wiesbaden, 1957), p. 5 of the Arabic text.

[42] N. Isfarayini, *Le Révélateur des mystères*, edited and translated into French by H. Landolt (Lagrasse, 1986), pp. 47-48.

The invocation with the breath stems from the emitting of the Arabic letter *h* (ه), which one pronounces starting from the lower abdomen, then going up towards the mouth, and releasing the sound into the air. This Arabic letter, whose circular form can be seen as an allusion to the mystic's heart, has precise functions in the invocation of *Lā ilāha illā Llāh* and *Allāh*. Sufis often invoke God using Names that are more elliptical such as *Huwa* ("He"), or *Hū;* the breath emitted by the letter *h* is crucial in these invocations. Sufis also invoke Him using just the breath alone: *"Ah."* This sound is the quintessence of the Name *Allāh* since it is composed of the first and the last letters of this Name. Being based on a prophetic tradition, Sufis regard this breath as a divine Name.[43] The sound *Ah* is also exhaled using various rhythms, depending on whether it is repeated individually or collectively. Certain jurists accepted the invocation of only *Lā ilāha illā Llāh*, but that did not prevent some important *ulama* from devoting themselves to all forms of *dhikr* at collective sessions.

— From the Dhikr of the Tongue to that of "Inner Consciousness". In Sufism, spiritual experience always departs from the phenomenal world in order to be gradually interiorized. The invocation generally comprises three levels of increasing depth:

The Invocation of the Tongue (Dhikr al-Lisān), in which one pronounces a formula vocally, corresponds to the corporeal dimension. This invocation should not be neglected because it produces physiological warmth even when one remains motionless, which is of a sort that can transmute the soul (*nafs*) into "spirit" (*rūh*). The Sufi must conserve this heat, and so he must not drink cool water during or after the *dhikr*. The invocation must be vigorous, so that its effect will penetrate all parts of the body, even "to the veins and the arteries." The *dhikr* of the tongue must be accompanied by the attention of the heart, without which it is useless. For the masters, this corresponds to the level of beginners and serves as a "sword" to release the heart from the stranglehold of the carnal soul. The aspirant must prove himself to be resolutely combative, because the fight is bitter. Even if he does not succeed in focusing himself, he should continue the invocation. "The intimacy gained through the invocation will be known only to he who has tasted the suffering of distraction," said Sha'rānī.[44]

---

[43] Najm al-Dīn Kubrā, *Les Éclosions de la beauté*, pp. 194-198; E. Geoffroy, *Les Voies d'Allah*, p. 515.

[44] *Anwār*, vol. I, p. 43.

The Invocation of the Heart (Dhikr al-Qalb) has for its seat the physical heart, the symbol of the spiritual heart. It is silent, because it must now be integrated into the beating of the heart and follow the flow of blood through the body. The human being can then feel a kind of liberation, an expansion of consciousness which is often accompanied by visions and supernatural auditions,[45] with the luminous phenomena leaving the most lasting impressions. Through the catharsis which it brings about, the *dhikr* is a "fire" which burns through the darkness of the superficial consciousness and transforms it into light. The disciple should not stop at these visual manifestations which are subordinate to the light he should seek, the principial Light evoked in this verse: "God is the Light of the heavens and the earth" (Koran 24:35). If one's attention slackens during the silent *dhikr*, it is necessary to return to the invocation of the tongue. Actually, the two levels are closely linked; they can be practiced together, or alternately.

The Invocation of the Inner Consciousness (Dhikr al-Sirr) can be compared with *ihsān*, the "excellence" which lies above "submission" (*islām*) and "faith" (*īmān*). At this level, any trace of duality disappears, the Sufi being extinguished in the Invoked.

These three degrees are very schematic, and the masters sometimes distinguish five to eight stages. For some Naqshbandis, progress in the *dhikr* is carried out in correlation with the subtle centers (*latā'if*) of man; these are generally five, each corresponding to a place in the body and to a particular color.

— Aloud, or in Silence? Naqshbandis are at the center of a debate which has taken on a major scale: is it necessary to practice the invocation aloud or in secrecy? Behind this question arises the problem of sincerity, for a disciple can let himself fall into the trap of simply acting out the intimate remembrance of God. Both forms of invocation have in fact a precedent in the actions of the Prophet since he initiated Abū Bakr into the "secret" and thus silent invocation (*dhikr khafī*), and 'Alī into the vocal invocation (*dhikr jahrī*). The Naqshbandis, whose initiatory chain passes through Abū Bakr, have generally chosen the silent invocation, which is still called the "invocation of the heart" (*dhikr qalbī*).

---

[45] See, for example, N. Kubrā, *Éclosions*, pp. 73-76; G. Anawati and L. Gardet, *Mystique musulmane* (Paris, 1961), pp. 223-226.

The detractors of the vocal invocation base themselves on verses such as: "Invoke your Lord within yourself, with fear and humility, and without raising your voice" (Koran 7:205). The supporters of this type of invocation reply that this verse concerns only the Prophet, who had already achieved spiritual realization, or that it is explained by the persecutions of the first Muslims in Mecca. Most Sufi masters today believe that beginners must invoke God aloud, to push back against the assault of the mind and to strengthen concentration. This practice also enables them to channel the spiritual energy which burns in them. It is reported that during a group gathering, some aspirants perished after having taken part in a session of silent *dhikr,* their livers, it is said, must have roasted as if they had been exposed to coals. The silent *dhikr* requires strict control on behalf of the initiating master and, although it is considered to be superior in theory, most Orders follow the vocal *dhikr.* Some groups practice the *dhikr* with tremendous volume. This is the case with the Rifāʿis, who have been called "howling dervishes" because of the raucous sounds which they emit during their ritual.

Sufis invoke the divine Names with an initiatory goal in mind. Each Name produces an effect on those who can, by invoking it, take on the quality of this Name themselves; each Name represents a tangible shape of the divinity and also a suitable remedy for each individual. Masters initiate their disciples into the invocation of one or another Name according to their personality, their spiritual evolution, their circumstances, etc. The disciple then repeats this Name a given number of times in a way that allows him to "realize" it within himself. Khalwatis practice an initiation into "the seven Names," which correspond to stages of the Path: *Lā ilāha illā Llāh, Allāh, Huwa, al-Haqq* ("the Real"), *al-Hayy* ("the Living"), *al-Qayyum* ("the Self-Subsisting"), and *al-Qahhār* ("the Victorious"). This initiatory process can last several years.

The invoked Names are preceded either by the particle *Yā,* or just by the vowel sound *A.* Thus the invocation *Yā Latīf* (O Gentle, Benevolent) has as its goal removing oneself from trials or ordeals. The subtlety of the *dhikr* has motivated certain masters to introduce particular types of invocation. Ibn Sabʿīn, for example, had his disciples repeat this short formula which is a metaphysical condensation of the profession of faith: *Laysa illā Llāh,* "There is only God."

— *Group Sessions of* Dhikr. All Sufis favor group invocation because it produces an energy that is much stronger and thus more likely to "melt hearts" and to "lift the veils" that separate us from the spiritual world. The group gatherings, whose practice spread after the appearance of the initiatory paths, quickly became the highlight of a *tarīqa's* life. These gatherings are called *majlis al-dhikr* ("session of invocation"), *hadra* ("presence" of the Prophet, and not specifically of God, for God is omnipresent), or *'imāra* ("filling oneself" with God). They are held once or twice a week in a mosque or the *zāwiya* of the Order, usually on Thursday evening,[46] and Friday after the prayer of *jumu'a*. A group session of *dhikr* sometimes gathers together several thousand people; for a large gathering, the brothers organize themselves to supply the means of transport.

The sequence of a gathering obviously varies from one *tarīqa* to another, but one always observes a progression in intensity. At the beginning of the gathering, with everyone sitting, the participants start by reciting the daily prayer (*wird*) particular to that path, some verses from the Koran, formulas of prayer on the Prophet or poems in his praise, or even some mystical poems composed by one of the masters of the path. This preparatory phase often lasts more than an hour. The spiritual tension increases, and the desire to give oneself to the *dhikr* is heightened. Suddenly, on a sign from the shaykh or from his representative, everyone stands: the upright position signifies the need for spiritual elevation. The participants place themselves in circles or rows, and take each other's hand by intersecting their fingers, which allows the flow of spiritual energy to circulate without interruption. The lights sometimes remain lit, or sometimes they are dimmed.

The *dhikr* often starts with the Name *Allāh* and then moves to *Huwa*, *Hū*, or even *Hayy* (this latter Name begins with the other letter "h" that exists in Arabic: ح; this sound is more guttural than the ه). Almost always, the participants then come to the invocation with the breath, *Ah*, the "*dhikr* of the saw," to an increasingly deep and staccato rhythm. The *dhikr* includes several sequences, each climax being followed by a lull, and so on until the final paroxysm.

The invocation is accompanied by movements of the body; these express the movements of the soul which is aspiring to find its spiritual homeland. Although they are accomplished nearly in unison by the assembly, these movements do not have anything artificial about them: some people move a great deal, others hardly at all. The shaykh often remains motionless because he has dominated his own spiritual state and because he is the axis around which the souls move. Junayd remained impassive during these gatherings and explained his attitude by quoting this verse: "You see the mountains; you believe them fixed, but they are passing at the speed of the clouds" (Koran 27:88). The ecstasy of accomplished spiritual seekers does not need to show itself: this is "enstasy." Sometimes, however, it is the shaykh, regardless of whether he is young or old, who gives the physical energy to the assembly.

---

[46] In Islam, the day begins at sunset. Friday, the day of group prayer, begins, therefore, on Thursday evening.

The movements can vary due to varying cadences, but also because of the group itself. Sometimes the participants hop in one place, bending their knees, swinging the torso back and forth, sometimes even completely bending over. They then finish by jumping, with the head raised and like one who is striving for the freedom of the air, because the soul-spirit seeks to take off, to escape from the world of matter. Sometimes they pivot the chest from left to right, then back again, in a pendulum-like movement that increases in pace; the arms remain loose, and follow the alternation naturally. During this, reciter-singers are chanting mystical poems, or invoking the Prophet or great saints; their voices do not follow the collective breath precisely, but they chant in a kind of counterpoint to it. The meaning of the words and the sounds help to transport the souls. There are designated people in the center of the circle who observe the revolution of each person. Their role is to make sure that each one is in rhythmic harmony with the others and to limit the inevitable excesses.

Let us point out here that the "trances" sought by certain groups, which are solely at a psychic level, have little to do with the spiritual emotion aroused by the *dhikr*. These groups sometimes combine the two levels while relying on shamanistic or animistic phenomena, whether this is conscious or not. It is for this reason that Naqshbandis are so attached to the silent *dhikr*, which they also practice in groups.

The standing invocation can last between about twenty minutes and several hours. At the end of the *dhikr* the participants sit down again in silence, and one of them recites verses of the Koran. This can be followed by a few words or a lesson from the shaykh, or tea or a meal might be served, and then discussions begin between the brethren. People who are not affiliated with the Order can often take part in the gatherings, and non-Muslims are sometimes allowed as spectators. At the gatherings, children move freely in the rows or in the center of the circle, but certain shaykhs forbid their presence in order to optimize the concentration of the participants. The gatherings of *dhikr* are usually mixed, but the women form their own circle (the separation can only be symbolic); they are led by the wife of the shaykh or one of his representatives. The women sometimes hold their own gatherings, preferably in a private place.

SPIRITUAL POETRY AND MUSIC: *SAMĀ‘*

The Echo of the Divine Word

Samā‘ works towards the same goal as the *dhikr*, because listening to music or song has the effect of reactualizing in the human being the original Pact, of making the primordial utterance, "Am I not your Lord?" (Koran 7:172) echo within him. For the mystic, the music that he hears in the here-below is like an echo of the divine Word and of celestial music. According to certain traditions, the angels managed to lock up the heart of Adam in a body only after having charmed it with the music. The progress of the initiate thus will consist in reascending the axis of Manifestation by liberating his soul through music. Because of its cosmic origin, it is a privileged means of spiritual awakening. The ecstasy into which the mystic is then plunged is called *wajd* in Arabic, which means that this person has "found" (*wajada*) God. *Samā'* is one of the methods by which one "strives to attain ecstasy," which the Sufis call *tawājud*, a word that comes from the same root as *wajd*.

To the "realized" being, all sounds, whether natural or artificial, evoke God because, in reality, they invoke Him: "The seven heavens, the earth and all that is in it glorify Him. There is nothing which does not celebrate His praises, but you do not comprehend their praise" (Koran 17:44). The accomplished Sufi is thus not only a visionary before whom the veils of the perceptible world rise; he also perceives terrestrial sounds as reminiscences of the spiritual world, which can lead him to a state of great nostalgia. This was in particular the path of Rūmī:

> Listen to the flute of reed [the *ney*], as it sings of separation:
> I have been cut from the rush bed, and since then my lamentation
>   makes man and woman groan.
> I call to a heart which separation has pierced to reveal to it the pain
>   of desire.
> Any being who lives far from his source aspires to the time when he
>   will be reunited with it.[47]

— **Subtlety and Ambiguity of Samā'**. Unlike *dhikr*, *samā'* is based on a profound ambiguity. It is easy to understand these days that not every kind of music makes for good listening. Instead of elevating the soul, some can lead it astray, or abandon it to "entertainment," the kind of worldly distraction stigmatized so much by the Koran. The difficulty lies in understanding what spiritual "listening" (*samā'*, in its proper sense) is, rather than the music or the poem which are simply used as supports; this is because they are not necessarily of a sacred nature. Similarly, for he who has achieved a "spiritual opening," it is not the world which changes, but his perception of it. The first Sufis who practiced spiritual listening hastened to differentiate their art, which they named *samā'*, from profane music, or *ghinā*.

---

[47] É. de Vitray, *Anthologie du soufisme*, p. 183.

In spite of these precautions, the question of *samā'* led to secular debates between Sufis and jurists, and even more between the various trends within Muslim mysticism. One even saw jurists authorizing the gatherings of *samā'*, and Sufi masters completely forbidding them to their disciples. Those who were opposed to *samā'* warned against the effect that music might produce on the soul; they sometimes also criticized the supposed influence of Greek philosophers (especially Pythagoras and Plato) on the theory of *samā'*, or even that of Ismā'īli esoterism of the "Brothers of Purity" (*Ikhwān al-safā*). Masters inclined to "sober" Sufism (Ibn 'Arabī, the Shādhili and Naqshbandi shaykhs, etc.) refused to "listen" to human speech, preferring the silence of the Absolute, which was perfectly eloquent for them. But saints of similar stature, such as Rūzbehān Baqlī and Rūmī, chose *samā'* as their spiritual vehicle.

Most masters agree that the practice of *samā'* should be reserved for an elite. *Samā'*, indeed, reveals things to the practitioner. Reflecting the private state of the listener, it accentuates both the coarseness of the layman and the subtlety of the mystic. Thus it is *prohibited* for beginners who still listen with their carnal soul; *permitted* for those who, though freed from passions, have stopped at the aesthetic aspect of the music, etc.; and it is *recommended* for initiates, who alone are ready to practice the spiritual alchemy of the word and the sound. Here again, Sufism adopted these three main categories from Muslim law. In addition, they adopted an essential principle from Islam in order to judge the admissibility of *samā'*: only the intention (*niyya*) of the listener constitutes a relevant criterion. Thus, for Ghazzālī, music and the sessions of *samā'* are neither good nor bad in themselves; it is the inner disposition of the listener and the level at which he listens which make them go in one direction or the other. Chanted poems, we will remember, often employ the erotic terminology of courtly poetry, and so listeners are supposed to transmute them onto a spiritual plane.

All of the ambiguity of *samā'* is summarized in this saying from Shiblī: "*Samā'* is seemingly a source of disorder, but it conceals a great spiritual teaching."[48]

— *A Joyful and Widespread Practice*. The various reservations expressed above must yield to reality: clearly, collective gatherings of "listening" were widely practiced during the medieval period. They were reported in Baghdad as of the ninth century, they then spread to Iran, and then to other areas of the Muslim world. A sign of the importance of this phenomenon

---

[48] Quoted by Sha'rānī, *Anwār*, vol. II, p. 180.

over many centuries has been that most Sufi authors have devoted a chapter or a book to the question of *samā'*.

The participants met in a mosque, a *zāwiya*, or in a private residence. The singers or reciters often recited their poems to the accompaniment of musical instruments. The most prized instruments were the tambourine and the flute; string instruments were more controversial. When emotion over-flowed and ecstasy overwhelmed the heart, the body itself began to move, but in a less ritualized way than in the *dhikr*: a person might stamp his feet or clap his hands, cry out, start to "dance," throw off his turban, hurl his robe towards the reciters or tear it, etc. One might faint from ecstasy and some-times, it has been said, die from it.

The sessions often ended with a dinner, even with a banquet. Some of the sessions obviously deviated from their spiritual objectives and degener-ated into excesses of all kinds, attracting the opprobrium of jurists as well as of Sufi masters. However, according to reports, major scholars such as the theologian Bāqillānī and the "sultan of the *ulama*" 'Izz Ibn 'Abd al-Salām took part in concerts of *samā'* and surrendered themselves to the "dance" (*raqs*). If these sources are to be believed, the grand sessions of *samā'* gath-ered together all who were considered scholars and *muftis* in such Islamic metropolises as Baghdad or Damascus. The position of the *ulama* on *samā'* is thus less cautious than one might expect. This is demonstrated by the fact that the current grand *mufti* of Syria has spoken very highly of music, in very mystical tones.[49]

Samā' became ritualized beginning in the fourteenth century, especially in the Orders which adopted it as a spiritual method. The best known exam-ple is still that of the Mevlevis, where music and dance have contributed to the formation of a veritable liturgy. But there the practice of *samā'* quickly merged with that of the *dhikr*; this latter term tends to take the place of the former, undoubtedly because it benefits from clearer scriptural supports. *Samā'* is now often performed as a concert usually open to the public, and even to tourists; however, it is still maintained in forms such as the Indo-Pa-kistani *qawwāli*. Some brotherhoods, such as the 'Alawiyya, have preserved the term *samā'* to indicate the *a capella* chanting of mystical poems which precedes and closes their gatherings of *dhikr*.

The therapeutic properties of music were already known in the hospi-tals (*bimāristān*) of the classical age of Islam. It is thus not surprising that its pedagogical and spiritual benefits would be widely accepted. With regard to mystical poetry, some scholars explained that one could experience more

---

[49] In his opening to a double CD devoted to the music of the *Whirling Dervishes of Damascus*, Le Chant du Monde (Paris, 2000) (English version).

emotion through listening to it than to Koranic verses; this is because the disproportion between the eternal divine Word and its ephemeral listener is so immense that it prevents this emotion. The listening to the Koran, as with any revealed text, triggers instead a meditative state and a reverential fear. According to the authors, this constitutes the exclusive sustenance of the prophets and the elect. The average believer and "Sufi" do not belong to these two categories and so they need, along with the reading of and the listening to the Koran, supports such as poetry and music.

Bibliography

Georges Anawati and Louis Gardet, *Mystique musulmane* (Paris, 1961), pp. 187-234 (insights on the *dhikr*, open to inter-religious comparisons, but sometimes confusing).

Rachida Chih, *Le Sufism au quotidien*, pp. 250-263.

Éric Geoffroy, *Le Sufism en Égypte et en Syrie*, pp. 407-422 (on the debates concerning the *dhikr* and *samā'*).

Ibn 'Ata' Allāh, *Traité sur le nom ALLĀH*, introduction and translation into French by M. Gloton (Paris, 1981).

Najm al-Din Kubra, *Les Eclosions de la beauté et les parfums de la majesté*, edited and translated into French by P. Ballanfat (Nimes, 2001).

Les Voies d'Allah, pp. 150-155, 157-172, 515 in particular.

Litanies and Prayers[50]

To strengthen his attachment to the *tarīqa* and to reinforce the bond which unites him with his shaykh, the member of a Sufi order must recite, usually morning and evening, a collection of prayer formulas called the *wird* (pl. *awrād*), which allows him to "recharge" himself each day. The founding masters of the *tarīqa* or their successors composed these litanies; some claimed to have received them from God or the Prophet. Most paths have adopted formulas of the *wird* which are ordered according to three degrees:

1. *The request for forgiveness* (*istighfār*). The disciple starts with his human nature, which he seeks to purify by withdrawing from the world inwardly.

2. *The prayer of blessing on the Prophet* (*al-salāt 'alā l-nabī*). There are many forms. Through his identification with the Prophet, the disciple lets his ego be absorbed into the Reality of Muhammad; he then attains his status of "representative of God on earth" and potentially realizes the state of "Perfect Man."

---

[50] For the sake of convenience, we have used these words with Christian connotations to translate the Arabic terms *awrād* and *ahzāb*.

3. *The assertion of divine Oneness (tahlīl).* The disciple repeats the formula *Lā ilāha illā Llāh* ("There is no god but God"), by itself or followed by a complementary formula. At this stage, the Prophet himself is absorbed into the divine Reality, because God alone is and, ultimately, He invokes Himself. After having passed through the previous degrees of purification and human perfection, the believer arrives at the degree of union.

Sufi masters sometimes present this spiritual scale as follows: the first formula calls to mind the symbolism of the mirror covered with rust—the soul which has not yet been purified—which cannot reflect the divine sun. The second suggests that of the cleansed mirror—the purified soul—which has become ready to receive the sun. The third corresponds to the sun without the mirror, that is to say, God envisioned in Himself, because divine reality is beyond human consciousness.

In certain brotherhoods, the reading of a Koranic chapter, or of several, precedes the repetition of the three formulas, which are also introduced by a Koranic verse. The *wird* is often closed with three repetitions of *sūra* 112, called "Oneness" or "Pure Religion." According to a *hadīth*, reciting this *sūra* is in fact equivalent to reciting a third of the Koran. The ritual of the *wird* is thus completely integrated into the texture of the Koran. It sometimes ends with a formula of prayer on the Prophet, a sign of the return from the divine to the human plane.

The disciple recites each formula thirty-three or one hundred times, counting with the fingers or using rosary beads. He performs the *wird* morning and evening in order to erase his sins and to protect himself during the coming hours. He carries it out either alone in silence, or aloud with other people (within the family, with some of the brethren, etc.). Certain formulas are repeated a very precise number of times, and the consequences can be serious if the rule is transgressed.[51] The group sessions of *dhikr* usually start with the recitation of the *wird* and related formulas. During his attachment, the beginner is initiated into "the common litany" (*al-wird al 'āmm*) of each member of the order. When he has progressed, or if the shaykh or his representative decide to do so, someone will communicate to him a "particular litany" (*al-wird al-khāss*) which he will have to recite in addition to the first. This *wird* does not allow of any carelessness.

The recitation of various prayers (*hizb*, pl. *ahzāb*) often accompanies that of the *wird*. Composed either by the founders of the brotherhoods or their successors, these prayers include Koranic verses as well as various invocations

---

[51] On this subject see the split which took place among the Tijānis between the followers of the practice of "eleven beads" and those who introduced "twelve beads": in Hampaté Bâ, *Vie et enseignement de Tierno Bokar*, p. 57 *et seq.* (English edition: *A Spirit of Tolerance: The Inspiring Life of Tierno Bokar* [World Wisdom, 2008].)

and petitions addressed to God. They are reputed to have great power. One of the most celebrated, "the Prayer of the Sea" (*hizb al-bahr*), was an inspiration through the Prophet to Abu 1-Hasan Shādhilī. It contains the "supreme Name of God," according to the Shaykh, who claimed that if the inhabitants of Baghdad had known it, their city would not have been plundered by the Mongols.[52]

The effectiveness of these prayers and litanies is such, according to certain masters, that the simple fact of reciting them introduces a believer into their spiritual family. Even today, the expression "to take the *wird*" is often employed to indicate initiatory affiliation. The collection of prayers to be recited daily (*awrād, ahzāb. . .*) is called in some Orders the *wazīfa* ("office"). Naqshbandis are distinguished by what they call the *khatm al-khwādjegān*, or "invocation of the masters" of the path; in it, one mentions the names of the shaykhs of the Naqshbandi lineage, and one recites the *Fātiha*, the prayer on the Prophet, and some *sūras* in a prescribed order.

Helped along by competition between brotherhoods, some have found that the repeated recitations of litanies and prayers that others practice are not effective for them. Obviously, for these daily recitations to be effective, it is necessary for the initiatory secret of the shaykh, whether he be dead or alive, to be present. In spite of the risk of routine, Sufi masters insist on the need for holding to it. They point out the interplay between the terms *wird* and *wārid* ("mystical inspiration"), which come from the same Arabic root: inspiration gives life to the practice of the *wird*, and this in turn makes the reoccurrence of inspiration more likely. "There is no spiritual state (*hāl*) without inspiration, and no inspiration without recitation," writes a Moroccan master.[53] Let us conclude with Junayd. Somebody seeing him one day with a rosary in his hand found this astonishing, because of his spiritual rank. "We will never let go of the thread which has led us to where we are now," Junayd answered.

The Retreat (Khalwa)

If "peregrination" (*siyāha*) constitutes a kind of traveling retreat, the "retreat," on the contrary, can be regarded as a motionless journey. This initiatory journey, which is carried out in a way that is more compressed than the conditions of ordinary life, must open the being to an expansion of

---

[52] In 1258. See *La Sagesse des maîtres soufis*, pp. 277-283, which contains a presentation and a translation of the *Hizb*.

[53] J. L. Michon, *Le Soufi marocain Ahmad Ibn ʿAjība*, p. 219. (English edition: *Autobiography of a Moroccan Soufi: Ahmad Ibn ʿAjiba* [1747-1809] [Fons Vitae, 1999].)

consciousness. In all spiritual traditions, retreats or periods of isolation support the concentration on God. The lives of the prophets provide the prototype for the retreat. God imposed a retreat of forty nights on Moses before speaking to him on Mt. Sinai (Koran 7:142), and Jonah understood the true meaning of his mission while in the belly of the whale (Koran 21:87). More directly, the *khalwa* has its basis in the frequent retreats which Muhammad took in the cave at Hirā' before receiving the call to prophecy. Following the example of the Prophet, who recommended this return journey into oneself, believers practice withdrawing themselves from society (*'uzla, i'tikāf*) for a given time, in a mosque or at home, particularly during the last ten days of the month of Ramadān.

The first ascetics and the Sufis who succeeded them withdraw into the deserts and the mountains, and written accounts of the "lives of saints" show them living among wild beasts. They liked to meditate among ruins and in cemeteries, which reminded them of the vanity of this world and recentered them on the essential. However, Sufis are distinguished from ascetics in the importance that they attach to community life and the consciousness they have of their social role. In addition, the first manuals of Sufism stipulated that only advanced disciples can devote themselves to isolation.

Those who meet these requirements, such as the founders of the initiatory paths, always begin their spiritual career with a demanding retreat; this is because it is necessary for the purification of the soul. They often stay in the desert for several years—'Abd al-Qādir Jilānī lived there for twenty-five years—before returning among men. In their loneliness, they face all the trials and temptations that have been reported to us concerning Christian hermits. Of these harsh "battles against the ego" (*jihād al-nafs*) and against the forces of darkness, we only know of those who have won. . .

— **Rules of the Retreat.** Ghazzālī (d. 1111) made retreats in a minaret of the Umayyad Mosque in Damascus or in the Dome of the Rock, in Jerusalem.[54] It was only around the thirteenth century, when the initiatory paths appeared, that the *khalwa* started to be the subject of specific regulations. It was carried out from that time on in cells intended for this use within Sufi establishments (*khānqāh, zāwiya*, etc.). Suhrawardī's manual, *The Gifts of Knowledge* (*'Awārif al-ma'ārif*), marked this change: it explained the benefits and the dangers of the *khalwa*, and outlined methods for it.

The cardinal rule that the Sufi must observe is sincerity (*ikhlās*), for he submits to the retreat in order to approach God, not to obtain some super-

---

[54] *Al-Munqidh min al-dalāl*, pp. 99-100 of the French text.

natural power or to enjoy an aura of mystique among people. One enters into retreat only with the permission of the shaykh and under his control because of the possible risks to the body and especially to the psyche. A *khalwa* that is badly conducted or done without the protection of a master can lead to madness, as many anecdotes have testified. In certain cases, the recluse must also visualize the image of his shaykh. When the shaykh comes to see him, the disciple tells him about his dreams or visions. The rules regarding the practice of the *khalwa* recall those which we mentioned concerning the *dhikr*: sitting in a darkened place, the recluse must remain in a state of ritual purity and, turned towards the *qibla*, he must invoke God constantly using the formulas *Lā ilāha illā Llāh* or *Allāh*. After the ritual prayers, he must recite particular formulas or engage in exercises of visualization. The *khalwa* always used to be done in a state of fasting, sometimes continuously for several days, but such rigor is not recommended any more nowadays, except if the retreat takes place during the month of fasting, Ramadān. In all cases, the recluse will eat very little (Suhrawardī limited food to bread and salt) and will avoid consuming animal flesh. He will sleep but little, and will stay awake as much as possible because the night is favorable to "illumination." He will avoid speaking, if the *khalwa* is carried out with several others. He will perform the ritual prayers with other recluses when he can, especially the Friday prayer if the *khalwa* is being done in a mosque.

The retreat used to last forty days, in theory. This number has an esoteric value recognized in all spiritual traditions. Sufis base this practice particularly on the forty nights during which Moses prepared himself for the Revelation and on this *hadīth*: "He who devotes himself completely to God for forty days will see wisdom gushing forth from his soul to his tongue."[55] The duration of the *khalwa* varies considerably according to the master, to the Order, and, of course, to the person doing the retreat. Some disciples obtain the hoped for results in a few hours; others will go back into retreat after having finished forty days. Some will never come to know that "illumination." Nowadays, the brotherhoods that practice *khalwa* recommend one that lasts three days and nights, or sometimes less. In former times the recluse was told not to think of the time that he was passing in *khalwa* nor of when he would finish. He was to consider his cell as the tomb he would have until the day of resurrection.

The descriptions which authors have given of the cell (it must be dark, narrow, and removed from any ambient noises) indeed suggest that entering into *khalwa* is like entering into one's tomb. Contrary to what occurs in

---

[55] Cited by Suhrawardī, *'Awārif*, p. 207.

ordinary life, the mind and body must be kept silent and the outward senses must be obliterated in order to develop the inward senses. The first Sufis dug their own tombs during their lifetimes and performed acts of worship there or stretched themselves out in them; they thus familiarized themselves with the ground in which they were going to rest.[56] To Satan, who asked one of these Sufis what he ate, what clothing he wore, and where he lived, the Sufi replied, "I feed on death, I dress myself in a shroud, and I live in a tomb." Shiblī recommended the *khalwa* in these terms: "Seek solitude, erase your name from the memory of people, and face the wall until you die." In their *zāwiyas*, shaykhs often had a hidden room, an underground cell into which they would withdraw for short or long periods of time.[57] Naqshbandis, for their part, practice "meditation on death," an exercise which consists of imagining oneself dead, buried, and in a state of advanced decomposition. The *khalwa* is thus a laboratory where initiatory death is transmuted into spiritual rebirth.

— *Not to Stop at Supernatural Phenomena*. The recluse thus should not think of the modalities of his retreat, but of God only. He will thus be able to drive away the bad or evil suggestions which will not fail to attack him, just as with supernatural perceptions which come to him. A master is necessary here because he can distinguish an authentic spiritual phenomenon from a simple hallucination. Sufi authors mention successive "unveilings" which can lead the recluse to a sometimes extraordinary expansion of consciousness, and which confirm the reality of his "illumination" (*fatḥ*). The initiate might see, for example, what people are doing in their houses; he may perceive the intrinsic truth of revealed laws or the degree of authenticity of the sayings of the Prophet, he may suddenly understand the various languages of humanity, as well as, perhaps, the language of the mineral, vegetable, and animal kingdoms, etc.[58] At the end of a retreat lasting seven years, Muhammad Hanafī, a Shādhili master of the fifteenth century, discovered that he had acquired the faculty of reading souls: he saw some people with luminous faces, others with the face of a pig or a monkey. He then returned to his cell to ask God to relieve him of this vision.

A person in retreat, indeed, cannot take pleasure in these unveilings; he must not stop at intermediate realities, which may certainly be tempting on

---

[56] É. Geoffroy, "La mort du saint en islam," *Revue de l'histoire des religions*, n° 215, 1998, pp. 17-34.

[57] One can still see the one of Abū l-Hasan Shādhilī in his sanctuary in Tunis, which, in addition, is in the middle of a large cemetery.

[58] Sha'rānī, *Anwār*, vol. II, pp. 105-117.

the spiritual level, but which can be the effect of a divine ruse. The medieval Islamic world, like any traditional civilization, was undoubtedly more receptive to supra-sensible phenomena than the modern Western world. Even so, such divinely conferred gifts were still exceptional in the past. Some masters believe that it would be better for a recluse who does not perceive any of these signs during his retreat to stop and to dedicate himself to exoteric religious sciences or to some worldly activity.

It seems, however, that in practice one frequently takes the means for the end. The *khalwa* was systematized starting in the fourteenth century. Even suggested for novices, the retreat in a cell is supposed to guarantee a minimum of "illumination" to any aspirant and to bring about the occurrence of spiritual states (*ahwāl*) to which they would not have access under normal circumstances. The Khalwatiyya Order has even taken its name from the *khalwa*, which it has set as a pillar of its method. This popularization roused criticisms from Sha'rānī, who believed that the visions experienced by the common run of disciples was the result of delirium.

For the masters of late Sufism, the *khalwa* remains a support that is much in favor. At the beginning of the nineteenth century, Shaykh Khālid introduced the retreat of forty days into the Naqshbandi path because he thought it more suitable to initiation than the traditional companionship between master and disciple (*suhba*). At the beginning of the twentieth century, the Algerian Shaykh Ahmad 'Alawī also brought this new practice to the Shādhili-Darqāwi path. Under his direction, the recluse invoked the Name *Allāh* for several days, or, if needed, even several months. The luminous visions and other phenomena such as levitation were, it appears, frequent, but one did not stop there.[59]

— **The "Retreat in the Midst of the Crowd."** The retreat in a cell can only be momentary, because the vocation of the Muslim spiritual seeker is to be among people. This presence in the world, stressed Ibn 'Arabī, is more beneficial to the spiritual seeker than his isolation. It is the same, with all the more reason, for a temporal leader: following the conquest of Constantinople by the Ottomans in 1453, Mehmet the Conqueror's shaykh refused to let him enter into *khalwa* because the pleasure that the sultan would have experienced might have led him to give up his power. The ideal thus lies in inner, perpetual retreat, a "retreat in the midst of the crowd" (*al-khalwa fī l-jalwa*), a Naqshbandi principle that other Orders have practiced in their

---

[59] J. Cartigny, *Cheikh Al Alawi. Documents et témoignages*, pp. 76, 86-87.

own ways. "The gnostic," noted Qushayrī, "is he who, while being near men, is far from them through his secret."

Rare, indeed, are the Muslim saints who have stayed recluses all their lives and whom one has not been able to visit. The great majority return to the world. After having experienced *fanā'*, the extinction in God, they try to achieve *baqā'*, "subsisting" in and through God, without that necessarily being apparent on the surface. For less realized beings, the "retreat in the midst of the crowd" is a constant challenge related to the outer demands of life. But this type of retreat is obviously more appropriate to modern life than the retreat in a cell.

In the end, should one not understand the *khalwa* as did Ibn 'Arabī, that is to say, as a return to the emptiness (*khalā'*) of our origin, a realization of our ontological emptiness that only the divine Presence can fill? In any event, wrote Ibn 'Arabi, "there is really no retreat in this world, for the very place where you find yourself is observing you."

Bibliography

Michel Chodkiewicz, "Les quatre morts du soufi," *Revue de l'histoire des religions*, Paris, January-March 1998, n°. 215, pp. 35-57.

Chapter 5

SUFISM AND INTERRELIGIOUS OPENNESS

"We consider the voices of various believers that rise up from all parts
of the earth as a symphony of praises addressing God, Who alone can be
Unique."

—Tierno Bokar

"Do not take a dislike to a Jew or a Christian, but rather to your ego. . ."

—Sufi adage

Religious Pluralism in Islam

According to the concept of cycles of time that Islam received from the
Revelation, each new prophetic message draws upon the spiritual heritage
of humanity. Islam is particularly aware of this inheritance since it presents
itself as the final expression of the divine will which has been revealed to
mankind since Adam, thus as the confirmation and the completion of the
revelations that preceded it. Because of this, it recognizes and takes up
again the messages of prophets who came before Muhammad. The Koran
is explicit on this legacy: "Say: 'We believe in God, in that which has been
revealed to Abraham, Isaac, Jacob, and to the tribes; to that which was
given to Moses and to Jesus; to that which was given to the prophets from
their Lord. We make no division between any of them; unto God do we
surrender" (Koran 2:136). Muhammad is the "seal"—meaning the last—of
the prophets, of which the number is 124,000, according to him. Now,
the Koran mentions only twenty-seven prophets, specifying that "for every
community there is a Messenger" (Koran 10:47). It must therefore search
on a vast scale for the others within the history of all humanity. Thus, certain Muslim scholars recognize Buddha, Zoroaster, or even Akhenaton as
prophets. They have noted three allusions to the Buddha in the Koran,[1] and
have seen the equivalent of the prophets of Islam in the "avatars," or the
incarnations of the divine within Buddhism. Similarly, some Indian *ulama*
regarded the Vedas, the sacred texts of Hinduism, as inspired by God and
have considered Hindus as among the "People of the Book," meaning the
peoples who have been granted a revealed scripture.

The Koran repeatedly mentions the "primordial" or "immutable" religion (*al-dīn al-qayyim*). All historical religions are said to stem from this

---

[1] Koran 21:85, 38:48, and *sūra* 95, titled "The Fig Tree."

nameless religion[2] and these would have a common genealogy. Therefore, Islam considers the diversity of peoples and religions as an expression of divine Wisdom.[3] Thus there exists a theology of religious pluralism in Islam, even in its most exoteric aspects. "To each of you, We have given a path and a perspective" (Koran 5:48): this verse justifies the diversity of religious traditions, which are united in what underlies them all, through the axis of the divine Oneness (*tawhīd*). Each believer will be paid for his faith and his observance of his own religion: "Those who believe, those who practice Judaism, those who are Christians or Sabians, those who believe in God and the Last Day, those who work righteousness: these are those who will find a reward beside their Lord. They will feel fear no more, nor will they grieve" (Koran 2:62).

The universalism of the Revelation was confirmed by the Prophet: "We prophets are all sons of the same family; our religion is but one" (Bukhārī). During a period when religious intransigence was accepted, the acknowledgment of religious pluralism had to result in a fundamental respect for other believers: "Whoever does evil to a Christian or a Jew will be my enemy on the Day of Judgment." Subsequently, issues of policy and economic interests, but also the Crusades, often undermined Islamic ideals in this area, and most of the *ulama* have restricted this broader perspective. According to these scholars, since the Islamic law repealed the laws which had been revealed previously, the religions which had come from those earlier laws were null and void. Endless dogmatic polemics, especially between Christians and Muslims, then came about. But even among theologians and jurists there were always minds which were inclined to a universal consciousness. Let us listen to Ibn Hazm (eleventh century): "Place your trust in a pious person, even if he does not share your religion, and distrust an impious person, even if he is of your religion," or indeed this fifteenth century *qādī* who stated: "Every man can be saved by his own faith, the one in which he was born, provided that he keeps it faithfully."

The Transcendent Unity of Religions

There are undoubtedly Sufis who are open to a broad interpretation of the Koranic theme of the "immutable Religion." They sense more keenly than others this community of worship that is composed of all humanity beyond the diversity of beliefs. Their openness to other faiths arises from an obvious metaphysical fact: "There can be only one doctrine of the divine Oneness" (*al-tawhīd wāhid*).

---

[2] See, for example, Koran 30:30.

[3] Koran 5:48, 30:22, 49:13.

The first ascetics were likely influenced by the Christian monks and hermits of the Middle East. It even appears that they took their example more from Jesus and his ascetical and peripatetic life than from Muhammad. In later times, it came to pass that many scholars and Sufis, with such as Ghazzālī among them, quoted profusely from the sayings of Christ, avowing their veneration for him. Christian monks have been respected throughout the history of Islam, apart from recent instances of terrorism, of course. Sufis have seen them as spiritual seekers following the path of Christ, and some shaykhs have pointed out to their followers the behavior of some monks as an ideal to be achieved.

Hallāj professed the universalism of the "primordial Religion." After having berated a Muslim who attacked a Jew in the Baghdad market, he said: "I have reflected on the different religious denominations and have made an effort to understand them, and I regard them as a single Principle that has many offshoots."[4] In the same vein, the Iranian Sufi master Ibn Abī l-Khayr said that "all religions and all thoughtful people recognize that He Who is worshiped universally and Who is the supreme Goal [for all] is one and the same Being."[5] Both through what they said and through their attitudes, Sufi masters such as Ahmad Rifā'ī and 'Abd al-Qādir Jīlānī, for example, would bear witness to a similar understanding of religious pluralism and of the universality of the worship of the divine.

It was once more Ibn 'Arabī who furnished a doctrinal framework for the concept of the "transcendent unity of religions" (*wahdat al-adyān*), although the term is not his. To him, all beliefs, and therefore all religions, are true because each is a response to the manifestation of a divine Name; however, all of these specific theophanies have their source in God, the "Real," the "True." There is thus a fundamental unity between all of the sacred laws, and each carries a portion of truth. The diversity of religions is due to the multiplicity of divine manifestations "which never repeat themselves." Basing himself on the *hadīth qudsī*, "I conform to the idea that My servant has of Me," Ibn 'Arabī first concludes that believers are conditioned by the different theophanies which have been received by human beings and by the necessarily fragmentary conceptions that everyone has of God; then that God accepts all beliefs—though not all to the same degree, of course—because human concepts cannot impose their own limits on the divine Being. Each religion, he said, unveils itself in actuality only as an aspect of divinity. Citing Junayd, he added that beliefs are like containers of different colors: in all cases,

---

[4] *Dīwān*, translated into French by L. Massignon (Paris, 1981), p. 108.

[5] M. Ebn E. Monawwar, *Les Étapes mystiques*, p. 65.

the water is initially colorless, but it takes on the color of each container.

Those who limit themselves to the stage that Ibn 'Arabī calls the "god created in beliefs" reject the credos of others, because they do not have access to divine Being, from which all theophanies emanate. The gnostic, however, recognizes God in any form because "Wheresoever you turn, there is the face of God" (Koran 2:115). Ibn 'Arabī gives this advice: "Take care not to tie yourself to a particular creed by renouncing all the rest. . . . May your soul be the substance of all beliefs, for God is too vast and too immense to be enclosed in one credo that excludes all the others."[6]

Ibn 'Arabī came to another conclusion: The form (God in His various appellations, but also nature, or idols) to which a man of a given religion devotes himself does not matter, it is still God that he loves, even if he is not aware of this. This is the meaning of his famous poem:

My heart has become capable of all forms,
A meadow for gazelles, a monastery for monks,
A temple for idols, a Ka'ba for the pilgrim,
The Tablets of the Torah, the Book of the Koran.
I profess the religion of Love, and whatever direction
Its mount may take, Love is my religion and my faith.[7]

One should not see in this poem a "flaccid syncretism"[8] but rather the expression of a spiritual realization carried out within a given tradition, in this case, Islam. The believer who has a superficial approach to religion remains on the circumference, at the level of the outer standard; He does not understand other beliefs and therefore seeks to impose his own. But he who attains realization within his own tradition reaches the level of universal Reality (*Haqīqa*), which transcends all beliefs and faiths.[9]

To practice the religion of Love is to recognize that "God has decreed that you [creature beings] worship none but Him" (Koran 17:23), and that man was created only for worship (Koran 51:56). After Ibn 'Arabī, several movements in Sufism have openly advocated this religion of Love, even

---

[6] *Fusūs al-Hikam* (Beirut, 1980), p. 113.

[7] Translation by H. Corbin, *L'Imagination créatrice dans le soufisme d'Ibn 'Arabī* (Paris, 1958), p. 109. (English edition: *Creative Imagination in the Sufism of Ibn 'Arabi* [Routledge, 2007].)

[8] C. Addas, *Ibn Arabi et le voyage sans retour*, p. 101. (English edition: *Ibn 'Arabī: The Voyage of No Return* [Islamic Texts Society, 2000].)

[9] See the diagram on p. 9.

though they may not specifically cite the *Shaykh al-Akbar*. During one public gathering, Ahmad Tijānī, for example, did not hesitate to maintain that "God loves the faithless," which shocked many in the audience. The Tijāni shaykh Tierno Bokar, called by Theodore Monod "the Saint Francis of Assisi of Bandiagara," taught in the middle of the African Sahel that there is only one primordial Religion, "comparable to a trunk from which the known historical religions branch off like the branches of a tree. It was this eternal Religion," he continued, "which was taught by all the great Messengers of God and which was molded to serve the necessities of each epoch."[10] Following the logic of Ibn 'Arabī, Tierno concluded that "to believe that one's race or one's religion is the only possessor of the truth is an error. . . . Indeed, in its nature, faith is like air. Like air, it is indispensable for human life and one could not find one man who does not believe truly and sincerely in something."[11] One of his disciples, Amadou Hampaté Bâ, manifested the veneration that a Muslim can have for Jesus, and he became one of the architects of Muslim-Christian dialogue.

For centuries, the school of Ibn 'Arabī, along with all those who have recognized their indebtedness to the Andalusian master, have resumed and adapted his doctrine to fit different historical contexts. 'Abd al-Karīm Jīlī explored the relationship between the Prophet Ibrāhīm (Abraham) and the *barāhima*, the "Brahmins" or priests of Hinduism: he believed that the similarity in sounds between the two words is not accidental because, according to him, Hindus claim that they descend from Abraham and that they belong to his religion.

Emir 'Abd al-Qādir was also a worthy emulator of Ibn 'Arabī in this area. Resisting the absolutism of personal beliefs, he stressed the divine Oneness that underlies the different creeds.[12] Despite his disillusionment with French imperialism, he advocated rapprochement with Christianity: "If Muslims and Christians would listen to me," he wrote, "I would stop their antagonism and they would become brothers outwardly and inwardly."[13] When he saved the lives of eleven thousand Christians being threatened by rioters in Damascus in 1860, he was only practicing the doctrine that he preached.

---

[10] A.Hamapaté Bâ, *Vie et enseignement de Tierno Bokar*, pp. 144, 153. (English edition: *A Spirit of Tolerance: The Inspiring Life of Tierno Bokar* [World Wisdom, 2008], p. 132.)

[11] Ibid., p. 129.

[12] M. Chodkiewicz, in his "Introduction" to the *Écrits spirituels*, p. 35 (English edition: *The Spiritual Writings of Amir 'Abd al-Kader* (SUNY, 1995]); 'Abd al-Qādir al-Jazā'irī, *Le Livre des haltes*, translated into French by M. Lagarde (Leiden, 2001), vol. II, pp. 114, 372-375.

[13] *Lettre aux Français* (Algiers, 2005), p. 69.

Motivated by the same spiritual humanism, Shaykh Ahmad 'Alawī always had an immense curiosity in regard to all religions. Knowing the Christian tradition,—he especially appreciated the Gospel of John—he preached understanding between Muslims and Christians throughout his life. "If I were to find a group that could interpret the European world for me, we would be surprised to see that nothing divides the West from Islam," he wrote in the midst of the colonial period. The Christ-like spirit that motivated him, and which we will examine shortly, was shared by his successors. Shaykh 'Adda Bentounes (d. 1952) exclaimed: "If the Christians knew the love for Jesus that ardently burns in my heart, they would rejoice that I live!"[14] and his son, Shaykh Mahdī, prescribed to a disciple "some prayer formulas that had to do with Christ" (*wird 'isawī*). Algerian members of the 'Alawiyya Order regularly met with Tibherine (Trappist) monks, who were later murdered; they had also warned them of the danger they faced from the G.I.A. (a violent Islamist group in Algeria).

René Guénon (d. 1951) also tried very hard to remind readers of the fundamental unity and identity of all spiritual traditions. It was precisely for this reason that his work deals more with Hindu doctrines, for example, than with Sufism, to which he was affiliated. Guénon's metaphysical affinities with Ibn 'Arabī are quite obvious since he further developed the doctrine of the "oneness of Being."[15]

Frithjof Schuon, whose spiritual lineage came through the 'Alawiyya, was also close to Guénon. He wrote a book having the specific title of *The Transcendent Unity of Religions*. Using Western terminology, it presents ideas which Ibn 'Arabī had mentioned, though he frequently did this in an allusive fashion. If one limits oneself solely to dogmas, Schuon explains, different beliefs appear antagonistic, and every sacred text seems to carry in itself internal contradictions. In fact, the differences between religions "do not undermine the single and universal Truth" since they are the expression of the divine Will.[16] Schuon, who took the name of "Shaykh 'Īsā (Jesus)," had a great influence on some Christian circles. The veneration that he had for Mary (Maryam) led him to name his initiatory path the Maryamiyya. "Mary personifies the non-formal Essence of all the Messages," he wrote, "She is therefore the 'mother of all the prophets'; consequently, she is identified with primordial

---

[14] *Le Chœur des prophètes. Enseignements soufis du cheikh Adda Bentounès* (Paris, 1999), p. 181.

[15] M. Vâlsan, *L'Islam et la fonction de René Guénon* (Paris, 1984), pp. 28-32.

[16] *The Transcendent Unity of Religions* (Quest Books, 1984); see the first chapter in particular.

and universal Wisdom, the *Religio Perennis.*"[17] Before Schuon, other Sufis had also meditated on the Koranic figure of Mary, and had claimed to be in subtle contact with the Virgin.

The Legacy of Prophetic Pluralism

This proximity between Muslim saints and prophets, which also includes some figures who pre-date Islamic history, must be understood within the perspective of the "prophetic legacy" which affects all Muslim saints.[18] This legacy in fact explains to a great extent the universalistic awareness which is characteristic of Sufis. All of the Westerners who approached Shaykh 'Alawī were struck by his Christ-like appearance, and one of them spoke of the "beautiful face of a sorrowful and tender Christ." This similarity was due to the emanation of the Shaykh's spiritual "station," which explains his wide-spread appeal to the Christian West. To the extent that one can judge this sort of thing, the Christ-like type seems to be one of the most widespread among Muslim saints, which is hardly surprising since Islam accords to Jesus a unique status and a major eschatological role. Sufis, however, have seen in him the "universal seal of sanctity."

Louis Massignon did certainly "Christianize" the figure of Hallāj to too great an extent, but it is true that Ibn 'Arabī considered Hallāj to be an heir of Jesus, within the Muhammadian sphere, of course.[19] Another Christ-like saint who was less well-known but was just as remarkable, was 'Ayn al-Qudāt Hamadhānī (d. 1131), who also suffered a similar "passion," since he was crucified at the age of thirty-three.[20] In Ottoman Turkey, where the influence of Ibn 'Arabī quickly spread, many shaykhs were distinguished by their Christ-like appearance; in the manner of 'Ayn al-Qudāt, some were even supposed to be able to resurrect the dead, which is a sign in Islam of a Christ-like disposition.[21] They were suspected of having secretly converted to Christianity. However, Ibn 'Arabī had specified that if a Sufi invokes Jesus, even on his deathbed, that this does not mean that he becomes a Christian.[22] But in a region where syncretism was flourishing, the exoteric authorities had reason to be wary.

---

[17] "Hagia Sophia," in *Marie et le mystère marial*, special edition of *Connaissance des religions*, n° 47-48, 1996, pp. 1-2.

[18] See *supra*, p. 18.

[19] M. Chodkiewicz, *Le Sceau des saints*, p. 103. (English edition: *Seal of the Saints* [Islamic Texts Society, 1993].)

[20] *Les Tentations métaphysiques*, from the "Introduction" by Ch. Tortel, p. 27.

[21] See Koran 5:110.

[22] *Le Sceau des saints*, p. 103.

More generally, the sources mention many saints who were supposed to be in contact with one prophet or another through the intermediary of his "spiritual entity." Visions of the prophet Ibrāhīm (Abraham) seem to have been particularly frequent.

The "Hidden Idolatry" of Common Believers

Many Persian mystics (Ibn Abī l-Khayr, 'Ayn al-Qudāt, Rūmī, Shabistarī, etc.) thought that the belief of the simple believer or even of the exoteric theologian was nothing but "hidden idolatry." A man who is not spiritually realized cannot be anything other than an idolater, or even an "infidel," because he does not love God in truth; he worships only what he *conceives* God to be. We find in this the teaching of Ibn 'Arabī, but the Persian Sufis proved to be more radical in their criticism of the "right-thinking" [i.e. conventionally orthodox] believer. They willingly engaged in this paradox of criticizing believers in order to awaken one's consciousness: faith and infidelity, good and evil are theophanies that are differentiated from the divine Being; since they spring from a single source, their opposition can only be something relative. 'Ayn al-Qudāt, who was a judge, declared in this regard:

> Alas, alas! This Law is the religion of stupidity,
> Our religion is impiety and the religion of the Christians. . . ;
> Impiety and faith are, to us, a single thing.[23]

While Sanā'ī said:

> Infidelity and faith run along His path,
> United in their praise:
> "He is one, with none like unto Him."

It is necessary to go beyond dogmatic barriers to better realize the universalistic essence of the Islamic message and to reach the primordial Religion. "I am neither Christian, nor Jew, nor Zoroastrian, nor Muslim," says Rūmī in a poem in which he denies all multiplicity and all duality in order to be reabsorbed into God alone.[24] Being very open to other faiths, Rūmī compared the diverse paths which lead to God to roads which all converge upon Mecca, and called forth: "Come, come, whoever you may be, infidel, religious, or pagan, it matters not!" During his funeral, "All the residents

---

[23] *Les Tentations métaphysiques*, p. 280.

[24] E. de Vitray-Meyerovitch, *Anthologie du soufisme*, p. 262.

were there, Muslims, but also Christians and Jews because all recognized themselves in him. . . . The Jews advanced in the cortège chanting the Psalms, the Christians proclaiming the Gospel, and no one thinking to exclude others." The Sultan had the leaders of the Jewish and Christian communities come to him, and he asked them why they were honoring a Muslim in that way. They replied: "When we saw him, we realized the true nature of Jesus, Moses, and of all the prophets."[25]

In his *Secret Rose Garden*, Shabistarī bore fruit from the doctrine of Ibn 'Arabī, in a Persian setting. Basing himself, like Ibn 'Arabī, on this verse: "The seven heavens, the earth and all that is in it glorify Him. There is nothing which does not celebrate His praises, but you do not comprehend their praise" (Koran 17:44), Shabistarī resolutely asserted the unity of religions, which arises from the "oneness of Being," and the unity of the diverse worshippers and seekers of God.

The Temptation of Syncretism

The boundary between an interreligious openness and syncretism is sometimes tenuous. The latter may be limited to the purely doctrinal dimension, such as with Suhrawardī Maqtūl, who taught a theosophy that blended together several sources, or with Ibn Sab'īn who drew from Plato and Hermes as well as from masters of *tasawwuf*. Ibn Hūd (d. 1300), a disciple of Ibn Sab'īn in Damascus, was called the "shaykh of the Jews" because of the influence he had on some representatives of that community. Moreover, he used to "greet the rising of the Sun by making the sign of the cross" and offered those wishing to place themselves under his direction a choice between three initiatory paths: those of Moses, Jesus, and Muhammad. He was seen as a syncretist by exoterists, but also by most Sufis. Some companions of Sadr al-Dīn Qūnawī would admit to the divinity of Jesus, which angered Rūmī himself.[26] Perhaps we should view Ibn Hūd as an "Abrahamic" Muslim saint drawing from the source of monotheism. In the Middle East, where for better or for worse Judaism, Christianity, and Islam coexist, the figure of the Patriarch can obviously play a beneficial role. In fact, there is in Israel-Palestine today an "Abrahamic initiatory path" (*tarīqa ibrāhīmiyya*) which draws upon Palestinian Sufis and Jewish spiritual seekers for its vitality.

Turco-Persian Sufism is distinguished by a greater tolerance than Sufism in Arabic-speaking environments. Although some Persian authors have

---

[25] E. de Vitray-Meyerovitch, *Islam, l'autre visage* (Paris, 1995), pp. 97-98.

[26] Rūmī, *Le Livre du Dedans* (Paris, 1982), pp. 164-165.

advocated a *supra-confessionalism* that is of a metaphysical nature, Anatolian dervishes willingly practice a kind of mysticism that is *trans-confessional*. Bektashism is a veritable crucible of various influences in which shamanism, Christianity, and heterodox Shī'a Islam coexist. At the end of the medieval era, the Bektashis were so close to the Greek monks that it was sometimes difficult to distinguish them apart. In Anatolia, the breaking down of religious barriers was shared by various faiths, and it was commonly said that "a saint is for everyone." Sufi groups have sometimes been accused of heterodoxy due to their flexibility regarding dogmas, but this has nevertheless also contributed without doubt to the Islamicization of others. Thus, Ibn Hūd brought some Jews in Damascus into Islam, and the Bektashis have widely contributed to the conversion of some Balkan populations.

Religious syncretism has sometimes had a directly political aspect. The most famous example is the dream of the Mughal Emperor Akbar (d. 1605), who wanted to free Hindus and Muslims of all denominational prejudice and who tried to promote a universal religion (*dīn-e ilahī*). For this purpose he founded a school for translators so that Sufism and the Hindu Vedānta would both be accessible. His great-grandson, prince Dara Shikoh was an intelligent connoisseur of both systems and he himself translated some major texts of Hinduism. In his *The Mingling of the Two Oceans* (*Majma' al-bahrayn*), he attempted to prove the unity of the principles of Islamic and Hindu metaphysics. Although he accomplished pioneering work on comparative mysticism, he cared little for politics and, accused of heresy by his own brothers, he was executed in 1659. Except in some Sufi circles, his example has hardly been kept alive in India by subsequent generations.

The Pressures of Exoterism and History

The interreligious openness that characterizes Sufism does, however, have its limits. First, not all Sufis adhere to the doctrine of the oneness of Being, on which the doctrine of the transcendent unity of religions is based in some ways. Those who support this doctrine are a minority and are often considered even within Sufism itself as being on the margins. A Muslim or a Sufi can have a dialogue with representatives or mystics of other religions without being convinced that there is some sort of "transcendent unity of religions." Furthermore, the Koranic principle of the "immutable Religion" often brings about criticism from Muslims that the religions which pre-dated Islam subjected the divine messages to "deviations." Islam criticizes Christianity in particular for the dogmas of the incarnation and the Trinity. The revealed books and the prophets that preceded Muhammad are recognized by many, but so are the dogmatic deviations that occurred over time in these other religions. On this point, the vast majority of Sufis align themselves with the official Islamic position.

In the past, before extensive contacts between civilizations had been established, each civilization or each religion was centered on itself, or was turned toward its own "sun." Even though each may have had knowledge of other solar systems, they perceived these as opposing their own. Each religion had its own internal coherence, and it was not necessary to adhere to all truth, but to its own truth.

This exclusivism was all the more justified in that the relations between different civilizations were often war-like. A great Christian mystic, Saint Bernard, himself called for a holy war against the "infidels." Even though the Crusades permitted contacts between Muslims and Christians, they also contributed to the deterioration of relations between the two. Although Ibn 'Arabī recommended that the Seljuk prince Kaykā'ūs show firmness in dealing with the Anatolian Christians, this was partly due to the progress of the Reconquista in Spain and the presence of Crusaders in the East. Moreover, this attitude is not surprising coming from a shaykh who focused so much of his attention on compliance with the Law. In addition, if Sufis such as Ibn 'Arabī were inspired by some type of universal consciousness, they could not be open about this with their contemporaries. They had to show their solidarity with the exoteric body to which they belonged; therefore, they could mention the fundamental unity of religious forms only in indirect terms.

Even Sufis who believed that Islam had not repealed the earlier religions were convinced of the superiority of their religion. For Ibn 'Arabī, Islam is comparable to the sun and the other religions to the stars: they do not die out with the sunrise, but their light is absorbed by the nearer star. One of his disciples, 'Abd al-Razzāq Qāshānī (fourteenth century), who was the author of an esoteric commentary on the Koran, conceded that Jews and Christians can attain the same spiritual degree and the same compensation as Muslim exoterists, which is already a considerable openness in the context of the time. But according to him, the knowledge of Unity, of the divine Essence, is reserved for the Muslim elite, that is to say, for the Sufis. The inherent limitations of Judaism and Christianity, explained Qāshānī, are resolved by Islam, which brings about a synthesis between their respective inclinations: The outer (*zāhir*) for Judaism and the inner (*bātin*) for Christianity. Islam thus represents "the absolute summit, and it remains qualitatively superior to other religious forms. To declare that all religions 'are alike' because they lead to a single Reality is only accurate up to a certain degree of spiritual realization. Beyond this there are no other paths to access full spiritual realization except for Islam, that is to say, the practice of Sufism to its highest degrees."[27]

---

[27] P. Lory, *Les Commentaires ésotériques du Coran*, p. 135.

Although some Sufis have admitted that all religious forms were still valid after the advent of Islam, the vast majority are aligned with the dominant position in Islam, namely that each religion has had its own reason for existing in its own time. Now, Islam is the last revealed religion. Thus, after Dara Shikoh (seventeenth century), Indian Sufis have admitted the truth of the Vedic doctrines and have occasionally used Hindu terms and symbols. Most, however, have proven to be skeptical about the possibilities for spiritual attainment within the Hinduism of their own time.

Since the twentieth century, the borders which separated civilizations and religions have collapsed. No one can ignore other "suns" any longer. Every believer is summoned to be faithful to his own tradition, while recognizing other religious forms as valid; if it were otherwise, he could lose faith in his own religion.[28] That is why in the last century authors such as René Guénon and Frithjof Schuon, but also Ananda Coomaraswamy and Aldous Huxley, were able to articulate the doctrine of universal Wisdom in its diverse modes of expression, regardless of the tradition to which they themselves belonged. The various fundamentalisms pose the problem of relations between the outward and inward dimensions within each revealed message, because the same religion can produce a blind dogmatism as well as an illuminating spirituality. The vocation of Sufism has been precisely to absorb multiplicity into unity, to go beyond the individual in order to access the universal.

Bibliography

Michel Balivet, "Derviches, papadhes et villageois: note sur la pérennité des contacts Islamo-chrétiens en Anatolie centrale," *Journal asiatique*, 1987, pp. 253-263.

———, "Chrétiens secrets et martyrs christiques en Islam turc," *Islamochristiana* 16, Rome, 1990, pp. 91-114.

Charles-André Gilis, *L'Esprit universel de l'Islam* (Beirut, 1998).

Seyyed Hossein Nasr, *Sufi Essays* (Kazi Publications, 1999).

---

[28] S.H. Nasr, *Essais sur le soufisme* (Paris, 1980), p. 176. (English edition: *Sufi Essays* [Kazi Publications, 1999].)

CONCLUSION

SUFISM YESTERDAY, SUFISM TODAY

The "Degeneration of Time"

> The real Sufis are gone
> And Sufism is but a desert.
> It now amounts to cries, the clapping of hands, a frenzied
> search for ecstasy. . . .
> The spiritual sciences, too, are gone.
> No more knowledge, nowadays, no more illuminated hearts.[1]

These lines of such finality do not come from a modern observer but from a tenth century shaykh. *Tasawwuf* was then just becoming an Islamic discipline and an initiatory school. In the following century, to hear Qushayrī tell it, the door had already closed, and authentic guides and real disciples had disappeared. Disciples no longer paid attention to the Law and greed replaced sincerity.[2] It was during this period that Būshanjī observed that "Sufism was formerly a reality without a name; it is now a name without a reality." In the centuries that followed, such statements multiplied under the pens of the Sufi masters as they added detail to the diagnosis or expanded the indictment.

We must put these judgments in the general framework of Islamic tradition, according to which each century is worse than the previous one: the further in time that the world moves away from the prophetic period, the more the world is expected to deteriorate. This *degeneration of time* applies to all fields of Islamic culture and Sufis cannot escape from this. Throughout the centuries, the bitter observations of shaykhs on the quality of Sufism being practiced during their time therefore depends in part on a "pious rhetoric"[3] intended to revive the inner flame of aspirants. The recurrence of such observations also testifies to the fact that during all eras Islam seemed to be tainted with deviations and decadence. Nevertheless, objective signs of degeneration have affected Sufism throughout the ages, as we have seen in the third part of this book.

---

[1] Sarrāj, *Lumaʿ*, p. 27.

[2] *Risāla*, p. 37.

[3] M. Chodkiewicz, in *Les Voies d'Allah*, p. 539.

The Illness of "Brotherhoodism"

The appearance of initiatory paths beginning in the twelfth and thirteenth centuries, as providential as they may have been, certainly had some negative effects. Although the first spiritual families provided a real spiritual presence, over time individual initiative atrophied alongside the group mentality. The quest for awakening, along with the spiritual audacity it presupposes, would seem to be transferred more and more to the person of the shaykh, as if he, whose function it is to bring his disciples to sanctity, was now the only "hero" likely to experience the spiritual adventure.

Would the institutionalization of the initiatory paths result in the loss of those aspirants who had affiliated themselves with those paths? In fact, as the history of Sufism would reveal, sympathizers seeking a shaykh's *baraka* became more numerous than those who were true aspirants to spiritual combat. Yet, there was always a core group of disciples who were limited in number but who gave life to and perpetuated the initiatory secret of their path. From the fifteenth century on, signs of ossification were clear. They were accompanied by a clear initiatory attrition which then led to the mass recruitment of followers; the self-absorption of certain paths which claimed their superiority over the others; shaykhs becoming "administrators of the sacred" but with little apparent interest in the initiatory secret; marabouts who met the demands of the crowd and distributed revenue and magical formulas; routine attachments to a path based on family customs, etc. All of these symptoms relate to what one can call the illness of "brotherhoodism," a form of degeneration inherited from the institutionalization of Sufism.

We frequently hear that "Islamicism is the enemy of Islam"; similarly, brotherhoodism undoubtedly represents the greatest danger to Sufism. The best-informed critics of brotherhoodism are not, in fact, Wahhabites or *salafis*, but Sufi masters themselves.[4] The principles of Sufism on this point are clear. The link between master and disciple must prevail over the sense of belonging to this or that brotherhood. The term "brotherhood," which is commonly used, is subject to confusion because it suggests that a *tarīqa* is an organization or association of a secular nature in which disciples would be linked by horizontal relationships, whereas the members of a *tarīqa* have as their goal sanctity, "proximity to God," and therefore they prefer the vertical relationship with their master. The term "order" is also unsuitable because it suggests that the *tarīqas* are structured like Christian monastic orders or certain Western esoteric organizations, which is rarely the case.

Sufis are supposed to form a single, large family since they follow the same Path of Muhammad which brings together all particular paths. Conse-

---

[4] For a contemporary example, see R. Chih, *Le Soufisme au quotidien*, pp. 176-177.

quently, the rivalries that exist between certain brotherhoods are contrary to the spirit of the Path if they go beyond the reflection of a simple spiritual incompatibility. The proselytism which is rampant in some brotherhoods is therefore the very antithesis of *tasawwuf*, which seeks quality and not quantity. Too great an expansion of an initiatory organization "is generally one of the principal causes of a certain degeneration."[5] Sufism has had some great saints who took only a few disciples, and, in general, the more advanced a Sufi is on the intellectual or spiritual plane, the less he emphasizes his affiliation. If the disciple must regard his shaykh as his "pole," this does not mean that he is *the* Pole. He must therefore include his shaykh in the community of Muslim saints while maintaining spiritual courtesy (*adab*) towards other shaykhs. When these codes of the Path are not respected, it leads to patterns of sectarian behavior that are the opposite of the spiritual and human "openness" which Sufism sets as one of its goals. In the name of a badly understood elitist doctrine, this discipline of awakening then becomes an instrument in encouraging the worst kinds of ostracism.

Nor should one reduce Sufism to the phenomenon of organized brotherhoods, which only appeared in a distinct form between the seventeenth and nineteenth centuries. Brotherhoodism has coexisted up to our own days with a Sufism of appropriate standards, but this does not easily lend itself to view. In addition, masters and disciples have always maintained informal relationships outside of any *tarīqa*. One could be a great spiritual figure, such as Kharrāz, and not be affiliated with an initiatory chain. In the domain of initiation, prudence is needed in regard to everything related to spontaneous generation, yet "the Spirit blows where It chooses"; in the end it is only the mandate of heaven that matters. Finally, Sufism has given rise to a culture, especially in the artistic (music, dance, architecture) and literary fields. Its radiance has, therefore, spread well beyond the environment of initiatory organizations.

Adapting to Cyclical Conditions

"It is related that every evening Shiblī used to have a bowl of salt water and a needle used for applying kohol brought to him and, whenever he was about to fall asleep, he would dip the needle in salt water and would spread it along his eyelids."[6] The early Sufis sometimes practiced a very rigorous asceticism. In Central Asia or India, some engaged in "overturned

---

[5] R. Guénon, *Aperçus sur l'initiation* (Paris, 1983), p. 74. (English edition: *Perspectives on Initiation* [Sophia Perennis, 2004], p. 69.)

[6] Hujwīrī, *Somme spirituelle*, p. 402.

prayer" (*al-salāt al-maqlūba*), which involves hanging by the feet, in a well for example, while reciting prayer formulas. There is even an account of an Egyptian Sufi staying in Mecca who ate only one raisin per day "for fear of defecating in the holy places."

Such mortifications are no longer accepted today and one who would devote himself to them would quickly lose his physiological and mental balance. The relationship between master and disciple has also changed considerably. Shaykhs are usually more accessible and they pay no heed to signs of deference that disciples used to show. They no longer test novices for fear that this will make them flee. If a true disciple was always a rarity, as the masters have said, he is virtually non-existent today. "Now," one often hears among Sufis, "it is the master who searches for a disciple." The shaykhs have always welcomed solid and motivated aspirants, but also souls that are distressed or restless. These masters are now working to counteract the temptations of materialism as well as the pull of fundamentalism in order to keep believers within an Islam that is still spiritual.

Disciples themselves often perceive that "they are not up to" the standards of the Path.[7] Modern life, in both the East and the West, is not conducive to contemplation and societal pressure pushes one towards activism. Islamic tradition says that during this end of the cycle we will witness time contracting, or rather that will be our perception. Followers of Sufism have had to adapt to these constraints. The practices have been simplified. Thus, the prayer portions that make up the *wird*, for example, are now often shortened, and the same holds true for the spiritual retreats (*khalwa*); in the twentieth century, some opponents of Sufism criticized those who practiced retreats for their "quietism." The practice of retreats has sometimes been entirely abandoned, while in some Orders they are reserved only for advanced disciples.

However, these changes should not undermine the essence of Sufism. "The Sufi is the son of his time," says the adage, and he can glimpse better than others the result of the divine Wisdom in any context whatsoever. He has to abandon those archaic forms which were valuable in the past, but which now hinder true initiation. "The effort of interpretation" (*ijtihād*) is required for that which relates to the outer Law, but this is also necessary in spirituality. Many masters have also engaged in these two modes of *ijtihād* so that they could maintain the vitality of the Law and the Path, even though it has been difficult for them to combat the growing inertia and formalism.

---

[7] R. Chih, *Le Soufisme au quotidien*, p. 243.

At the beginning of the third millennium, those who claim to follow Sufism must focus on the essential, the *dhikr* for example, and on ancient methods such as "constant vigilance" (*muraqāba*) or the Naqshbandi principle of "the retreat in the midst of the crowd," none of which have lost their relevance.

Towards a Restructuring of the Roles of Sufism

As it has in the past, only now more explicitly, Sufism has taken on several roles of varying scope. Its purely initiatory function should live on, while continuing to limit itself. Some shaykhs believe that the Path is closed; others, on the contrary, ensure that it is not: the route of the Path has adapted itself to cyclical conditions and therefore no longer knows the harsh aspects of yesteryear. In broad terms, Sufism has the vocation of spiritualizing Islamic life. Ghazzālī successfully undertook this, as have shaykhs and Sufi *ulama* throughout the history of Islam. At a time when humanity faces major challenges, when confessional self-absorption no longer has a place, will Islam follow this slow pendulum-like movement that swings between politics and mysticism, as Malraux suggested? Far from being a fleeting fashion, the current quest for spirituality corresponds to a need felt by at least a portion of humanity. In this regard, Sufism contributes to opening up Muslims' field of vision through its encouragement of interreligious exchanges and the intermingling of cultures.

The virulent *salafī* attacks against Sufism, which claim that it is "modernist," have apparently caused Sufism to fall into disgrace, and even up to the 1970s Orientalists were prophesying its demise. A revival clearly took place in the 1980s and especially in 1990. This was due to the failure of various ideologies that the Arabo-Muslim world had known in the twentieth century (nationalism, Marxism, Islamicism, etc.), as well as to the disenchantment of those who followed the Western model. Despite the critical phase that it has passed through, Sufism has maintained its anchoring in Islamic culture. In 1989, Sa'īd Hawwā was able to declare that ninety percent of all Muslims had, in one way or another, a link with Sufism over the course of the centuries.[8] Ninety percent of the Senegalese have been affiliated with a brotherhood, and it has been suggested that a third of all Egyptians and two thirds of all Pakistanis have been as well. (But we wonder if this is still true after the spread of the Wahhabite-Taliban virus. . . .)

Sufism is currently experiencing a resurgence of its vitality in Muslim countries, while it also arouses growing interest in the West. There is, how-

---

[8] *Tarbiyatu-nā al-rūhiyya* (*The Spiritual Education that We Propose*) (Beirut, 1989), p. 12.

ever, a great deal of contrast in the situation within different Muslim lands. In most countries, large numbers of young people are joining brotherhoods, while twenty years ago the average age of the members was quite advanced. In other countries, however, Sufism appears to be relatively in retreat. Clearly, spiritual aspirations move into the background when the mind is monopolized by material preoccupations and the concern for subsistence, when the international context and the media promote the emergence of ideologies that are easy to consume, and when fundamentalism in whatever form has mined the ground.

The form of the brotherhoods, however, does not now show signs of good health. Thus, in many cases when a shaykh dies, either he is not replaced, or the succession is a purely hereditary one, relating more to the administration of property than to spiritual direction. Some *tarīqas* that are important in terms of the number of their members might succumb at one time to an ideology that is Islamist, and then at another time to a messianic sectarianism. It is now, therefore, more than ever important to distinguish between Sufism and brotherhoodism. Some shaykhs are aware of this, and so they try to break the routine practices of the *zāwiyas* to encourage their disciples to engage in other forms of spiritual work. The various disenchantments mentioned above push a certain number of believers to a discovery or a rediscovery of the spirituality within Islam, but in an environment that is often broader than that of the brotherhoods. This process occurs in social and intellectual circles that are often more advanced than those to which "popular" Sufism is accustomed. If there was a Sufism before the brotherhoods, there may a Sufism after them as well. Does the future belong to "limited groups," to an "anonymous Sufism?"[9] Nevertheless, people in Sufism as elsewhere like to be supported and surrounded by structures which reassure them.

The Messianic Adventure

According to most of the *ulama*, we are entering into the "end of time," the period which the Prophet had discussed in great detail. This advent had already been announced several times in the past, but at present the allusions are becoming more precise. Roughly speaking, the scenario would be the following: various geological and human disturbances would announce the revolt of the Antichrist (*al-Dajjāl*), the incarnation of the forces of evil. Aided by the righteous among Muslims, the Mahdī would then rise up to combat the Antichrist and to prepare for the coming of Jesus on earth. He

---

[9] M. Chodkiewicz, "Le soufisme au XXIᵉ siècle," in *Les Voies d'Allah*, p. 543.

would assist Jesus in his mission to kill the Antichrist, and to "fill the earth with equity and justice" for seven years, according to some sources, before Jesus himself would establish a messianic reign before the end of the world and the Last Judgment.

Some shaykhs maintain that the Mahdī is already among us, and they suggest that they are among his "ministers" mentioned by the Prophet. However, Sufi groups who openly claim their participation in messianic events which are already happening or are still to come sometimes adopt behaviors that are sectarian, and they pin their hopes on a conflict between the Muslim world and the West. One shaykh in particular regularly used to announce the Third World War to his disciples and the advent of the Mahdī, which should have occurred, according to him, as early as the 1980s. Each time, the disciples gathered supplies for the ninety days that the war was supposed to last. What could this shaykh have been trying to accomplish by raising an eschatological expectation like this? Thus, the messianic doctrine of Islam is today susceptible to being appropriated and to giving rise to incredible ideological manipulations.

Sufism in the West

Throughout history, Sufism has sometimes preceded and at other times accompanied Islam in its expansion. Its universalistic character has led it to adapt to new contexts and to radiate outward from the lands of Islam. It certainly influenced Jewish and Christian mystics of the medieval era and perhaps even authors such as Dante and the Catalan mystic Raymond Lully. Holding the place of honor in Orientalism since the nineteenth century, it was not unknown to a certain intellectual or artistic elite in Europe. Other factors led it to spread into the West in the twentieth century. Colonialism precipitated the encounter between Islam and the West in an atmosphere that swung between fascination and repulsion. In the middle of the colonial period, Westerners fleeing a mechanistic civilization and the ideology of progress had already been won over by the "mystique of the desert." Deploring the secularization of Christianity and its reduction to a religious morality that adapted well to European imperialism, some have searched in Sufism for a kind of metaphysical rejuvenation.

After participating in various esoteric cliques in Paris, René Guénon was initiated into Sufi Islam in 1912. Having settled in Cairo in 1930, the "Shaykh 'Abd al-Wāhid Yahyā" followed the Shādhilī path while he continued editing a work in which he wished to warn the West against the "obscurantism" of modernity and to remind it of the universal doctrine of the "primordial Tradition." He dealt less with Islam than with some other traditions, but Guénon thought that Islam had the most effective initiatory possibilities since it was the last revealed religion. Through this work and through the advice that he tirelessly shared with others in his correspondences, Guénon caused a leap of consciousness among Westerners, whether they were believers in various religions or followers of initiatory organizations such as masonry; of these, some opted for Islam. Although he completed his "simple life" in Cairo in 1951,[10] Guénon continues to exercise a singular influence in the West and in a few circles in Muslim countries.

From Guénon came the "traditionalist" movement of Sufism in the West, whose main figure was the Swiss Frithjof Schuon (d. 1998). An artist and a poet, he wrote powerful doctrinal works. The Maryamiyya path that he founded has experienced various divisions, but Schuon's initiatory radiance in the West and in some parts of the Muslim world is undeniable. Several of his disciples or his ex-disciples have been among those responsible for a major movement in the study and translation of Sufi texts: Titus Burckhardt (d. 1984), Martin Lings (d. 2005), Seyyed Hossein Nasr or even Michel Vâlsan (d. 1974), who spread the study of Ibn ʿArabī in the West; at the instigation of Guénon, Vâlsan created his own path in France. For its part, the ʿAlawiyya, through which Schuon came, expanded into Europe as early as the 1920s, before the first wave of Maghrebian emigration.

Since the 1970s, several Sufi groups from major paths—Shādhiliyya, Tijāniyya, then Naqshbandiyya, Qādiriyya, Burhāniyya, Niʿmatullahiyya—have emerged in the West. This expansion was not a simple consequence of emigration, for "Oriental" shaykhs had long since regarded the West as a providential land. Observing that socio-political pressures in their countries were hindering individual development, they saw in the West a space for freedom and they noted a real expectancy in the spiritual domain. People of Muslim origin, perhaps students or workers, thus discovered in the West a Sufism in which they saw only superstition or routine. Some "Eastern" masters soon settled there, while a small number of trained Westerners acted as representatives for a foreign spiritual master, or themselves rose to the status of shaykh.

All in this circle take advantage of orthodox Sufism, since affiliates remain faithful to the requirements of Islam and are sometimes versed in the Islamic sciences. Most members retain a link with one Muslim country or another. The issue of adaptation to the Western context is not resolved in all cases: among those who have been initiated and educated in the East, some tend to import Arab, African, or other customs. Sufism remains an important factor in people converting to Islam, even though the profiles of Westerners

---

[10] See P. Chacornac, *La Vie simple de René Guénon* (Paris, 1958). (English edition: *The Simple Life of René Guénon* [Sophia Perennis, 2004].)

embracing this religion now vary greatly.

Other groups, however, have removed themselves from the Islamic form to better set free, in their opinion, the universalism contained within Sufi wisdom. Opening the door to syncretism, these groups pin their hopes on a sort of "globalization" of the Spirit. The "Universel," which came from the Indian Chishtiyya brotherhood led by Pir Vilayat Khan (d. 2004) and now by his son, is part of all this. For his part, Idries Shah (d. 1996), who was of Afghani origin, taught a philosophy that was inspired by his own vision of Sufism, but which some people have described as charlatanism. Disciples of these various groups rarely enter Islam. Followers of "Islamic" Sufism obviously condemn this syncretism. Recalling that initiation can only exist within a definite religious form, and that it is dangerous to diffuse this initiation here and there, they believe that respect for the spiritual traditions of mankind obliges them to follow only one tradition at a time.

In the West, Sufism is now exposed to commercialism: here and there, brochures promise trances or even "possession." The "Sufi business" is doing well. Although some individuals may present Sufism with the safeguards necessary in any spiritual approach, it is likely that the West will transform Sufism into an object of consumption as has been done with other oriental techniques. "Eso-tourism" has even touched the Muslim world. In North Africa, for example, the Aïssaouas (of the popular ʿIsawiyya brotherhood), who are known for their possession rites and self-mutilation, are exhibited quite officially so as to attract customers, while in Istanbul Westerners are quickly "initiated" by Mevlevi whirling dervishes.[11] Between the extreme openness which dilutes the boundaries of religious membership and the sectarianism that claims the exclusivity of salvation, Western Sufism sometimes has difficulty finding its balance. It is again necessary to distinguish American Sufism, which can sometimes be outlandish, from European Sufism, which is deemed more sober and is certainly more Islamicized.[12]

In our rather unstructured societies with their dizzying diversity of individual experiences, Sufism has more than ever taken on a therapeutic role, a situation which it shares, of course, with other spiritual paths. "The first stage of the path consists of calming and then dispersing psychic conflicts, complexes, and frustrations, as well as the negative and destructive tendencies within the disciple, so that he can reach a psychological, mental, and emotional equilibrium. And then during the second stage, the disciple

---

[11] See the observations made by T. Zarcone (*Les Voies d'Allah*, pp. 377-378).

[12] M. Hermansen, "Hybrid Identity Formations in Muslim America: The Case of American Sufi Movements," *The Muslim World* 90, n° 1-2, 2000, p. 187.

recovers the divine attributes," confided Javad Nūrbakhsh, master of the Niʿmatullāhiyya and a psychiatrist by trade.[13] There are many significant traumas that can stem from the established religions, which aspirants may have experienced as shackles; there is also the problem of the bloated Western ego that claims to have reached the highest degrees of sanctity without having integrated into itself the basic rules of Sufi courtesy.

As it has in Muslim countries, Sufism in the West can also contribute to the spiritualization of daily Islam, which is now followed by millions of individuals there, and it can offer initiatory nourishment to some; it can promote the emergence of an essentialized Islam that has been freed from allegiances to countries of origin or from reflexes of identity; it can also offer a different view of Islam, which can help establish a kind of bridge between East and West.[14]

If during current times it is possible for everyone to doubt the presence of any form of sanctity, we should recall that according to Sufi doctrine the saints dress themselves in the clothing of their time and that they conceal themselves when conditions require this. "All times are the mirror of God."[15] Mankind will have run its course when the cycle of sainthood will itself have completed its term.

Bibliography

Michel Chodkiewicz, "Le Sufisme au XXIe siècle," in *Les Voies d'Allah* (Paris, 1996), pp. 532-543.

Eric Geoffroy, "L'attraction du soufisme," in *Histoire de l'islam et des musulmans en France, du Moyen Âge à nos jours*, edited by M. Arkoun (Paris, 2006), pp. 827-836.

Constant Hamès, "Situation présente et perspectives d'avenir," in *Les Voies d'Allah*, pp. 521-531.

The journal *Les Cahiers de l'Institut des hautes études Islamiques*, edited in Milan.

The journal *Soufisme d'Orient et d'Occident*, edited in Paris.

---

[13] *Dans la taverne de la ruine. Manuel du soufisme traditionnel* (Cabrières d'Avignon, 1997), p. 21.

[14] M. Lings, *What is Sufism?* (Islamic Texts Society, 1993), p. 24.

[15] *Le Chœur des prophètes. Enseignements soufis du cheikh ʿAdda Bentounès* (Paris, 1999), p. 158.

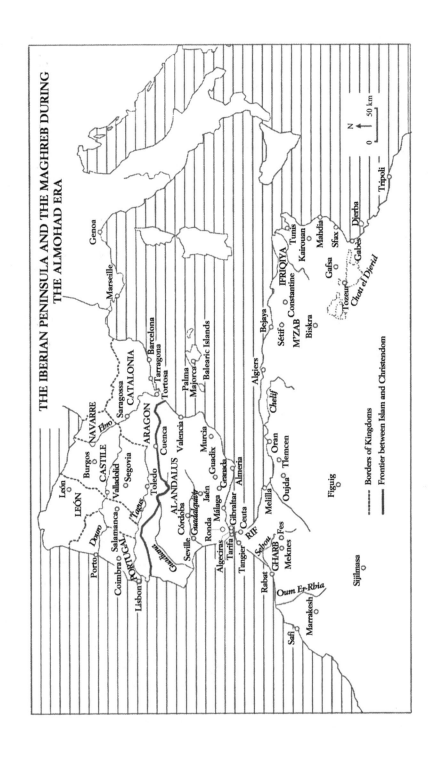

THE IBERIAN PENINSULA AND THE MAGHREB DURING
THE ALMOHAD ERA

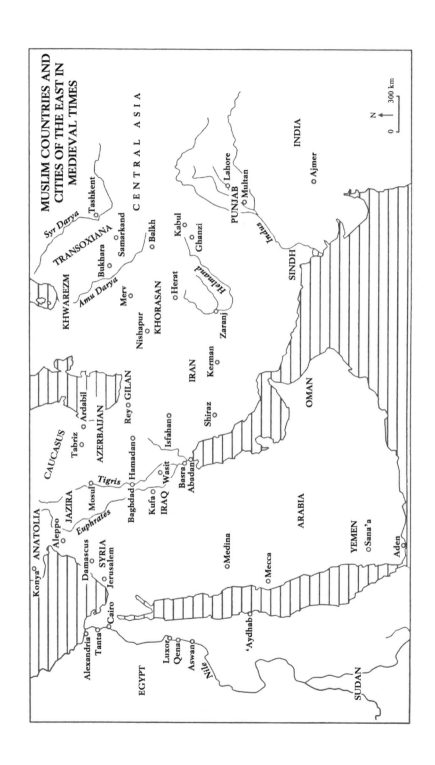

MUSLIM COUNTRIES AND
CITIES OF THE EAST IN
MEDIEVAL TIMES

GLOSSARY AND INDEX OF TECHNICAL TERMS
(Islamic and Sufi)

abdāl: "substitutes," a category of the esoteric hierarchy of saints, 17, 77, 121, 125

adab: code of spiritual courtesy governing both inner attitude and outer behavior, 12, 145, 196

ādāb (pl. of *adab*): rules of conduct in the spiritual life, 51, 158, 160

'ahd: initiatory pact, 121, 154

ahkām: legal statutes, 160

al-'āmma: ordinary, or "average" believers, 9, 40

awtād: "pillars," a category of the esoteric hierarchy of saints, 17, 121, 125

baqā' (after *fanā'*): the state of "subsisting" in God, 15, 17, 72, 181

baraka: divine or Muhammadian spiritual influx; blessing, protection, 2, 49-50, 111, 124, 148-149, 152-153, 156, 195

bātin: "inner," esoteric, 1, 7, 19, 41, 192

bay'a: allegiance, initiatory pact, 137, 154

bid'a: innovation in religious matters, 53, 125

dawla bātiniyya: the "esoteric State of the saints", 125

dhawq: spiritual "taste," knowledge through "taste", 8, 84

dhikr: remembrance, reminder, invocation of God, 22, 57, 61, 77, 79, 82, 107, 113, 119, 123, 135, 138, 143, 149, 155-156, 162-171, 173-175, 178, 198

dhikr jahrī: invocation with the voice, aloud, 167

dhikr khafī: silent invocation, also called *dhikr qalbī*, invocation of the heart, 107, 167-168

al-dīn al-qayyim: the "primordial" or "immutable" Religion, 1, 182

falsafa: Hellenistic philosophy, 120

fanā': "extinction," annihilation of individual consciousness in the divine Presence:
  al-fanā' fī Llāh, 14-15, 17, 35, 51-52, 56, 72, 144, 164, 181

al-fanā' fī l-rasūl: "extinction in the Messenger", 51, 144

al-fanā' fī l-shaykh: "extinction of the disciple in the master", 144

al-fanā' fī l-tawhīd: "extinction of the ego in the divine Oneness", 56, 72, 85

faqīh (pl. *fuqahā'*): a "jurist" (lawyer), a specialist in Muslim law, 78-79

faqr: "poverty," consciousness of one's poverty in God, 5

fath: spiritual "opening," illumination, 147, 179

fikr: meditation, 164

fiqh: law, jurisprudence in Islam, 55, 59, 78-79

fuqarā' (sing. *faqīr*): the "poor in God," the Sufis, 5, 17, 108; see *faqr*

futuwwa: spiritual chivalry, companionship, 100-101

ghazal: originally a secular love poem, transposed onto the mystical plane, 94

habs-i dam: holding of the breath, 165

hadra: "presence" of the Prophet, a group session of *dhikr*, 169

hāl (pl. *ahwāl*): spiritual "state", 10, 37, 62, 67, 176, 180

Haqīqa: the inner Reality of everything that has been created, of every Law, and of every religion, 9, 59-61, 86, 185

khatm al-awliyā': "seal of the saints", 73, 131

khawātir: extrinsic or extraneous thoughts, 150

khilāf: Islamic principle of "divergence", 17

khirqa: initiatory robe or cloak, 23-24, 28, 79-80, 153-154

khuluq (pl. *akhlāq*): noble character, 12, 97, 137

latā'if: subtle centers of the human body, 106, 167

madad: spiritual support emanating from the Prophet or from a shaykh, 149

madrasa: a college of higher education in Islamic sciences, 27, 49, 79-80, 84, 86, 90, 103, 117, 121, 123-124

mahabba: reciprocal love between God and man, 3, 37, 68, 70

majdhūb: "enraptured in God," ecstatic, 11, 17, 114, 120, 145

majlis al-dhikr: a session of invocation done in a group, 169

majlis salāt 'alā l-nabī: a session of prayer on the Prophet, 124

malāma: "the path of blame", 67-68, 81

maqām (pl. *maqāmāt*): initiatory "station", 10-11, 37

maqām (or *mazār*): tomb or shrine of a saint, 124

ma'rifa: knowledge of God, gnosis, 3, 13, 41, 68

mawlid (*mulud* in Maghrebian dialect): celebration of the birthday of the Prophet, 53, 99, 124

Mi'rāj: celestial Ascent of the Prophet, 8, 48

mīthāq: the Pact sealed between God and humanity in the spiritual world before creation, 11, 163

mujaddid: "reviver" or "renewer" of the Islamic religion, 108

muqaddam, moqaddem: a delegate who represents a shaykh, 132, 152

murād: he who is "desired" by God, 3, 11

murāqaba: unceasing vigilance, 38, 198

muraqqa'a: patched robe, 79, 154

murīd: aspirant on the Path, 3, 11, 154

murshid: spiritual guide, 137, 142

musāfaha: rite of "taking of the hand", 49, 154

mushāhada: contemplation, 14

nabī: prophet, 18, 48

nafs: the carnal soul; the ego; seat of the passions, 12, 67, 149, 166, 177

nubuwwa: prophecy, 23, 28

al-nūr al-muhammadī: the "Light of Muhammad", 44, 46, 85

qibla: the direction for prayer, towards Mecca, 144, 160, 164, 178

qurb: the proximity of God, 37

qutb: spiritual pole; the "Supreme Pole" is at the summit of the esoteric hierarchy of saints, 17, 24, 121, 125, 196

rābitat al-shaykh: attachment to one's master, 107, 144

raqs: spiritual "dance", 173

ribāt: an establishment for Sufis, 67, 103, 122

ridā: contentment towards God, 38

rūhāniyya: an "entity" or form that is in the spiritual realm, 52, 107, 146, 158

rujuliyya: spiritual virility, 28, 146

tawhīd: assertion or recognition of the divine Oneness, which is the foundation of the Muslim creed; the inward realization of this doctrine by Sufis, 14, 56, 72, 83, 85, 90, 158, 183

ta'wīl: "restoring a scriptural verse to its original meaning"; esoteric interpretation, 41, 93

tekke (Turkish term): the same thing as *zāwiya*, 123, 162

'ubūdiyya: man's fundamental servitude to God, 15, 56

uwaysī: a mode of private and individual initiation, 52, 157

al-wahda al-mutlaqa: the absolute Oneness, 83, 98

wahdat al-adyān: the transcendent unity of religions, 184

wahdat al-shuhūd: the unity of "witness" or of "contemplation", 56

wahdat al-wujūd: the oneness of divine Being, 15, 56, 85, 90, 96

wahy: Revelation, 7, 63

wajd: ecstasy, or rather "enstasy", 171

walāya: God's "taking care" of His creation, from which His proximity to man derives; in return, man's gaining of proximity to God, and thus "sanctity" or "holiness", 23-24, 37-38, 73, 81, 150

walī: friend of God; one close to God; a "saint", 18, 37, 48

wārid: mystical inspiration, 176

wazīfa: the set of prayers to be recited daily, 137, 176

wird (pl. *awrād*): "daily spiritual renewal"; prayer formulas one typically recites twice per day; a litany, 169, 174-176, 187, 197

al-wird al-'āmm: common or typical litany, 175

al-wird al-khāss: private litany, 175

yaqīn: certainty; certain vision, 7, 39, 55, 63, 84

zāhid: one who engages in *zuhd*, 17

zāhir: outward; exoteric, 7, 47, 192

zakāt: purifying alms, 54, 57, 61

zāwiya: an establishment for Sufis, 30, 104, 110-111, 120, 123-124, 126, 139, 147, 159, 161-162, 169, 173, 177, 179, 199

ziyāra: a visit to the shrine of a saint, 124

zuhd: detachment; ascetical renunciation of the world, 20, 65-66, 68-69, 132

For a glossary of all key foreign words used in books published by World Wisdom, including metaphysical terms in English, consult:
www.DictionaryofSpiritualTerms.org.
This on-line Dictionary of Spiritual Terms provides extensive definitions, examples and related terms in other languages.

INDEX OF PROPER NAMES
(Major People, Groups, Ethnic Groups, and Dynasties)

BIOGRAPHICAL NOTES

ÉRIC GEOFFROY is a scholar, translator, educator, and writer who is Professor of Islamic Studies in the Department of Arabic and Islamic Studies at the University of Strasbourg, France. He also teaches at the Open University of Catalonia, at the Catholic University of Louvain (Belgium), and at the International Institute of Islamic Thought (Paris). Dr. Geoffroy specializes in Islam and its mystical dimension, Sufism, often focusing on aspects of sainthood. Among others areas, his research also extends to comparative mysticism, and to issues of spirituality in the contemporary world (e.g. spirituality and globalization; spirituality and ecology, etc.). In addition, he is a member of an international research group on Science and Religion in Islam, through the Université Interdisciplinaire of Paris.

Dr. Geoffroy gives many lectures all over the world (Europe, the Arab world, USA, Indonesia, and elsewhere) on subjects related to Sufism, and, more generally, to Islamic culture. Besides this, he has also participated in many international conferences. Geoffroy himself works on organizing conferences and seminars (for example for the Bibliotheca Alexandrina in Alexandria or the European Council in Strasbourg, etc.), and has written materials for a traveling exhibition on Sufism directed by the Arabic World Institute in Paris.

To date, Éric Geoffroy has had seven books published. He has published numerous articles in journals on Islamic studies but also in some magazines such as *Le Monde des Religions, Le Point Hors Série*, and *La Vie*. He has contributed some fifteen articles to the *Encyclopedia of Islam* (2nd and 3rd editions), and others to key reference books such as *Les voies d'Allah, Dictionnaire critique de l'ésotérisme*, and *Dictionnaire du Coran*. Dr. Geoffroy is the official consultant on Islam for the French dictionary *Le Petit Larousse*.

Besides this, Éric Geoffroy has on many occasions been the guest on some national and international radio and television broadcasts in Europe and in the Muslim world. His own web site, www.eric-geffroy.net, has links to some of his writings online, as well as to video and other links of interest.

ROGER GAETANI is a professional editor, translator, and educator. He was co-editor, with Jean-Louis Michon, of the World Wisdom anthology *Sufism: Love and Wisdom*, and he later edited the award-winning *A Spirit of Tolerance: The Inspiring Life of Tierno Bokar*, which details the life of the renowned African Sufi. In addition, Mr. Gaetani directed and co-produced the DVD compilation of highlights of the 2006 conference on Traditionalism, *Tradition in the Modern World: Sacred Web 2006 Conference*. While living and traveling in the Muslim world for some years, he came into contact with a number of leading Sufi figures and was able to see first-hand the remnants of Sufism's impact on Islamic civilization, but also its effect on the lives of those Muslims who still follow its path. He lives in Bloomington, Indiana with his wife.

Titles on Islam by World Wisdom

Art of Islam, Language and Meaning: Commemorative Edition,
by Titus Burckhardt, 2009

Christianity/Islam: Perspectives on Esoteric Ecumenism,
by Frithjof Schuon, 2008

Introduction to Sufi Doctrine, by Titus Burckhardt, 2008

Introduction to Traditional Islam, Illustrated: Foundations, Art, and Spirituality,
by Jean-Louis Michon, 2008

Islam, Fundamentalism, and the Betrayal of Tradition, Revised and Expanded:
Essays by Western Muslim Scholars,
edited by Joseph E.B. Lumbard, 2009

The Mystics of Islam, by Reynold A. Nicholson, 2002

The Path of Muhammad: A Book on Islamic Morals and Ethics by Imam Birgivi,
interpreted by Shaykh Tosun Bayrak, 2005

Paths to the Heart: Sufism and the Christian East,
edited by James S. Cutsinger, 2003

Paths to Transcendence: According to Shankara, Ibn Arabi, and Meister Eckhart,
by Reza Shah-Kazemi, 2006

The Sacred Foundations of Justice in Islam: The Teachings of 'Ali ibn Abi Talib,
edited by M. Ali Lakhani, 2006

A Spirit of Tolerance: The Inspiring Life of Tierno Bokar,
by Amadou Hampaté Bâ, 2008

The Sufi Doctrine of Rumi: Illustrated Edition,
by William C. Chittick, 2005

Sufism: Love and Wisdom,
edited by Jean-Louis Michon and Roger Gaetani, 2006

Sufism: Veil and Quintessence, by Frithjof Schuon, 2007

Understanding Islam, by Frithjof Schuon, 1998

The Universal Spirit of Islam: From the Koran and Hadith,
edited by Judith and Michael Oren Fitzgerald, 2006

Unveiling the Garden of Love:
Mystical Symbolism in Layla Majnun & Gita Govinda,
by Lalita Sinha, 2008